On the Breakout of Chinese Economy

This book is part of the Peter Lang Regional Studies list.
Every volume is peer reviewed and meets
the highest quality standards for content and production.

PETER LANG
New York • Berlin • Brussels • Lausanne • Oxford

Qiren Zhou

On the Breakout of Chinese Economy

A Breakout Collection

PETER LANG
New York • Berlin • Brussels • Lausanne • Oxford

Library of Congress Cataloging-in-Publication Control Number: 2022006286

Bibliographic information published by **Die Deutsche Nationalbibliothek**.
Die Deutsche Nationalbibliothek lists this publication in the "Deutsche Nationalbibliografie"; detailed bibliographic data are available on the Internet at http://dnb.d-nb.de/.

ISBN 978-1-4331-7294-6 (hardcover)
ISBN 978-1-4331-9050-6 (ebook pdf)
ISBN 978-1-4331-9051-3 (epub)
DOI 10.3726/b18628

Translator: Luo Xiaoping

中信出版集团
CITIC Press Group

This edition is an authorized translation from the Chinese language edition
Published by arrangement with CITIC Press Corporation
(B&R Program)

80 Broad Street, 5th floor, New York, NY 10004
www.peterlang.com

Contents

Preface

Enhancing the Penetration Power of Reform[1]

Reform is a global trend, and now many countries are upholding the banner of reform. However, reforms undertaken by different countries are remarkably different. In particular, the reforms of large countries have their distinctive characteristics; because large countries have multiple levels and uneven development, it is not easy to reach consensus on the reform and it is also more difficult to implement the reform decisions. On the other hand, once a reform in a large country is implemented, its dividends are considerable. To study the reforms of large countries, the important part is to learn how the consensus is formed and how the reforms are then put in place. A critical question in this is the penetration power: After consensus is reached and reform decisions are made, can the reform penetrate through all the multiple levels of organization from the top to the bottom? This is a challenge. A large country is called "large" because it takes a long journey to go from the top to the bottom. For the reform experience and the endeavors from the bottom of a large country to enter the top-level design, the journey is even much, much longer. Is it possible to achieve penetration both

1 This essay is adapted from the keynote speech given by the author on December 19, 2014, at the 5th Caixin Summit themed "New Normal and New Reform."—Editor's Note.

ways? This is a question we will confront as we review 2014 and look ahead to China's reform situation for 2015.

We all agree that the decision to comprehensively deepen the reform made at the Third Plenary Session of the Eighteenth CPC Central Committee and the decision to rule the country by law at the Fourth Plenary Session are correct. If there are any concerns or misgiving, it is about whether or not these decisions will be effectively implemented and achieve effective penetration. This penetration is bidirectional: Not only must decisions from the top penetrate down to the bottom, but also the actual situation at the bottom and the reform experience created at the bottom also percolate up toward the top. The penetration power has a decisive significance for a large country's reform. As to how to enhance the penetration power of China's reform, different people might have different views. I personally believe the following points will probably be helpful.

First, reform goals must be clear and simple. Only when the goals are clear and simple can the penetration power be strong. Taking the economy as an example, the goal of the reform is for the market to play a decisive role in resource allocation. This is a general outline which drives all aspects, including a better role from the government. In the fields of politics and society, the goal is democracy and the rule of law; in particular, public or government power should be put into the cage of institutional constraints to bring the country onto the track of rule of law and to motivate more members of the society to participate in social governance. The market, democracy, and the rule of law as goals are adequately simple and should not be burdened by adding more and more complications. What is passed on from China's culture is also actually quite simple; this is because China is a very large country, and it is difficult for too-complicated things to have penetration power. From the top to the bottom, too-complicated things might change as they pass along the way and can thus be difficult to be truly implemented.

When the goals are correct, adequately simple, and adequately clear, the only thing left is persistence. Only when the simple and clear reform goals are upheld can the penetration power be strong. Not all changes can be called reforms; a reform must have a clear direction and clear connotations. It cannot be willy-nilly, heading east for a while, then going west. The reform of a large country must follow with perseverance an exceptionally simple and clear direction, and only by doing this can the penetration be powerful.

Second, the number of potential interpretations to reform decisions and goals should be reduced as much as possible. This is because the reform decision is a program of action, not a set of complicated theories or rhetoric. In particular, the various levels and departments do not need to "interpret" reform decision, because it is not difficult to understand. We can simply let people read the original text of the *Decision*[2] of the Central Government and take actions immediately after the reading. In particular, no complicated interpretations are needed; otherwise one sentence becomes five sentences, five sentences become fifty sentences, patches are added onto patches, and finally no one understands what is being talked out and people do not know what to do, then nothing at all can be achieved. Some interpretations go in the opposite way of the intent and content of the *Decision,* so which one should prevail? It should be the *Decision*.

Let us take the land system reform, which I am familiar with, as an example. In this case, the structure of the reform scheme ratified by the Central Leadership Group for Deepening the Reform is very clear by itself: do not touch the "three bottom lines"; local governments are encouraged to do more exploration, practice, and creation; and its goal is a land market, a unified urban and rural land market. However, after various interpretations, it seems that the "bottom line" has been changed into a closed loop, which can only circulate within itself and cannot break any boundaries, and the local explorations and the goal of building the market are all disappearing. This makes it very difficult to accomplish the reform. The way out - is to minimize interpretations. In particular, departmental interests, vested interests, and outdated concepts should be prevented from taking advantage of the interpretation and turn the originally correct, clear, and understandable decision into a muddled and ambiguous puzzle. The information puzzle for a big country's reform is obstructing the penetration like a haze.

Third, there should be more exchange of actual hands-on reform experience. The *Decision* is correct and concise, but its implementation will often encounter all sorts of actual situations. What should be done to put the implementation in place, and what new problems need to be resolved? This is a very important step to enhance the penetration power of the reform. According to my research and observations, this aspect is very likely the weakest one. While the Central Committee's *Decision* has been talked about and emphasized multiple times, which actions have been taken at the grassroots level? Did these actions happen after the Third Plenary Session of the Eighteenth CPC Central Committee? What are the universally applicable experiences? What are the setbacks, and what are the deviations?

2 The Decision by CPC Central Committee on Several Major Questions Related to Comprehensively Deepening the Reform.

In fact, at the bottom, there are many moves toward the direction of marketization and many actions toward the expansion of democracy and the rule of law. To give an example, in 1999 when the internet started to become popular, internet telephony appeared on the scene. The regulatory departments in place at the time were of the opinion that network communications conducted directly by the private sector was violating relevant communication laws and regulations; as a result, the innovator not only got his property confiscated but also lost personal freedom for a while. Fuzhou Intermediate People's Court tried this case and decided that the judgment by the court of first instance had no legal basis and that the case should be returned for retrial. The implication from this case is clear: For things not expressly prohibited by law, some space can and should be left for innovation behaviors.

This is a good case. If it gets transmitted to the super structure, it will provide a substantial push to many things, such as preventing administrative monopoly, strengthening market competition, and following the same rules of the game in interest distribution. It is often said that China does not have many excellent judges or many excellent lawyers, and that the number of people with the concept of the modern rule of law is even smaller. However, we still have some, even if "not many." Sometimes, a single counter-example has great penetration power. If we can seize such counter examples and instigate a discussion in the whole society, the penetration power of the reform can be enhanced.

Fourth, new systems should be formed in some critical locations. Currently, the general belief is that China's product market is better developed than its factors market. What exactly is the factors market, though? Take the land market as an example: It isn't necessary for every village to become a place for land transactions, because factors trading and their price discovery need to be relatively concentrated at certain locations. "Global oil prices" are often discussed in the news. What are global oil prices? Are they something decided by the whole globe? No; they are decided at a small location, namely the high-end oil market. To enhance the penetration power of China's reform, we must seize key locations, namely high-end markets, because as long as the new system can stand on its own and successfully operate in these locations, the original system can be broken and the new system will have a huge radiation power.

Shanghai Free Trade Zone policy has spread to Tianjin and Shenzhen; this obviously has shown some penetration power, but it seems not strong enough. Why was Shanghai's financial reform put at the port and warehouse area? Wouldn't the radiation be stronger if it had been put in Lujiazui? Later on, a sentence was added to extend the free trade zone policy to Pudong New District.

It is hoped that relevant financial service policies will not only play a role in the warehouse areas of the trade port but also be proactively expanded Pudong's core urban areas so as to generate more radiation throughout the Yangtze River basin, the southern part of China, the whole of China, and even the Asia–Pacific region. This is an important move to strengthen the penetration power of the reform.

Fifth, remove some difficult obstacles. Currently, administration according to law is being emphasized; this means that administration should follow existing laws and legal regulations. However, some of the content of existing laws and regulations conflicts with the reform decisions made by the Third Plenary Session of the Eighteenth CPC Central Committee. To move toward the market mechanism and build a country governed by the rule of law, it is imperative to touch some previously formulated laws and regulations; frictions will therefore be unavoidable, which is a significant difference in comparison with the reform of the early 1980s. Therefore, the current reform should go hand in hand with legal revisions. It would be best to have a list of legal revisions together with a timetable. If the existing laws and regulations do not get changed at all, the reform cannot be advanced.

1 Reform's Next Step

Redefining State Capacity[3]

In the early 1990s, a new definition for state capacity was proposed—"State capacity is the ability of a country to translate its will and goals into reality"—embodying the country's extractive, regulatory, legalization, and coercive capacities. The proposers emphasized in particular: "only the central government can represent the will of the country." Therefore, state capacity is not the so-called "comprehensive national strength," and still less is it the capacity of general public authorities or local governments—it can only be the capacity of the central government.[4]

The backdrop for this new definition is that the reform and opening-up starting in the 1980s touched the old system of highly centralized power by

3 This section is adapted from the text of the author's lecture given at the 4th Caixin Summit on December 18, 2013.—Editor's note.

4 Wang Shaoguang and Hu Angang, *A Study of China's State Capacity* (Liaoning People's Press, 1993). For the latest commentaries, see *Commemorating the 20th Anniversary of the Publishing of A Study of China's State Capacity*, "Sina History," July 22, 2013.

decentralization, activated the economic and social vitality, and inspired people to explore new paths for economic growth. As reflected in the distribution of national income, the proportion of fiscal revenue in the GDP fell and the proportion of the central government's fiscal revenue to the total fiscal revenue also fell. By the early 1990s, when people noticed that the proportion of the central government's fiscal revenue was too small, they re-emphasized that the financial resources should be centralized, especially into the hands of the central government, and therefore came up with relevant concepts, theories, and policy recommendations.

More than twenty years have passed since the 1990s, and although China has accumulated new experiences in development, it also needs to face new problems. From the perspective of the actual situation, it is necessary to correctly define state capacity, so as to ensure that major reform continue to progress without deviating from the proper course. In terms of the definition itself, I personally think that equating the concept of "the state" to the government, or the central government, is, in and of itself a significant deviation. If the state really can truly be equated to the government, then surely it would be sufficient to directly discuss "government capacity" or "central government capacity"; why take all the trouble to come up with "state capacity," which is a synonym?

It must be made clear that the "state/country" is not equivalent to the "government." In concept, a state is first and foremost a territory, which has clear spatial scope and borders. The people who live in the territory of a country (its citizens) are the foundation of that country because "To the country people is all-important." A country without its people is an empty shell; thus, it would be nonsensical to talk about any capacity or capability. The citizens of a country are the masses, and public affairs between the masses must be coordinated and managed; otherwise, there will be disputes and conflicts and the country will be put into unrest and trouble. Therefore, a system of laws and regulations must be formulated so as to define normative behavior and draw the boundaries for every person's freedom. The system, with the soft part being the culture and customs, and the hard part being the legal coercive force, is used to prevent some people (whether external or internal) from invading others. The government is the enforcement agency of this legal coercive force, or—as described by some economists—"the only organization that owns the legal coercive force."[5]

5 Such as North (1973) and Barzel (2002).

In this sense, a country is the trinity of territory, people, and society (regulatory systems); the absence of any one of these elements means there is not a country. The government is important because territorial integrity, the well-being of the people, and social order cannot be separated from the effective exercise of the legal coercive force. However, in any case, it is unreasonable to define a country only as a government.

At most, it can be said that the government is the agent of the state. This agent is the artificial person, and government workers are the legal representatives. However, whenever there is an agent, there is a principal, and without a principal, there will be no agent. In the concept of the country there is an implied principal–agent relationship. In the final analysis, the government is entrusted by the country, the people, and the society to exercise the power of legal coercion; this is also why power must be constrained. Putting the principal–agent relationship aside, we come to the question: What is "the will of the state," and where does it originate? If the will of the state is simply the will of the government, or even the will of leaders or officials, with no regard for the requirements, likes, and dislikes of the people, then this kind of will of the state is suspicious in terms of ideology and dangerous in terms of practice. The stronger the "state capacity" to realize this kind of will is, the greater will be the danger of the abuse of power.

If the connotation of the definition the country or state is deviated, state capacity will also follow. For example, the aforementioned quotation simplifies "the state's capacity to mobilize socioeconomic resources" into "the state's [actually the government's] capacity to extract fiscal revenue" or "fiscal capacity." Then with a further simplification to quantify, it becomes "the proportion of the government's fiscal revenue in GDP," and the more representative "proportion of the fiscal revenue of the central government" in the eyes of the opinion holder. To put it straight, this is to treat the amount of fiscal revenue extracted by the government as the core indicator to measure the state capacity.

But can the state (the government) capacity be measured his way? In the common sense, we don't define athletes' abilities based on how much meat they eat or how much milk they drink and ignore how fast they run or how high they jump. To measure only the input but not the output, or only the ingestion and consumption but not the contribution in defining the athlete's capability, is a deviation; it would be equally so in defining the government or the state capacity. It is just a game of figures to enumerate the proportions of fiscal income of all the countries without consideration to the concept of public finance, to the source and destination of the revenue, and to its service targets, evaluation standards, extraction procedures, and degree of supervision.

Moving on to the "legalization capacity," which is referred to as "the ability of a country to use political symbols to create consensus among its people and then to consolidate its ruling position," the question becomes: Where does the "consensus" come from? Shouldn't it be based on practical experience? And, shouldn't the virgin creations by the civilians and grassroots be respected so as to timely incorporate the institutional reforms which are suitable for the development of productivity into the legal framework? Per the above-cited definition, none of these seems necessary; all that is needed is the "political symbols" to "create" the "consensus," which serves to "consolidate its ruling position." And yet, this theory is a total fallacy.

Further, "the coercive capacity" "refers to a country's ability to use methods, organs, or deterrence of violence to maintain its ruling position." Such coercion is dangerous is because once the people and the meaning of authorization and entrustment are removed from the concept of the country, the abuse of power or abuse of legal coercive force can easily become a danger in the reality. In theory, public affairs cannot be regulated without legal coercive force. Nonetheless, legal coercive force is a sharp weapon of the state, which must be used with caution according to strict procedures and with supervision. The key to shut the power into the cage is to put legal coercive force into the confines of rule of law. It is a pity that these substantive constraints are largely ignored in the above-quoted explanation as if the door of the tiger cage could be left perpetually wide open just to "maintain the ruling position."

Based on the above discussions, I believe that the aforementioned definition of "state capacity" in the early 1990s is incorrect, connotatively incomplete, and unable to withstand the test of experience. Conceptual deviation objectively affects the actual operations of state power such that certain deviated use of power also takes place. Based on personal observations, I believe the following points are worth noting.

First, in the distribution of national income, the share taken by government departments rises too quickly. According to published statistics, between 1990 and 2012 fiscal revenue increased by a factor of 38.9 (of that, central government fiscal revenue increased by a factor of 55.6); however, during the same time period, the total GDP as calculated using current prices only increased by a factor of 26.6, and urban residents' disposable income and the per capita net income of rural residents only saw increases by a factor of 15.3 and 10.5, respectively.[6] The

6 Calculated as per data on P44/328/376 of China Statistical Yearbook, 2013.

distribution with increased share for the state and decreased share for the people squeezes private consumption and private investment—which then leads to weak domestic demand. Furthermore, the aforementioned fiscal revenue does not include the government's "land finance" or its benefits from state-owned enterprises (SOEs); therefore, the actual share by the government is even larger. The problems here all have their own causes and cannot be generalized. However, it is undeniable that this conceptual deviation—the mistaken belief that higher government revenue naturally represents stronger "state capacity"—has enhanced the situation.

An even more serious problem is that the rapid increase in government financial strength has not come with relevant restraints or supervision. In recent years, why have the corruption, hedonism, and extravagance suffusing the officialdom become worse? The economic foundation of the problem is that the unrestricted "state (government) extractive capacity" has been growing by leaps and bounds. If we do not press the brake, the more gets extracted by (government) power, the more danger the country will face.

A second consideration is the boundaries of the government's administrative power. The government has more and more power after several rounds of reform. A general observation suggests that our products market has taken shape, whereas the factors market is far away from reaching its reform goal. A closer look reveals that there is still excessive improper government control and approvals in the product market, and—at the same time—inadequate quality supervision. As for the factors market, the problem is even worse. In the past, under the planned economy, "factories were managed by ministries." Currently, however, it's mostly a case of "ministries regulate [factor] markets." Every important factor market is directly managed by a certain ministry; but what about the methods of managing? They are a bit different from the ways of managing factories in the past, but still without much progress. The consequence, just as expected, is that today's frequent economic problems are precisely concentrated with the factors markets, which are directly managed by the ministries—land, real estate, currency, banks, capital, and foreign exchange. Otherwise, why would the government bother to keep themselves so busy regulating, regulating, and regulating?

Third, the scope of "legalization" is overly narrow. The country's capacity for legalization is not—nor should it be—limited to serving the government, its departments, and its officials. For the original creations by civilians, businesses and enterprises, markets, and grassroots, as long as they do not infringe on the freedom of others and social interest, the attitude should be open and inclusive and to give them timely legal recognition. We must avoid such practices by which anything without approval—or even without the nod of officials—is illegal. As we must see, "legalization of departmental interests" and the arbitrary behavior of some officials in squeezing the civilian's freedom of operation are continuously suppressing innovation and suffocating the economic vitality of the society. Rampant rent-seeking and rent-setting not only poisons the social atmosphere but also increases the system's operating costs and ends up harming a good number of officials as well. Empirically, the world beyond the law is brilliant and nobody will respect the law.

Fourth, the legal coercive force is improperly used and goes beyond the reasonable boundaries. In times past, there was a concept of "internal contradictions among the people," emphasizing that the means of dictatorship should not be arbitrarily used on the people. In more recent years, the boundaries of power have been blurred; episodes have been heard about forced demolitions and relocations and violent law enforcement in some places. It is necessary to crack down any underworld, but to use violence in enforcement is an even more serious problem because it is like the un-caged tiger biting people. If the tiger of power is not contained, how could there be the people's support, justice, order, and rule of law?

These deviations are not the mainstream in China after the reform and opening-up. However, they do exist, and we must be vigilant of their presence. If corrections are delayed for too long, they will endanger our national foundations. To get to the bottom, I believe that deviant definitions of the "country" and "state capacity" hinder people from soberly assessing the degree of danger of deviated use of power. This is not to say that all disturbing behaviors are the result of having read and been convinced by the definition of state capacity as criticized by this chapter. Instead, my point of view is that the deviations in the definitions of the "country" and "state capacity" are the public opinion and theoretical expression for the deviated power. The deviations make the tendencies that may produce long-term adverse consequences seem not dangerous, or even very correct and very necessary such that the circumstances do not need, or even should not be allowed, to change.

The present chapter argues that it is necessary to redefine state and state capacity. The concept of the state includes the territory, the people, and the institution of governance. Of this, government power, built on the legal coercive force, is not God-given or obtained by heavenly mandate. Instead, it comes from the people's choice, it should be supervised by the people, and it should serve the people on the trajectory of rule of law. Therefore, the state does not equate to the government, and state capacity does not equate to government capacity and still less to fiscal resource extraction capability. State capacity, in the first place, is the ability to govern the power entrustment relationship, whereby the government is entrusted to obtain financial resources, to administer in accordance with the law, to safeguard the independence of national sovereignty and protect the safety of people's lives and property, and to maintain social justice and order. Is this understanding also a deviation? Readers are welcome to make comments and explore together.

Establishment of Rights Cannot Be Circumvented[7]

The Third Plenary Session of the Eighteenth CPC Central Committee made the decision to comprehensively deepen the Reform. As explained by General Secretary Xi Jinping, this decision "brings together new ideology, new judgments, and new measures for comprehensively deepening the Reform; reflects the voice, demands, and expectations of the society; and pools together the ideological consensus and the wisdom of action from the entire Party and the entire society on comprehensively deepening the Reform."[8] The present chapter will just offer the author's understanding of the statement of "Improving the Property Right System" as a part of the *Decision by CPC Central Committee on Several Major Questions Related to Comprehensively Deepening the Reform* (hereafter, the *Decision*).

In the past, popular belief was that after public ownership is established in socialism, there would no longer be issues with property rights. China's experience proves that this kind of understanding is wrong. Looking at things from the current perspective, we can see that both the state ownership system in cities and the collective ownership system in rural areas are just the initial choices of the early stages of socialism; not only do they need to be further improved, but also they need to be reformed. In reforming the system of public ownership property rights, the essence is to establish all the actual rights of the property so as to lay a solid foundation for the market economy.

7 The original title of this section was "Establishment of Rights Cannot Be Circumvented—An Understanding from Studying the *Decision,*" as published in 2014 in the first issue of the *Economic Research Journal*.—Editor's note.

8 Quoted from Xi Jinping's Explanations on the Decision by CPC Central Committee on Several Major Questions Related to Comprehensively Deepening the Reform.—Editor's note.

First, let us look at the state ownership system in cities. Nominally, state-owned assets belong to the entire people. But in point of fact, technically the state-owned assets belonging to the entire people cannot be integrated with the whole people, and they can only be engaged in production and operation when part of the asset is combined with a portion of the people (i.e., workers and managers). So this presents a challenge: How should the boundary of rights be set between the people actually using some of state-owned assets and the entire people nominally owning all the state assets? The old method was for the administrative government agencies to manage state-owned enterprises "on behalf of the whole people." As a result, the property rights of the whole people evolved into highly centralized administrative control, and the entire national economy became like a single super company which rejected market relations and the autonomy of state-owned enterprises.

Switching to the rural collective ownership system, from the perspective of legal ownership rural land and other productive resources belong to farmers' collectives. But in point of fact, the relationship of rights between the farmers' collective and the rights of the state was never clearly defined. Although the land, labor animals, and the productive labor force all belonged to the collective, what to grow, what to raise, and to whom and at what prices to sell agricultural products must be controlled by government instructions. Within the collective, the rights boundary of members remained yet to be delineated. As a matter of fact, the institutional arrangement had it that the collective did not have the power to determine various rights of its own members. For example, the decision by the production team to contract farm land to farmers was illegal for quite a while, and the production team was not allowed to transfer its own resources.

The reforms undertaken since the Third Plenary Session of the Eleventh CPC Central Committee have touched both the urban state ownership system and the rural collective system. With regard to the reform of state-owned enterprises, China's experience was to start with expanding the autonomy of enterprises, introduce various types of contract responsibility systems, and allow state-owned enterprises to go bankrupt and restructure, and then take the standardized path towards joint-stock enterprises. The essence was to push state-owned enterprises into an increasingly open market, to try to break administrative monopoly, and—within the general framework of the market economy—to redefine the rights boundary between state-owned enterprises and the state, between state-owned enterprises and other state-owned enterprises, and between state-owned enterprises and domestic and foreign private-owned enterprises. The reform of the rural collective system was done via the household responsibility system for collective land to establish the rights of rural households as members of the collective, such as the planting rights, operating rights, income rights, and transfer rights. The contracting system was also extended to collectively owned mountain forests, water surfaces, township enterprises, and land for construction. The farmers' enthusiasm for production was greatly stimulated.

This opening-up was mainly intended to open up to the global market and allow all sorts of foreign private capital to set up factories and enterprises or to invest in the mainland. In addition, with the lawful status granted to the domestic private economy, some of the income from different types of contracting in the urban and rural areas and private savings continuously became domestic private capital. The Chinese economy has finally broken the monotonic public ownership and has formed a new property rights landscape where public ownership serves as the mainstay, with multiple forms of ownership competing under co-existence.

The new policy of reform and opening-up must be adhered to, and new experiences must be affirmed, but it is also necessary to face new problems squarely. Because of the gradualist reform strategy, what's easy has been reformed and what's difficult has remained unchanged. As a result, there are still frequent frictions and conflicts in the arrangement of the property rights system. The most prominent problem is that the market status for entities with different types of ownership is not equal, and the boundaries for multiple types of property rights are not clearly delineated, which, in turn, limits the healthy development of the market system.

Targeted at the aforementioned reality, the *Decision* proposes to "improve the property rights protection system," points out that "property rights are the core of ownership," and clearly states that "[we must] improve to have a sound modern property rights system with clear attribution of ownership, clearly determined rights and responsibilities, strict protections, and smooth circulation .... [Under this system] the property rights of public ownership economy shall not be infringed, and equally the same of non-public ownership economy shall not be infringed." This statement is the program of action for comprehensively deepening property rights reform in the next step.

My take on this is that there are three main points. First, not only must the ownership be clearly ascribed, but the right to actually control, use, operate, and dispose of the property in various types of ownership systems must also be clearly delineated––with clearly determined rights and responsibilities as well as strict protections. To deepen the reform, the problems left behind by previous halfway property rights reforms must be targeted and resolved. We must ensure that there will be clear property rights boundaries for everyone, be it the managers or employees of SOEs, joint-stock enterprises or private enterprises, or the contracting household of the rural collective economy. Only by doing this can the expectations become more stable and behaviors more standardized.

Second, all types of ownership systems and all types of actual property rights must be equal before the law. The task of the state is not to prioritize the protection of any one kind of ownership or any one category of property right and discriminate or ignore other types of ownership and property rights. For a country governed by the rule of law, the most important thing is the equal protection of all lawful ownership and property rights. This is also the institutional foundation to achieve the goal of "motivating all types of labor, knowledge, technology, management, and capital to give full play to their vigor, and encouraging every fountain of social wealth to surge." The existing fruits of reform have established multiple types of ownership and multiple types of property rights, but they are still far from being equality under the rule of law. This is the goal to be achieved by deepening the reforms.

Third, in effective protection of property rights, not only must the right of stable long-term use be protected but also the right of smooth transfer must be protected even better. This is because any resource has many possible ways of use; this includes the situation whereby the same entity uses the resources in different ways to produce different benefits, and also the situation whereby different entities use the resources to produce different benefits. Protecting property rights means protecting the owner of the property rights in their choice of different ways of resources use, which include giving up the right of use and transferring it to someone else. This protection of rights is the foundation of the market economy. We cannot see that protecting property rights means that resources can never change hands or be transferred. Such strict adherence to the ideal of self-sufficiency with regard to resources will actually serve to jeopardize the development of the division of labor and transactions, and this—in point of fact—can never be allowed to happen. It must be clear that—on the basis of open, equitable and impartial transactions—the "smooth flow" of all resources, including both state-owned assets and collective assets, is a must in property rights protection.

None of the above three points can be dispensable. For "the market to play a decisive role in the allocation of resources," the foundation is precisely a sound modern property rights system. This explains why the establishment of rights cannot be circumvented in adopting the market economy. To "improve the system of property rights protection" is a cornerstone projects for the comprehensive deepening of the reforms.

Let More People Benefit from the Reform[9]

Nowadays everyone is interested in knowing how to firmly push forward the reform in accordance with the *Decision* made by the Third Plenary Session of the Eighteenth CPC Central Committee. I think everyone knows that to advance the reform there must be many difficulties. But why is advancing reform so difficult? Because, first and foremost, the reforms will touch the vested interest and change the existing interest structure. Reform is not the same as revolution in that it offends the vested interest but gives more or less some compensation. Many times a reform fails to be initiated because there is not enough principal to pay the compensation, then after delays the reform gets a rushed start but quite easily leads to social conflicts. This has happened throughout history. At present, China's reform has entered deep waters, so the vested interest to be offended is quite large. Although China's national strength is much greater than thirty years ago, the price to compensate the vested interest has also gone up. I'm afraid that no one can afford to compensation for everything. Given this situation, do we still need to reform? How can we effectively push forward the reform? From previous experience I think there may be one method, or one path, that is worthy of attention. That is to say, in addition to resolutely offending the vested interest which is unavoidable, the reform should, to the best of its ability, allow as many people as possible to benefit from it, rapidly form new vested interest, and form beneficiary groups that are consistent with the direction of the reform.

Let us take a look at the experience after the Third Plenary Session of the Eleventh CPC Central Committee. At that time, the reform to the people's commune system also bumped up against vested interest. Under the "big rice pot" system, the people who gave orders in rural production—the ones who had the power to distribute grain and grass—had lots of power and they were able to determine the fates of others' families. After the implementation of the household contract responsibility system, this power was eradicated, and, of course, the vested interest was contravened. The conditions back then didn't allow for compensation because the production team and the nation were poor and unable to pay compensation. With that being the case, how was the reform advanced? Built on the successes of local trials and experiments, the household contract

9 This section is based on a speech given by the author at the 15th Anniversary Dinner of *Caijing Magazine* on November 20, 2013, and was originally published in *Caijing* 2014, Volume 1.—Editor's note.

responsibility system was rolled out across the country chunk by chunk. Soon every household produced more food and sold the excess for more money, and thus the starvation problem of even the farmers themselves was resolved. Most farmers benefited from the reform and became a new vested interest group related to the household contract responsibility system. Once a tipping point in the number of people had been reached, the reform became unstoppable. The former grassroots-level village cadres—those capable ones—quickly switched to sideline businesses or set up township enterprises, which was way better than ringing the bell to tell the farmers to go to work. And they also became a new vested interest. A small number of the incapable of them could only blame themselves for being good for nothing.

This is the case with reforms in other aspects. Take a moment and think back—why do we say that the pre-1985 period is the golden age of China's reform? Because most people benefit from the reform. The reform in the rural areas benefited hundreds of millions of farmers. The legalization of self-employed businesses and private enterprises benefited more than a 100 million people. The resumption of *gaokao*, or the college-entrance exam, brought hopes to several million young people every year. These young people, plus their family members, are no small percentage of the population. Tens of thousands of intellectual elites are encouraged every year by liberalizing overseas study. The "four qualities" policy for cadres (per Deng Xiaoping's speech on August 18, 1980, they are to be revolutionary, youthful, knowledgeable, and professional) has led to a large number of young and promising officials standing out from the crowd. Each time a market is opened up, a new batch of first-movers will benefit. Experience proves that the greater the number of people benefiting from the reform, the harder it will be for the reform to be reversed or negated. There will always be people dissatisfied with the reform, but they are the outnumbered minority and have to gradually adapt themselves.

To go back and ask ourselves, have all of Deng Xiaoping's decisions been fully kept up with and supported? Probably not, because it is not possible. However, on the whole I support the reform and the opening-up. Why? Because I, myself, was a new college student for Grade 1978 (by year of entrance). If it were not for Deng's decisive call to resume the college entrance examination, I would never have had the opportunity to attend college! I have no choice, as I myself am a beneficiary of the reform!

SOE reform is difficult. However, so long as we attend to it, the reform will bring along some new interests. In market competition, there will always be some SOEs that are able to make money, and along with this there will always be entrepreneurs who earn new social status. Lenovo, Haier, Gree, and TCL are all fruits of SOE restructuring. Without restructuring and reform, these good companies would not exist. China's capital market opened in 1990, when Deng Xiaoping said that we can go ahead and close it if it doesn't work. The results of practical experience have shown that this market cannot be closed after opening. Why? Because folks like Yang Huaiding (a legendary stock trader, who became a millionaire by trading stocks) wouldn't agree. So many new interest groups are reaping the benefits or hoping to benefit from the capital market, how could it be possible to close it?

Of course, it is also possible for the benefiting vested interest to become the obstacles for further reform, so it is necessary to continue with the reform. To continue, attention should be paid to the rapid formation of new vested interests and push forward rounds after rounds. To make just one shot and bring the reform to success is a beautiful dream that cannot achieve real progress. These experiences only serve to show that no matter how conceptually or theoretically correct the established goals are, it is actually quite difficult to move the reform forward without forming new vested interests. The success of the reforms in the early 1980s lies in that new beneficiary groups were quickly formed during the reform process with sufficient number of people. I believe that this experience will also work in the process of comprehensively deepening the reform.

We have many friends coming to this *Caijing* event today, and all of us care about whether these new reform decisions can be implemented and what we can do to achieve real progress in the reform. I can think of a few points for your reference:

First of all, today's reform is different from years ago. We have many existing laws that must be followed. But what to do when some legal provisions go against the full-scale deepening of the reform? If this question is not resolved, a decision is just a decision and it will be difficult to get implemented. Taking the land system as an example, the legal text says that rural collective land cannot be sold or bought, rented, leased, or transferred and that farmers' houses cannot be collateralized. All of these are written in black and white into the existing law. To this end, I would like to call on the legislature, including people from all walks of life, to do a sorting to existing laws and legal regulations and benchmark with the *Decision* of the plenary session, list all the severely conflicting clauses, and then revise them through legal revisions and amendment procedures. And I suggest to abolish some of them (if needed). Otherwise, it will not work to violate the law to push forward the reform. If the law does not get revised or amended after the *Decision* is taken, the decision will remains as decisions, and the law and regulation remains what it was—we can talk about it for several years but the reform doesn't get moving. Time passes very quickly!

Second, the *Decision* has clearly pointed out that the market should play a decisive role, and that the market system should be improved with a focus on factor markets. This is also a key threshold so far for economic development. In this direction, attention should be focused on intensively advancing reform in certain areas on increasing the concentration of reform elements and the density of reform measures. Because the factor market is different from the product market, fanning out the reform is ineffective; there is no need to open up markets in every township and every county. The factor markets is relatively concentrated, financial markets are even more concentrated, and price discovery has to take place in the central market. This is very important for China. Because China does not have enough talents, enough lawyers, and still fewer numbers of qualified supervisors, if high-end factor market construction gets scattered, it will be turned into nothing wherever it is attempted. Therefore, the strategy needs to focus and aggregate and do a good job in building the factor markets in the central metropolises.

Third, in implementing the *Decision,* in addition to abstract principles and guidelines, it is even more important to pay attention to "live pictures," namely real stories and real scenarios. From the perspective of communication, pictures speak louder than abstract text. The emphasis on the private economy has been raised to the highest level in its history. This is very important, because it is a decision by the central government. But regarding the question of whether the *Decision* can be effectively implemented, lots of talking will not be as convincing as real stories. An example: When Deng Xiaoping affirmed the private economy, he seized the story of the "Fool's Melon Seeds."[10] He said "don't touch him" over and over again for several years, and so everyone knew he was serious. Currently, when it comes to implementing reforms, we need pictures badly. We hope *Caijing* can report a number of good stories about the reform so that people will be able not only to understand the provisions but also take them seriously and not end up with empty talking. For example, on the topic of disaffiliating universities, public institutions, and hospitals from the administrative system, it is useless to just talk about, and few early-mover examples will always be necessary to form a wave of

10 In general, the "fool's melon seeds" refers to private businesses which were considered capitalist and owned by members of the proletariat. It is specifically a reference to the tycoon Nian Guangjiu, who had started out as an illiterate sunflower seed roaster.

momentum for the reform. Otherwise, people will no more believe it if we talk about it for years without doing anything.

Fourth, people usually think that reforms will move the vested interest and compartmental interest; this is correct. However, the actual situation is that both vertically at different rankings or horizontally across different functions or regions, there is also a force within government agencies which advocates reform. The question is how to create an atmosphere or a public opinion that helps to motivate the power of governmental departments and reduce their resistance to reform. One important aspect may be to formulate a real accountability mechanism related to pushing forward the reform after the central government's decision taken to comprehensively deepen the reform. Over the past few years, we have seen a bad phenomenon—to see the reform as the business for the local level. Some senior officials are used to finding faults and saying this is not right, that is not right. It just seems that they themselves have no responsibility for ensuring the implementation of reform decisions. In the 1980s, not a few pilot reform areas were set up at the local regions, the relevant central government departments also actively participated. Whether it was the Shenzhen Special Economic Zone, or the later opening-up of Shanghai, it was never only a local responsibility. Ameliorating the dangers of deep waters via reform cannot be achieved by local governments alone; it must be done via interactions between the top and bottom with aligned efforts. As we can see from the experiences, it is necessary to put more responsibility on the relevant central government departments in relation to advancing the reform. Only when such a public opinion and atmosphere are formed can the power to advocate reform within the departments rise up and the reformist cadres take over.

Crossing the River by Feeling the Stones

Before the Eighteenth CPC National Congress, people were having all sorts of heated discussions about the path which China should take in the future. The Eighteenth CPC National Congress concluded: "[We must] continue to comprehensively deepen the reform." On the same road in Shenzhen as Deng Xiaoping had walked on, General Secretary Xi Jinping said: "The reforms should not stop, the opening-up should continue to move forward." So the question is, what methods should be used to advance the reform and opening-up?

Crossing the River by Feeling the Stones: Top-Level Design and Virgin Creation From Practice

From experience, there were several methods. In the early days of the reform and opening-up, "crossing the river by feeling the stones" was proposed as the methodology for the reform back in the 1980s and originally related to the rural reform. In a period around the Third Plenary Session of the Eleventh CPC Central Committee, the output quota was contracted to households in many places at the grass-root level because the farmers were impoverished and could not have enough food to feed themselves for many years. The phenomenon was investigated, studied, and analyzed by some provinces such as Anhui and Sichuan, and some local policies were formulated to support this reform. Afterwards, the practice was accepted and affirmed by the central government with five successive No.1 Documents.[11] This is the first typical example of crossing the river by feeling the stones.

The second stone to get touched was the private economy. Once the problem of food and clothing was solved, where should the surplus labor, who loafed on their job within the commune system, now go? State-owned and collective enterprises did not have such a large absorption capacity, so the private economy was put on the agenda. At its earliest, the private economy was also something popping up from the bottom level. The story of Chen Zhixiong and his fish ponds[12] in Guangdong or "the Fool's Melon Seeds" in Wuhu both involved hiring workers by private enterprises. This was unacceptable according to previous concepts, which believed that such actions were incompatible with socialism. The central leadership's opinions toward this were also inconsistent. So Deng Xiaoping made the decision to hold for a longer while and see what would happen, and the policy recognition was not granted until 1987.

11 Between 1982 and 1986, the CPC Central Committee successively published five "No.1 Documents": *The Minutes of Meeting of the National Conference on Rural Work*, *Several Questions Facing Current Rural Economic Policies*, *Notice Regarding Rural Work in 1984*, *Ten Policies on Further Energizing the Rural Economy*, and *Deployment on Rural Work in 1986*.

12 A farmer in the Shapu Commune #6 Production Team, Chen Zhixiong's initial contracting of fish ponds during the early years of reform and opening-up led to a dispute over hiring workers and whether or not he had moved so far from collectivism as to be purely capitalist. Because it was one of the earlier cases of its kind, it would end up being a landmark event.

When the reform was extended from villages into cities, the question became complicated because a slight move of one small thing could affect the whole system. Therefore, around 1986 or so, a comprehensive overall reform was planned for the entire economic system, covering prices, taxation, commerce, import and export, fiscal revenue, and SOEs. The decision on economic system restructuring adopted at the Third Plenary Session of the Twelfth CPC Central Committee is quite systematic, and Deng Xiaoping said his impression was that it is a new book of political economics. The phrase "top-level design" was not used, but the content was already there. At the same time, systematic reform of the political system was also brought on the agenda; the relevant departments made lots of investigation and study and prepared a plan, which they submitted to the Thirteenth National Party Congress for discussion and approval.

By the 1990s, particularly after Deng Xiaoping made the inspection tour to South China and mentioned the question of market economy, which covered a more extensive scope, the reform decision adopted by the Third Plenary Session of the Fourteenth CPC Central Committee set the goals for a socialist market economy and proposed a systemic reform that would allow the market mechanism to become the basis for resource allocation.

Another dozen years passed, and around the time to set the "Twelfth Five-Year Plan" the formal proposal was made to "strengthen top-level design." The meaning of this is that reforms should not conflict with each other, that we need to avoid having the reforms work here but not work elsewhere, and that we need to consider the overall picture.

These experiences are very meaningful. Among these, there is one thing that is worth thinking: Why do we still need to launch the reform again and again after it has been planned with all aspects having been taken into account? Was it because the original design was incomplete or because the reform was delayed as a result of resistance during implementation? As we can currently see, determining the goals, the scheme design, and the implementation of the reform are three interrelated links in a chain. The goals must be clear; they can't go first one way only to turn around and then go the other way. The scheme must be systematic and comprehensive and, as much as possible, take all aspects into consideration. Implementation depends on both the environment and the timing, and it's important to select a good breakthrough point.

Facing the Flying Stone

We also need to see that now the situation is no longer what it was back in the 1980s or the 1990s, or at the beginning of the new century. China has been through the reform for more than three decades, and many new situations have emerged. The central and local governments, the grassroots, the general public, enterprises, and all sorts of organizations––all of them have encountered new problems. In particular, the information received by young people, their demands, their awareness of rights, and their views on social issues are all very different from the previous generation.

Can it be said that for the people in power it is not just a matter of feeling for the stones beneath the water to design the scheme to advance the reform—some stones, large and small, have risen above the surface to test the decision makers every day? Many sharp questions have actually risen out of the water for a long time; do we need to face them, and how? Sometimes, a phenomenon occurs again and again. Sometimes, the outbreak of a contingent event, like throwing a stone into the water and causing ripples, affects many aspects and attracts the attention of the entire society, which demands answers and responses and wants to see whether positive energy can be absorbed from the event into policy and institution formulation.

To give an example, how much has happened to the land relationships between farmers? Even though reforms in this aspect started very early, the stones are quite big. Everyone says the household responsibility contracting system will stay there over the long term, and it seems that the problem has already been resolved. The earliest saying was the will remain for fifteen years, then for thirty years, then it became long-term at the time of the Third Plenary Session of the Seventeenth CPC Central Committee. In answering questions from a foreign journalist, Premier Wen Jiabao stated that "long-term" means "forever." All these sayings are correct, because practice has proven that the effective economic system should not be changed. However, if we walk into the countryside and take a look, it is not so difficult to see that land relationships are, in actuality, often "changed." Why is this happening? Because even though the people's commune system has been abolished, the genes of the collective system are still there.

To clarify, the (rural) collective economy is not the post–Land Reform when land became the farmer's private property, nor is it a cooperative economic system based on farmer's private property and voluntary agreements. After the Land Reform, the boundary of farmers' private property was very clear; it was impossible to take some land from someone else and give it to you just because your family population grows quickly. The cooperative works the same way. Joining a cooperative is like injecting equity into a company; an increase or decrease in family population does not change the property rights within the cooperative. But in the "collective," everyone is put together in one single pot: all the people of the village—those already born and those to be born—enjoy a share in the land rights. As a result, the land rights boundary between farmers gets changed as the population changes. This is the essence of the collective system. After the implementation of the household contract responsibility system, the central government says the policy will not change. However, in point of fact, as the population of rural households change, there are always requirements for land adjustment in accordance with the rules of the collective economy. Adjusting the land is a change; therefore, we haven't achieved the goal of "no change forever."

Midway through the 1980s, Meitan County of Guizhou Province, as a pilot reform area, brought up this question. Guizhou was relatively backward, with a very large rural productive force concentrated on farming; if the land was adjusted and changed every year, why would anyone do good farming and invest into the land? Therefore, the local government proposed the idea that "the land will not be increased with population increase, or decreased with population decrease." This is to say, to draw a clear boundary for the land property rights of rural households. This experiment proved to work in the region and was later promoted in central government documents and was even written into *the Law on Rural Land Contracting of the People's Republic of China* in 2002. The problem is that it was not implemented across all parts of the country; at least half of the rural communities make adjustments to contracted land every few years. So what exactly is the problem all about? Is it because the law is wrong? Or is it a problem that the law is not followed? If this is not sorted out, the land circulation (transfer) will be restricted because the entire population—both current and future—of a specific geographic area are locked together by a physical asset, namely the small piece of land, forming a permanent debt chain. Under this chain, to transfer a piece of land equals to have also transferred the rights of other households for future land adjustment.

Even the farmers' house sites in the rural areas are treated as a physical fringe benefit and isolated from lawful circulation, transaction, and the market. House sites in themselves are means of subsistence and do not need to be included in the scope of socialist transformation. However, after the people's commune movement, in 1961 a red-letter document (namely official document, usually from the central government) abolished the Land Reform Law and announced that residence sites are also collective land of the production team. Because the land belongs to the collective, the aforementioned guidelines for all the people to continuously share the physical benefit is applicable, and when every farmer gets married and establishes a household, he is assigned a piece of land as home site. In the past, with the separation between urban and rural areas, this would seem to be no big deal. However, as farmers move into cities as migrant workers, countless empty villages and empty houses are left unused, but there is no lawful channel for circulation. Premier Wen says that land is a property right of the farmers, and he is right. However, property rights include (or should include) the right of transfer, so leasing, buying and selling, and mortgaging should be allowed. Yet, up till now, all these rights remain unlawful. Is this one of the stones?

Along with the free economic expansion, industrialization and urbanization are also accelerating. But the collective genes from the people's commune are still a hindrance for farmers, preventing them from responding to higher income opportunities. My personal view is that this stone has risen out of the water for a long time, and the key is how our philosophies, policies, and regulations will deal with it. Turning a blind eye or pretending that the problem does not exist will only cause the problem to become a slap in the face every day.

An even bigger stone is the land relationship between government and farmers. Currently, social contradictions in this aspect are very acute; many mass incidents, major corruption cases, even the approbation or reprobation of the people, are all somewhat related to this. The basic framework has a problem, such as "all urban land being state-owned," the existence of a unilateral land acquisition system which does not distinguish land use, as well as the determination of land acquisition compensation by administrative orders. This is just the way the system is, and we can not blame local government or cadres for not solving the problem. To get down to the bottom, we see that the problem involves multiple facets, such as the split of administrative power and fiscal income between central and local governments, the separation between government and enterprises, between government and capital, and between government and land, and so on—are all among the causes. This stone is not easy to handle, and this problem is a tough one because there is yet no overall consideration.

Unexpected Encounters

Currently, the number of stones exposed above the water is actually quite large. To stick to the reform, we must respond to these problems. Facing the stones flying at us, we certainly need to make investigations, studies, evaluations, and analyses and touch them to get a feel. We need to have holistic considerations and prioritize them. Therefore, there is no contradiction between catching the stones and the top-level design, or "crossing the river by feeling the stones."

Has Wenzhou's development in these recent years also encountered such "stones"? I have not made any systematic investigation, so I cannot make a judgment. However, I have come to Wenzhou several times, and I know that a good number of Wenzhou friends are rather unsatisfied with the development of their city. Looking from afar, it is definitely not because of lack of money. Wenzhou is the earliest cradle for China's private economy; however, later it seems unable to aggregate greater wealth; or, in other words, the framework has not formed for the aggregation of more wealth. It's not that there has been no impulse to do so. For example, some ten or fifteen years ago a Wenzhou-based interest group wanted to join forces with private capital to invest in urban infrastructure. Even earlier, the town of Longgang emerged as "a small town run by farmers," trying to come up with a new system for urbanization. However, most regrettably, neither of the two projects came into reality. Without a larger framework for development, Wenzhou also finds it very difficult to reach a higher stage.

An example is private banks, which was brought up as early as in 1984 when we accompanied Du Runsheng[13] to Wenzhou on an investigative trip. With so much private capital, and so many industrial enterprises, why is it that Wenzhou couldn't have lawful and standardized private banks? In this aspect Wenzhou is not as good as Taizhou. Several private banks have been established in Taizhou, and one of them is Tailong, which is a commercial bank created by the expansion of a privately operated small credit cooperative. Now this bank has ten branches in cities such as Shanghai, Hangzhou, and Ningbo and total assets of Ren Min Bi (RMB) 36.5 billion, and it provides excellent services to grassroots micro-enterprises. In the end we have to ask: Is it that Wenzhou doesn't have enough money or enough talents, or is it something else? Perhaps the reason is that we didn't confront and catch the stone flying at us so as to open a new road.

From example, (we can see that) it is very important to respect the local initiative spirit. China is a large country; for many problems related to local practice we cannot purely count on the central government for all the solutions. For local practices to be adopted as globally legitimate, overall holistic consideration must also be made under a clear global goal. Therefore, "crossing the river by feeling the stones" should be combined with top-level design. Can't we add another

13 Du Runsheng (July 18, 1913–October 9, 2015) was a Chinese military officer, revolutionary leader, politician, and economist. He is hailed as "father of China's rural reform."

point? Regarding those problems that long ago floated to the surface, we must not often evade them; rather, we need face them squarely. As Albert Einstein said, "To do scientific research, we shouldn't drill many holes at the thin part of a piece of wood but have no courage to the thick part." The reform works in the same way. For the key issues hindering the long-term development of the national economy, the harder they are, the more we need to address them.

In short, to the advance reform, I am afraid that we need to fight the war in all sorts of forms, including positional fight, guerrilla warfare, and skirmishes. Currently, many problems are coming at us; the "stones" have long been protruding out of the water. Whoever evades will lose the initiative. The trend for the future might probably be that China's reform and transformation will be pushed forward in interactions, including the interactions between the top and the bottom, between concepts and practice, and between design and implementation.

Why Do Profitable State-Owned Enterprises Still Need Deep Reform?[14]

Reviewing the Experience of State-Owned Enterprise Reform

The reform of SOEs has been going on for a long time. The process of reform has been complicated and, up to now, hasn't yet been completed. Discussions on SOE reform particularly need to be based on observable experience. For both science and politics, the starting point of discussion should be the actual situation, the problem and the possible choices available. *The Annals of State-Owned Enterprise Reform from 1998 to 2008* (published by the Economics Science Press in April 2014, hereinafter referred to as *The Annals*) is based on the real stories of frontline experiencers and provides a clear line of history of SOE reform. *The Annals* also summarizes existing experiences and discusses the problems to be resolved in SOE reform. Obviously, because it was written mainly from the perspective of government agencies, the book focuses on the background for reform policy and its formulation, and it records the author's understanding of the logic for SOE reform. I am sure it will be more rewarding if we examine this book together with real-world examples and stories of grassroots-level reform.

14 This section is the author's commentary on Shao Ning's keynote speech delivered at the Second Session of "CF40·Sun Yefang Book Club."—Editor's note.

In theory, SOE reform is almost the "everything" of the reform of the socialist economic system. The concept of the socialist system, on its initial establishment, was for the Bolsheviks to take control of the state machine to create a super state company for the state to employ everyone and implement the planned economy. The market theory emphasizes competition between enterprises, whereas the market economy emphasizes turning the national economy into a super state company. In this sense, the socialist economic system reform and the SOE reform are basically the same topic.

The Annals describes the reform of state-owned enterprises under the jurisdiction of SASAC (State-Owned Assets Supervision and Administration Commission). However, from a broader perspective, finance and other state-owned systems as well as local (governmental) companies are also the products of the decentralization reform of the "super state company." Obviously, because both the Soviet Union and China were underdeveloped, it was therefore impossible, in practice, for the super state company to be pure. The Soviet Union had collective farms; the majority of China's population were farmers, and it was impractical to make each and everything purely state-owned, so the rural collective economy was in existence for a long time. Nonetheless, the non–state-owned part of the rural economy also followed the country's mandatory plan and also served the country's industrialization.

Encircling the City with the Countryside and the SOEs with the Market

In the planned economy, the rural areas supported the low wage, low cost, and high levels of accumulation of SOEs by way of providing cheap agricultural products. As introduced in *The Annals*, at a general discussion meeting on the economy in 1978—when China was still preparing for the reform—an idea was put forward that excessive concentration of power has led to economic inefficiency. At that time China's leaders went out to see the rest of the world and discovered not only that the gap had widened between China and the developed countries but also that quite a number of countries and regions that were less developed than China had become developed after the war. This created a sense of urgency for that generation of leaders, who then hoped that China's economy could accelerate its modernization and put forward the idea of decentralization for the reform. On the basis of experience gained in Sichuan, the Third Plenary Session of the Eleventh CPC Central Committee incorporated strengthening the autonomy of state-owned enterprises into the *Resolution*. This was the first voice of SOE reform. The Third Plenary Session adopted a recuperation policy on the countryside and decided to spend foreign exchange (forex) and import food to alleviate the poverty of farmers. Yet in actual practice, rural villages in Anhui, Guizhou, Sichuan, and Inner Mongolia adopted the household contract responsibility system and became the top runners in the reform; then township enterprises suddenly rose as a new player, and the situation of "cities being encircled by the countryside" was formed for the reform. In this competitive environment, state-owned enterprises would not be stabilized if they didn't get reformed.

The pressure from the opening-up was even greater. In the early years, special economic zones started up on "frontiers" such as Guangdong and Fujian have let in enterprises from Taiwan, Hong Kong, Japan, and Korea. Plus for the domestic township enterprises and domestic private enterprises, whose lawful status was recognized by the 1988 Amendments to the Constitution, competition in the domestic product market became fierce, and SOEs were no longer able to control the situation. The logic behind market competition is really quite simple: Consumers will just select whoever has both high quality and good prices. In the past, the SOEs were superior because they were the only supplier and consumers had no choice. Now the SOEs had competitors, and they couldn't win the game just by talking. What's more, the competition will be transmitted from the product market to the factor market. As a result, the new rule of allocating resources by the price mechanism came into play and a series of market pricing issues was put on the agenda. In point of fact, resource pricing eventually comes down to the delineation of property rights, because in the final analysis, questions like the right to ask for prices, the right to bargain, and which party must bear the operations pressure from price decisions are all just a matter of delineation of property rights. It was precisely in the competitive market environment that the reform to the right of the control, operation, and even legal ownership of the SOEs was put on the agenda.

The pathway for SOE reform formed in this way is very different from that of the Soviet Union. China's experience is to first open a market, push the SOEs into that market, and then use the logic of market competition to push forward the SOE reform. Initially, people accepted the autonomy of the enterprise, then they saw the product pricing rights and the factor pricing rights, and the final analysis went deep down to the delineation of property rights of the enterprise. The people's perception on SOE reform deepens along with the rhythm of the deepening of market reform.

The Desperate Battle, Invigorating Big SOEs and Relaxing Control on Small Ones

At the end of 1997, China crossed the final hurdle for World Trade Organization (WTO) accession. After a five-year preparatory period, China would begin its full-scale integration into the historical process of globalization. Right at this time many SOEs were experiencing huge losses. The challenges were severe: In an environment with limited opening, SOE already lacked competitiveness; how could they survive when the market become fully opened up? China was forced to advance SOE reform, and it was like starting a desperate win-or-die battle.

This is also the highlight of *The Annals*. It should be noted that the peak workforce of China's SOEs back then amounted to more than 100 million. Already the losses experienced by vast numbers of SOEs had nothing to do with the workers in terms of the reason because it was not they who made decisions on the mechanism and management. However, at a time when overburden was common for many SOEs, it was difficult to change the customary practice, the government's pockets were not deep enough to provide the minimum assurance, the banks were unable to help them out, and the stock market didn't have enough capacity, a large number of SOEs had to go bankrupt or be restructured. The number of laid-off workers was tens of millions. For many well-established old SOEs, the whole family of some workers worked in the same factory. So when the enterprises lost money, had wage arrears, or laid off workers, it affected the livelihoods of thousands of families. For China to be able to move itself out of the trouble, the difficulties by no means just arose from the economic aspects; there were also challenges from the perspectives of mindset, social life, and even political framework. As an eyewitness to this arduous and significant reform, I have noted down the situation, the choices faced, the strategies and methods adopted, the difficulties encountered, and the solutions. Even today, it is still soul-stirring to read these records.

As mentioned in the book, the main move was to evaluate the different status of the SOEs in the market competition and seek different ways of breaking out the siege based on actual constraints. Shao Ning's description is very vivid: by no means should they be dealt with in the same way because they are all "state-owned enterprises," but rather small pieces and small pieces were torn off from the big paper of SOEs to seek the solutions for actual problem. In other words, the huge number of SOEs must be split into details to come up with specific solutions, just like the way that the famous butcher Paoding dismembers an ox.

Then the SOEs were categorized. The first category was the majority of small and medium-sized SOEs, with outdated mechanisms, heavy burdens, weak competitiveness, and even severe insolvency. Objectively, it is impossible to for all these enterprises to be reversed from losing money to making profits and to earn a space in the fierce market competition by restoring their SOE identity. The method was first tried and found by Zhucheng in Shandong Province: contracting, disposal, and asset and debt reorganizing, and SOE restructuring were used to put a number of SOEs that had no hope to reverse the money-losing situation back into the market. What they did also included allowing state-owned enterprises to go bankrupt or to be changed into non–state-owned enterprises, and clearing historical debts so that they could start anew in the market environment. You may ask: How big was this piece of paper? As recorded in *The Annals*, there were around one million enterprises and tens of millions of employees. To use the buzz word of those times, this is to release the small ones (namely to relax control on small SOEs).

The second category was larger SOEs operating in a competitive market environment but with poor performance. The relax control approach was not suitable for them because they had large amounts of assets; to sell them at high prices there were few enterprises that could afford to pay, and to sell them at a low price is a violation of the provision on loss of state-owned assets. Anyway, the transformation approach of Zhucheng wouldn't work. For this type of SOE, basically later the framework of the joint-stock system was adopted, which allowed non–state-owned capital to participate as incremental equity and gradually changed their full state ownership. The size of this category? According to *The Annals*, the rough number is about 5,000 big SOEs and tens of million employees.

After the reform of the above two types, the pressure on SOEs to stop losing money was eased. Obviously, eliminating the situation of losing many for the large number of SOEs was achieved not fully under the SOE framework but by restructuring them into non-SOEs or not fully state-owned enterprises. The third and last category is the large SOEs, which underwent merger and reorganization then issued a small portion of equity into overseas of domestic capital market with the state being the controlling shareholder. For this category, SASAC was established to manage the people, the business, and the assets and improve corporate governance. By benchmarking against Fortune 500, this approach has created a number of world-class SOEs or state controlled enterprises.

Why Profitable SOEs Need Deep Reform

The central task for previous wave of SOE reform is to reverse the money-losing situation and increase the profit. This also leads to a perception that whenever SOEs are turned profitable, the remaining task is to grow bigger and stronger, so no further reform is needed. When most SOEs are profitable, especially when the central government-owned enterprises make a total annual profit of several trillion RMB and a number of them become Fortune 500 companies, it is not so pleasant to the ear to say that the reform still needs to be deepened for the SOEs.

The way I see it, it is necessary to make a deep dive into SOE's profitability. First, their paper profit is not always completely the same as the profit in the sense of economics, because part of it might be the rents from their occupied resources. For example, resource-type enterprises often occupy (or have the rights to) a large quantity of exploitable resources, and national telecommunication companies occupy the communications infrastructure. Whosoever occupies these extremely scarce resources will be able to generate income. Therefore, if competition is opened up, any of the non–state-owned enterprises or any of the enterprises that are not controlled by the central government would offer a price and compete for these resources. This price quotation is the rent for the resources rather than profit, and it ought to be deducted from the profit in the financial books of central government–controlled enterprises because it does not represent the true contribution from their efforts in business decision-making or operations.

Second, in the market economy, profit has the orientation function for resource allocation; this is because no matter how profit is generated, it always means that "more resources needs to be invested towards profit generation." In other words, only profit orientation and market access are bound to work together, and only in this way can the fruits of innovation from an enterprise continuously "overflow" to the entire industry, the market, and the national economy. However, under our country's actual conditions, some central government–controlled enterprises obtain high "profits," but their market access is not opened up; other enterprises can only look at the exorbitant profit but cannot join the competition. This type of "closed-market profit" has no positive meaning for the overall economy because it actually constitutes a cost to all other businesses and to consumers. As everyone can see, currently China's cost advance in the global market is fading away quickly. One of the reasons is that for large numbers of China's enterprises, their cost includes the "hard and indigestible" bits. These days, the products and services provided by quite a few central government–controlled enterprises are priced too high, so that it even becomes necessary for central government leaders to call for lower rates. This rightly shows that the "closed-door profit" as a result of inaccessible markets is not a boon but rather a cost burden to the national economy.

Third, the largest part of the huge paper profit of central government–controlled enterprises is retained by themselves for its own disposal. In terms of distribution, the profit is not handed in in full as national fiscal revenue, not to mention to repay the property rights owner, which is the people of the whole country. As for the appropriation of a small part of the profits or assets of central government–owned enterprises as social security, it is essentially nothing more than a compensation for historical debt; the shortfall of China's social security is mainly caused by the fact that workers working for SOE in the days of low salary do not have enough pension, and it was also impossible to withhold enough money. However, state-owned assets did not come only from the contributions of the workers at SOEs; people across the country (including farmers) also contributed to the formation of state assets. Over many years, the low price for the handed-in grains and agriculture tax were also a source for state-owned assets. If we ask what real benefits the farmers have gained from the huge profits from central government–controlled enterprises, I'm afraid the answer is nil. This kind of distribution simply cannot be justified without change.

Fourth, the recent corruption cases with high-ranking people (such as Zhou Yongkang, CNPC, and Ling Jihua) and the result of inspection to a number of central government–controlled enterprises by the Central Disciplinary Inspection Group have exposed a big problem: While enjoying huge profits, assets, and numerous "tangible benefits," SOEs are, to a large extent, a big fat cat locked up inside a bullpen.[15] Morally, logically, and legally on paper, central government–controlled enterprises are obviously SOEs and thus they belong to entire population of the country. However, from the perspective of actual control, the lack of effective supervision from the policy is the common Achilles' Heel for super large SOEs.

To sum things up, that SOEs become profitable is admittedly the result of the previous reform, but this does not mean that the further deepening of reforms is no longer necessary. In terms of urgency, the current situation is no less imperative than the environment for the previous wave of SOE reform back in the 1990s. This is because—from the perspective of opportunity cost analysis—if

15 This is an analogy to say corruption can occur very easily. Because the opening of the bullpen is very large, the cat can escape very easily. This is to say, the system has so many big loopholes that leaders can get corrupt easily.

the reform is not deepened for the currently profitable SOEs, the price will not just be with a certain economic sector but also with the overall national economy; further, it will not only be economic but also social and political.

As for how to deepen SOE reform, reading *The Annals* I find it still enlightening to what we are doing today. The basic line of thinking, as Shao Ning explains, is to categorize the problems and find the answers from practice of reform. I think this approach will still work. Time permitting, we would like to hear Zhao Ning's thoughts on how to categorize the current SOEs and advance the reform in the future.

On-site Interaction

Shao Ning: Different roles and responsibilities lead to different angles of looking at questions. Scholars often see problems more from the perspective of rationalization, such as how should the SOEs be reformed? From the department perspective, they think more about whether the reform path is feasible or not and whether there are risks. Therefore, from a scholar's perspective, we might simply think that there is no problem with privatization. But from a departmental perspective, SOE reform is not so simple and it must be operable. Presently, it is already a fact that our country has so many SOEs. Therefore, the question now is not how to reform the SOEs, and it won't be as easy as most people imagine for the state to withdraw the controlling shares. In fact, our reform of the large SOEs adopts the same approach as Thatcher's and Reagan's governments; that is, to change large SOEs through initial public offering (IPO) into publicly listed companies and gradually ease the burden on the country. The only difference is that after the IPO, the British and American governments sell all the state-owned shares, but China does not. That does not mean these shares cannot be sold; from a long-term perspective, selling can be done.

Just now Qiren Zhou touched on categorized reform. This will be the approach for the next step of SOE reform. To be simple, there will be two categories. The first category is to reform the monopoly SOEs. For example, some state-owned enterprises (Sinopec, CNPC, telecommunication and power grid) currently do not have the authority to set prices on their own; instead, these prices are set completely by the government. NDRC (National Development and Reform Commission) gives the guiding price, and these enterprises—just within the scope of government concessions—provide services to society at the prices set by the government. These kind of enterprises need to be transformed into special enterprises in the market economy which are governed by special law and specific forms of social supervision. The second type is large competitive SOEs. The reform can be done by changing them into companies and IPO. The burden of state ownership can be gradually absorbed. If necessary, the state-owned shares can be reduced. Therefore, I think the prospects for SOE reform are still very clear.

Qiren Zhou: Mr. Shao's wrap-up was brilliant. SOE was compared with a giant sheet of paper, which should be torn off by little pieces. And this is also how SOE reform was done over the past thirty years. Just now Mr. Ren Zhiqiang[16] said why take all the trouble, simply burn them off? My personal point of view is somewhere between the two of them. What kind of property rights system is compatible with the market economy? For a period of time, we reached some consensus, but now we have different opinions. Lu Xun says if a room is too dark, we need to open a window. No one agrees with the approach. But if someone says remove the roof of the house, then people find it easier to accept to open a window. Therefore, sometimes aggressive and radical reform propositions can be helpful in advancing a mild reform. The reform is pushed forward by multiple forces from different angles.

Of course, sharp viewpoints invite sharp oppositions. Historically, during the rural reform, the debate on the household contracting system also went awry. Frequent intense debate made people unable to decide. The intensity decreased when the topic was changed to some concrete practical questions. Therefore, we might need to change the question into "what to do?" and draw the attention of most people toward the problems that need to be solved; doing this will push the reform toward real progress.

16 Ren Zhiqiang (born March 8, 1951) is a former real estate tycoon and member of the Beijing Municipal Committee of the Chinese People's Political Consultative Conference, known for his outspoken criticism of the Communist Party.

2

Economy's Dependence on Megatrend

Economic Dilemma and Breakout[17]

The Chinese economy is facing immense downward pressure. Let's look at the annual rate converted from quarterly rate: To go from the highest growth of 15% in 2007 to the current 7%—and it is still a question mark whether this rate can be maintained and stabilized or not—the growth rate of the world's second largest economy has been cut by half. This is no trivial matter.

So how should we see the economic trend as high growth goes downward?

First, regarding the high growth: No one can deny that more than 14% is an unusually high rate; it is quite rare to maintain greater than 10% annual growth even for small economies, not to mention for a large economy such as China. So, where does the high growth rate come from for this large country of ours? China has a large population and was rather poor before the reform and opening-up; even the farmers didn't have enough to eat. So what is the driving force behind the enormous changes in China? To obtain new insights we need to review the past. There have been three waves of reform to drive China's economic growth.

17 This section is based on the author's speech given at the 3rd ChinaStone October Management Forum on October 31, 2015.—Editor's note.

The first wave was the rural reform coming after the Third Plenary Session of the Eleventh CPC Central Committee, which solved the food and clothing problem for farmers, started to supply sufficient food and agricultural products to the domestic market, and supported the development of light industry and cities.

The second wave was the legalization of private enterprise. Especially after 1992, the rope binding China with the question "if the reform is socialist or capitalist" was untied.

The third wave was the opening-up. From the earliest four special economic zones and fourteen open coastal cities all the way to World Trade Organization (WTO) accession, China became open across the board; this was the biggest push to China's economic growth.

To use a vivid analogy to describe this, the three waves have connected two sea levels. One is the high sea level, namely the United States, Japan, and Europe, with high levels of modernization and a per-capita GDP ranging from 10,000 to several dozen thousand U.S. dollars (USD). These countries have large domestic markets with strong purchasing power. The other is the low seal level, which is the emerging developing countries. Most of them became independent after World War II and put a great deal of emphasis on national sovereignty. And as they were influenced by the then-dominant economic thinking, they also believed that sovereignty could only be maintained by the close-the-door construction and developing the economy by import substitution, so they did not have much dealings with developed countries. Therefore, for many years, international trade and international investment primarily took place between developed countries. Between the sea levels, the per capita income difference was a factor of nearly 100 times, and the potential gap was huge.

China's opening and reform, led by Deng Xiaoping, and the subsequent opening of India and the disintegration of the Soviet Union, worked together to open up a channel between the world's two seal levels. Because the water-head gap was so large, once the two levels became connected, the largest wave of global economic potential since the Industrial Revolution was released. This led to a significant change in the global landscape.

First and foremost was the capital and technology falling down from the high sea level. Capital and technology always go to places with a high degree of scarcity because the returns are higher; this is in line with the logic of economics. For the Chinese economy to be as it is today, our own efforts are important but not sufficient; we also need large amounts of capital, technology, business models, and information from overseas. Before the opening-up, Chinese people worked equally hard; however, to close the door to build the economy, no matter how hard the efforts were, the key bottlenecks could not be resolved and therefore high growth was impossible.

Obviously, the low seal level also needs to reform itself and change the system and the mechanism that restrict development so as to emancipate the productive forces. It may be hard to imagine, but China's total export in 1980 was only USD 10 billion, and most of that was from resource products. Along with the opening and reform, especially with the development of the private economy, labor-intensive businesses and small and medium-sized enterprises started to export large volumes of products; the comparative cost advantage was fully leveraged to form a huge convection between the high and low seal levels and allowed "Made in China" to establish its foothold throughout the world.

Within this development, there are three key elements:

First, China has lots of low-cost labor. China suffered for a long time from poverty before it was opened up, and it didn't realize that "poverty" was also a kind of competitiveness until its opening-up. Because of the poverty, the wages and the labor costs were also low. For the same products, of course, low costs means competitiveness. The prices for production factors were also very low, but in fact that was just the result of long-lasting poverty. As a result of China's huge population and labor force, once the potential gets released, the change in the global market is drastic.

Second, China learned from the Soviet Union in the past and tied its own limbs with an ossified institutional mechanism. After the emancipation of minds and the opening and the reform, Chinese people were willing to venture and try, and so the market economy got built, the improper controls were gradually removed, the lawful existence of private enterprises was acknowledged, and thus the system operation cost and organizational cost for the national economy were significantly reduced.

Third, activities of the market economy highlighted the importance of knowledge and skills, motivating people to learn by doing and to invest more into human capital; as a result, the Chinese people's learning curve continued to rise, and in all aspects the quality of products was soon brought up to close to the world's advanced level.

The rise of China's economy from the low sea level is attributable to the comparative cost advantage formed by the combination of the above three items.

Around the year 2000, developed countries started to invest heavily in China. The Ford Motor Company asked itself to locate a factory in the United States or in China when it decided to increase the auto production capacity. Investors and entrepreneurs will make comparisons across the globe and look at the market capacity and the cost advantage; China's rapid export-oriented growth was formed within this context.

Of course, globalization also can foster new problems. The rise of emerging market economies could not help but change the original global landscape. In 2007, the financial crisis detonated from the United States swept across the world; the external demand of developed countries dropped and their imports fell, and correspondingly China's export annual growth fell from 20% to 30% in previous years to -20%, for a drop of nearly 50 percentage points. For years, the export-oriented economy went on pretty well, but in 2008 China's economy experienced tremendous downward pressure.

Domestically, the challenge was the continuous build-up of unstable and unsustainable elements in the transformation and the high growth; in addition, there were more improper administrative controls and approvals from the macro control. In combination, these factors added up together and operating cost of the economic system started to increase again.

Moreover, with many years of increased money supply, the real interest rates became very low or even negative, stimulating higher demand for loans, and the national economy was moving towards the direction of increased leverage ratio. In particular, enterprises with government background were under high debt ratios. Once the external demand shrunk, export became difficult and the price index decreased accordingly; consequently, the real interest rates rose sharply, the pressure of repaying interest was increased for enterprises with high volumes of liabilities, and the economy was pulled towards a downward direction.

Therefore, this wave of economic downturn has three major causes: the shrinking of external demand, the higher system costs caused by administrative control, and the real interest rate turning positive.

In response to this wave of financial crisis, the U.S. Federal Reserve has drawn lessons from the past and concluded that tightening during depression would only take the situation from bad to worse. So it started to save the market and adopted the quantitative easing policy. In terms of the effect, the economy got supported; at least there was no such big depression akin to that from 1929–1933.

The average global growth was 5.2% for 2010, which was not bad. However, it was 4% for 2011, 3.2% for 2012, and estimated to be around 3% for 2015 (the actual was 2.47%). This means that the stamina for the government to save the market was limited. The European debt crisis appears to be a bigger problem than the United States financial situation. The logical problem is this: If the government comes to the rescue when the market has problems, who will be there to help out the government if the government's debt is too high? There is no answer at present; Europe is muddling along to deal with today and they have no time available to care about the future.

Under monetary easing, it feels great to increase the leverage because the government can get everything it wants. But the economy has its law; once the high debts encounter a decline in real interest rates, it is fatal for enterprises, local governments, and industries. Nowadays all countries of the world are saying that external demand is weak, and the worst situation is with China: Starting from May 2010, exports from China began to slow down. Although it rebounded a little at the beginning of 2015, the growth was only 1% for May and 3.1% for June, and no one can be sure whether it will slump again or not.

The greatest challenges, actually, come from home. Just as the old Chinese saying goes, it is easy to climb uphill but difficult to go downhill; when the high-level economy goes downwards, there is a strong inertia, it will probably dash out of the slide-way if not stabilized. Additionally, when the economy is at a high level and growing, many stones are hidden beneath the water surface; yet as soon as the water recedes, these hard stones will become exposed.

In the short term, we will have to deal with three big stones. The first one is cost. Economic growth is a continuous process, and this year's income constitutes (as it gets spent) next year's cost; this an obvious truth. After so many years of high growth, the cost curve of China's economy has gone back upwards after the decline and it is continuously moving up. Currently, the stone of "cost" has long been a big cause of suffering for many enterprises, especially those lacking cost control capabilities. Currently, every enterprise is trying to get through this, or the business has to be closed down if it fails; enterprises are pinched from both sides, one side being lack of order from the market, the other, too high costs.

The second stone is debt: The reversal of the real interest rate is a significant problem. Debt is a long chain, and debt default by one single company will put a large number of companies, and perhaps even an entire region, in trouble. Currently, people are paying attention to China's local government debts. My opinion is that the most dangerous thing is not the total debt but rather the quality of the investments over the years made with these debts. If it is just a question of high debt ratio, but the future return is high, then any challenge will be relatively easy to handle. The problem is, the quality of administration-led "investment" projects is worrisome, decision-makers who pat the head to make decisions and will probably leave the current position when projects get built do not care whether there will be investment return or not. And the reform to the investment and financing mechanism has a long way yet to go. The risks here are not small.

The third big stone is overcapacity. When things go well, people become overly optimistic about the future and rush to expand capacity. They are not aware that there will be overcapacity until the downturn comes and the expectation gets reversed. Based on past experience, to reduce the capacity involves big adjustments to asset prices as well as layoffs,; so everyone hopes the capacity cutting is on others so that he can get through the bad times himself. The problem is that everyone's hope is the same, the overcapacity suppresses producers' prices, and so the adjustment is artificially prolonged.

Because the water level of the high growth goes down, the three large stones get exposed above the surface of the water. This is the predicament of China's current economy. As can be seen currently, China's economy must be transformed; this is because the previous pillars are no longer able to support sustainable, rapid growth. As mentioned above, China's high growth comes from its active participation in globalization; therefore, if developed economies become sluggish, it is difficult for China to be immunized, and this is because the two sea levels are so closely linked.

On the whole, it is necessary for China's economy to rely more on domestic demand. It is a must to let domestic demand play a larger role in guiding sustainable economic growth. To achieve this transformation, we must implement in-depth structural reform and start a new impetus for economic growth. Over the coming ten or twenty years, large economies like China must rely more on domestic demand to support the growth.

There is not much disagreement on this judgment, but it is likely that domestic demand may not pick up so quickly. By 2012, industry still accounted for 47% of China's total GDP. China's massive manufacturing capacity was born to satisfy the global demand, and it cannot be digested by the current domestic demand. The potential domestic demand cannot come without structural reform, especially reform on income distribution structure, and this reform won't be released immediately as we have hoped. Although we have been talking about it for years, it is still difficult for domestic demand to act as the mainstay; the fundamental reason is that the people's income still occupies a too-low proportion of the national income. If this problem is not resolved, our country's domestic demand will only be potential.

It sounds reasonable to say that urbanization is the largest domestic demand, because China's urbanization index has just, after all, passed 50%, and the ratio of real urban residents is lower than this. But we also must understand that "the great leap forward in the administrative-led urbanization" is unreliable—this is because the critical system remains unchanged. The administrative-led investment, the confined resource allocation, the land system, and the household registration, or *Hukou* system, and the fiscal relationship between the central and local governments are all problems; if no solid reforms are implemented, the inefficient resource allocation in the "urbanization" will go beyond the tolerance of the economy, the society, and the political system before the urbanization rate reaches the desired level.

It takes time for the reform to unlock its dividends; namely, there is a process to go from sowing to harvest. We plant the trees today, and they won't bear fruit until a few years later. This is the current dilemma: We already no longer have the conditions to sustain the high growth from the past, but the transformation is difficult. Even if there is consensus and measures are correctly put in place, it will still take time to see the effects.

Reality imposes constraints on us; but no matter how difficult the situation is, we must persist in opening up. First and foremost, we must see that although globalization is having problems, the opening-up still has potential. Since the global financial crisis, the world's average growth has declined, but the share of the emerging economies in the world has increased. During the early stage of China's opening-up, it was necessary to target the market of developed countries; this is because their purchasing power was not only high but also readily available, and their commercial channels, infrastructure, credit, and financial services were also readily available. Therefore, what China needed to do was to focus on building itself into the world's factory and the world's workshop without worrying about markets for its products.

But precisely because China and a batch of emerging market economies took the road of opening-up, the global landscape has already changed. In 2000, China accounted for only 3.7% of the total global economy; today, it accounts for 11.5%. The share of emerging economies has grown 15.4% to 29.7%, whereas the share of the G7 Group has dropped from 65.4% to 47.3%. The way for slicing the global "cake" has changed.

Of course, not a few developing countries lack readily available purchasing power, but they have potential purchasing power, just like the China of some years ago. For them the restriction from the current reality is lack of sound infrastructure facilities and production services; but, as the opening-up continues, there is an opportunity for the potential demand to turn into actual demand. China should respond to this potential in a proactive way.

China's share in the added value of the global manufacturing has grown from 6.3% in 2000 to 17.4% in 2011 and 19% in 2012. But China's industrial capabilities do not match with its market development capabilities. On the one hand, our manufacturing capability is strong; with plenty of human resources, willingness to work hard and learn, plus imported equipment, it is as easy for us to build large factories to form new production capacity. But comparatively speaking, our ability to develop the global market is weak and we mainly live on orders from developed countries. Once the big tide sweeps the high sea level, we will have overcapacity. In point of fact, if we put developed economies aside and only look at the markets of India and Russia, not so many things are from China.

When I went on an investigative trip to Xinjiang to study the opening-up of western China, I saw several local private enterprises going to Kazakhstan and other Central Asian countries to build electrical substations and power distribution networks, proactively participating in local infrastructure investment and construction. Didn't China rise in the same way, namely by making up the years of weakness such as the infrastructure through the opening-up? Right now, to continue along this line of thinking is still perfectly feasible; that is, to push foreign trade with outbound investment by leveraging the accumulation of China's foreign exchange, investment, and production service capabilities. To go to other countries to build power stations, most of the equipment comes from China. To build highways, the concrete, asphalt, rebar, and equipment are also made in China. Therefore, it makes sense to study how foreign capital entered China and learn from it as to how China's economy should go overseas.

Of course, there will also be also risks. Chinese enterprises have gone to Vietnam and Myanmar. They not only sell products but also lend these countries money to buy Chinese products and to invest in roads and other infrastructure. This will drive trade and help with the digestion of domestic production capacity. This is a direction to strive for, and it is an upgraded version of China's economic opening-up. If we look to the west, to the Middle East, and to the south, we can see that there are more than one billion people in the Islamic world with unique cultural requirements; to the west of Xinjiang, there are tremendous amounts of resources and potential purchasing power; Association of Southeast Asian Nations (ASEAN) countries also have development opportunities.

The second direction to work on is industrial upgrading. Currently some people are publicly saying that China's demographic dividend is no longer there and that this is why the growth cannot be maintained; the worker's salary has gone up, so China's economy will be a problem. This seems to be a popular opinion. But, in reality, there is still the other side of the coin: in 2015, China's per capita GDP was only USD 8,000. Even though the gap with the high seal level has been narrowed a great deal in comparison with the beginning of the opening-up, the gap in per capita income is still several folds as compared with developed countries. So how could it be possible that China would no longer be able to grow well, just as some people have claimed?

The Netherlands has a per capita GDP of USD 50,000, but it is one of the world's three major exporters of agricultural products. Of this, flowers alone account for more than half of the world's total exports. The people of The Netherlands have such a high income that the labor cost is also certainly high; but why do their agricultural products still have export competitiveness? It must be understood that comparative advantage is not determined by the absolute level of wages; rather, what needs to be compared also are productivity, product types, materials, craftsmanship, processes, quality, and business models, and the background behind all these is education, training, and improvement to the overall quality of people. According to economic logic, as long as productivity improvement outpaces wage growth, there will still be advantages and opportunities.

Therefore, we should not look at problems with inertia, nor should we get used to seeing a salary of Ren Min Bi (RMB) 1,000 to 2,000 for workers; only by doing so can we be able to gain a foothold in the market. Economic growth must, in the end, come down to the continuous growth of per capita income, and the comparative advantages, therefore, must change. However, the decisive factor is not the absolute level of wages; rather, it is the growth in productivity.

Recently, I have been telling the story of "Mr. Swatch" (Nicolas Hayek) to entrepreneurs. The background was that the rise of low-cost quartz and electronic watch industry in Japan and Hong Kong put Swiss precision watch-making into the corner. The labor in Switzerland was more expensive than in Japan. The Swiss entrepreneur Nicolas Hayek stepped forward and devoted energy to innovating the watchmaking industry. By combining functional products with fashion, the innovation-driven productivity improvement enabled Swiss precision manufacturing to stand the test. Even up to today, Swiss watchmaking has not been relocated to low-cost countries, but it still maintains a foothold across the globe. This story illustrates that an upward cost curve does not necessarily mean a dead end. If products and industries are upgraded, there is still a lot that can be achieved.

The third consideration is aggregation and concentration. The connotation of urbanization is a spatial redistribution of the population and the "aggregation and concentration" of population and economic resources. The global urban population accounts for more than half of the total population, but cities only occupy a very small part of the earth's surface. The general trend is that a smaller and smaller land will have the aggregation of more and more people to produce an increasingly larger economic output. The United States has an urbanization rate of nearly 80%, but cities only take up 3% of its land. Of this, New York City accounts for 7.5% of the country's population and 10.1% of the GDP. How much land does New York City take up? Manhattan is less than 60 km^2 (only 87.5 km^2 if water surface is included), and the total area of all New York City's five boroughs is less than 800 km^2. Japan's three major metropolitan areas concentrate nearly 70% of its population and one-third of its total economy. How much land do they take up? The greater Tokyo metropolitan area covers 13,000 km^2, which is smaller than Beijing Municipality!

As soon as China allowed free movement of the population, the trend of gathering and concentration already comes into play, and in this there are tremendous opportunities. However, our level of aggregation and concentration is still at the primary level, and the obvious manifestation is that there is still room for higher density; that is to say, the economic output per unit of land area is still not very high, so there is great potential. The problem is, to fully release the potential for aggregation, the current system is far from well-adapted. Once the deepening of the reform, the urbanization expressed in aggregation and concentration, not the "urbanization" featured by administrative separation and the style of "rolling out the pan-cake," will drive more sustainable investment and economic growth. To summarize, the reality is that we have encountered the dilemma of transformation after the high growth rate, but the possibility of breakout co-exists.

First, changes, like it or not, are inevitable. Along with the new normalization of low growth rates for developed economies at the high sea level, China's export-oriented high growth rate from the past few decades is bound to change.

Second, stones will be inevitably exposed when the water recedes. The exposed stones are merciless; all that we can do is to reduce the costs, restructure the debts, and apply the law of the survival of the fittest to reduce the capacity to get through the difficulties.

Third, there are three directions for future breakout: The first is to use outbound investment to drive foreign trade and open up new frontiers of globalization; the second is for the already-established Chinese manufacturing to continue to seek comparative advantages and to initiate technological upgrading of both products and industries; and the third is to deepen the reform and remove the obstacles that prevent the flow and aggregation of resources in a bigger scope so as to further unlock the potential from urbanization.

To this end, it is of decisive significance to inspire the spirit of reformers, entrepreneurs, and careerists—for every one of us to look ahead. There are reasons for optimism, and there are reasons for pessimism. However, the future will not be shaped by looking on but solely by actions. I do not believe I have the magic to predict the future. What on earth will China's future economy look like? It all depends on the judgment, decisions, and actions of the team of industrialists, entrepreneurs, and investors that has formed since the opening-up and the reform. Different actions will lead to a different future.

Looking at China from the Perspective of System Costs[18]

Interpreting the Ups and Downs of China's Economy

The topic for today is to look at China's economy from the perspective of system costs. Currently, not only Chinese people ourselves but also many people around the world care about China's economy. I'd like to start from 2008.

The year 2008 was a very important year for China's economy. Ever since the beginning of the opening and the reform, China's economy has experienced a long period of rapid growth, and by 2008 the high growth had been there for thirty years. The academic community has done lots of review to this thirty years. For example, in January 2008 a seminar on the opening and reform was included into the "the New Year Forum" organized by Guanghua School of Management at Peking University; in July 2008 the centenarian Professor Ronald Coase organized an international academic seminar in Chicago on the thirtieth anniversary of China's change to its economic system. According to a report published by National Bureau of Statistics, in 2008 the annual growth of China's economy was 9.8%, down from the previous year but still reaching the thirty-year average since 1979. In 2009, China surpassed Japan to become the world's second largest economy; in 2010, China became the world's largest exporter; and in 2013, China became the world's largest trader. In 2014 the International Monetary Fund used the purchasing power parity, or PPP, to do the math and concluded that China had overtaken the United States to become the largest economy in the world.

These achievements have also stimulated the ambition of the academic community to summarize China's experience. Indeed, some heroic statements have also popped up; for example, Steven N. S. Cheung points out with his unique exaggeration that China's institution is the best economic system in human

18 This section is adapted from the author's speech on March 20, 2016, delivered at the Ninth Humanities and Economics Forum.—Editor's note.

history to his knowledge. In short, the academic ambition stimulated by developments of the practice seems to have begun.

Let us look back and see what kind of foundation of the British economy was followed by Adam Smith for his study. When Smith published *The Wealth of Nations* in 1776, the British economy had experienced a long period of only slow growth. At the time, most enterprises were quite small; there were only a few very large enterprises, such as British East India Company, with franchised trading rights granted by the royal family.

By today's standards, the living conditions of ordinary British people back then were quite bad. In 1773, Smith was working at the Edinburgh Customs House and he needed to go to London to prepare for the publication of *The Wealth of Nations*. The distance from Edinburgh to London was only 410 miles (about 650 km), but there was usually only one public carriage in a month between the two cities, the whole trip took between ten and fifteen days, and a will needed to be written before getting on the carriage because it was dangerous. As a result, when we revisit the background, experience, and economic achievements of the time of this foundational work of modern economics, there seems to be nothing unusual.

Therefore, it is fair to say that China's economy in 2008 should be qualified to come up with decent thoughts and theories. Only that the bigger the ambition, the more challenges we will be facing. Right after 2008, China's economy was faced with immense downward pressure that was rarely seen before: In 2007, China's GDP growth reached as high as 14.2%, but it then fell all the way down very badly. Although the 2009 stimulus policy maintained the growth, the downward trend was not fundamentally reversed. In 2015, the GDP growth rate was at 6.9%, and the target annual growth for the next five years was set at 6.5%. In other words, as compared with the highest point in 2007, the growth rate for the world's second largest economy has been cut by half.

This brings up a new question: Is there a concise framework to explain the ups and downs of China's economy? Of course we can also look at things separately—the rapid growth has its reasons and so does the sharp decline. However, I still hope to give them a consistent explanation, and this is what we are discussing today.

(A). Comparative Advantage Includes System Costs

The comparative advantage theorem was proposed by a classical economist named David Ricardo after Adam Smith. Before Ricardo, the popular opinion was that the difference in absolute costs is what caused trading behavior. Why do people trade? They do so because they can exchange with each other what they have for what they do not have. But why are there differences between what they have and what they do not? Because the absolute costs are different. Place A may dig out coal very easily, but Place B needs to dig to the other side of the earth; as the cost for the latter hits a certain high level, it is bound to have no coal. Ricardo moved on with the above analysis and believed that transactions are not necessarily based on absolute cost advantage; even if both places produce coal, and they both also produce tea, as long as there is a relative difference in their production costs for coal and tea, each of them can still produce the product with its respective cost advantage and obtain the maximum total output through trade.

The comparative advantage theory has extraordinary explanatory power. But we have another question: Do people compare only the production cost? Think about it for a moment—the "comparison" is made to establish mutual connection and trade with each other; but whether free trade is achievable or not, since ancient times, has to do with two prevailing mindset: trade policies and a large set of related institutional arrangements. In his original book, Ricardo used wine and wool coats as examples to analyze comparative advantage. Why didn't he use grain and steel? Because the United Kingdom had not yet repealed their Corn Laws until after Ricardo's death, and free import of grains was not permitted in the United Kingdom by the objection from landlords. Ricardo did not see the freedom in grain trade before his death, not because Britain did not have the comparative cost advantage from producing steel and importing grain but rather because there were other costs in the real world above and beyond production costs.

However, for quite a long time, economists only paid attention to production costs. It was not until 1937 that young Ronald Coase discovered that there are still "transaction costs" involved to enter into the transaction after products are produced. The expansion of the concept of "costs" improved the ability of economics to analyze real-world phenomena. After this, in 1969, Kenneth Arrow noted that transaction costs are actually the costs of operating the entire economic system; then in 1987, Steven N.S. Cheung posited that "transaction fees" are actually "system costs." According to the linguistic habits in China since the opening and reform, I think we might as well use the term "institutional costs"—"institution" connotes a system of policies, and its operation must consume resources. When we put "institutional costs" into an analysis framework of comparative advantage, it is not difficult to see that what gets compared in the real world is not limited to production costs, nor is it limited to the narrow sense of transaction costs because it also includes institutional costs. We can try this out below.

(B) When Institutional Costs Go Down, China's Economy Goes Up

The current downward pressure faced by China's economy is, of course, relative to its rapid growth. So, where does the high growth come from, and what is the force to drive China's rapid economic growth?

Breakthrough in Food and Clothing: Hunger Must Be Resolved Before Talking about Development

The secret for the high growth of China's economy is to systematically and persistently cut its institutional costs. I came to Beijing to study in 1978, and in 1980 China was formulating the Sixth Five-Year Plan, which covered from 1981 to 1986. As I remember, the economic growth target was to "strive for 5% and ensure 4%," meaning to strive for 5% in the average annual growth but to make sure that at least 4% growth was achieved. Looking at it now, both the growth rate and the expectation were very low. Why was it so low then? Because the national economy was greeted by many problems that were very difficult to solve. The first major problem was the shortage of food; the total population was about one billion and about 800 million of them were farmers, but still there was not enough food. Back then the foreign exchange reserve was very small, and it was impossible to import large volumes of grains. This created a huge bottleneck for the development of the national economy.

Let's look at how this problem was solved. To solve the problem, first the root of the problem must be identified; 800 million people worked on farming but were unable to produce enough food because the enthusiasm of farmers was low. Back when the starting point to choose the People's Commune system was to create an economy of scale, adopt collective labor, and facilitate fair distribution, everything sounded so nice. But when the idea was put into practice, the results couldn't stand the test; from a micro perspective, the zeal of the farmers could not be motivated by the collective system.

As an educated youth, I was assigned to the countryside, and I found that the real farmers were different from what we had learned from radio broadcasting, newspapers, and model operas. They worked really hard on their private plots, but the efforts got discounted a lot in the collective big plots because there was not good measurement and distribution and more labor did not mean more reward. Centralized management does have the benefit of economy of scale, but if wrong orders are issued in the centralized system, the scale effect will be negative. The system back then did not have the ability to restrict cadres of various levels to give blind commands, so the efficiency of resource allocation was low and, as a result, there was a long-term food supply shortage.

In the end, the way to solve this problem was to reform the system and change the "big rice pot" to the household contract responsibility system. If this shortcoming is not overcome, the grains will remain inadequate; how then can the industry be developed? If the farmers are poor, even if the industry get developed there will be no domestic market, and the efficiency of the entire national economy will be very low. The target was set to "strive for 5% and ensure for 4%" back then; the drag from agriculture, farmers, and rural areas was the decisive factor.

The Combination of Capital and Labor: From Burden to Bonus

A new problem immediately followed after the grain shortfall was resolved: the surplus rural labor. Previously, for the 800 million farmers out of the total one billion population, this 80% of the population had no opportunities to work in cities, nor did they have the little grain pamphlet and housing in the urban setting. The household contract responsibility system liberated massive amounts of labor, but where could they go to look for work? In any case, state-owned enterprises certainly did not have the capability to recruit so many workers. The answer, which popped up later on, was to rely on self-employed households, private economy, and township enterprises. If this hurdle had not been crossed, the issue of surplus rural labor would remain unresolved even today. In recent years, the demographic bonus has become a popular topic. Actually, solely from the perspective of demographics, once the war was over and the environment calmed down, the marriage rate rose sharply; it only takes sixteen years after a child is born to have an adult labor, so the ratio of labor force out of the total population would of course go up. However, did China enjoy demographic bonus in the 1960s and 1970s? After 1968, why were such a great many urban educated youth sent to the countryside? Because there was surplus labor. The demographic dividend hypothesis assumes that all members of the working-age population are effectively used, but such an assumption does not automatically exist in the real world. If the institution is not correct, the working-age population will only become the employment pressure for the society, and there won't be any dividend at all.

The development of non-public economy went through numerous difficulties and hardships. The debate over "socialism or capitalism" as the nature of reform went on for many years. Fortunately, the Third Plenary Session of the Eleventh CPC Central Committee set the ideological line that "practice is the sole criterion for testing truth," so we no longer had to live on textbooks and doctrines. In retrospect, if in those years the institutional costs in this aspect had not been systematically and significantly decreased, then a large part of China's current total economic output, total employment, or total tax revenue would not have existed at all!

The policy allowed to set up non–publicly owned enterprises, but to set them up needed capital. After so many years of poverty, China had little capital in its society. The solution was to open up and attract investment. Back in those years, there were many incidents in Guangdong involving large numbers of ordinary mainland residents escaping to Hong Kong to work there. At that time, Hong Kong and other members of the "Four Asian Tigers" were experiencing rapid growth, and there was a severe shortage of labor. Blocking the stowaway as the only method to restrict movement of workers could not ultimately resolve the problem. In 1977, the escape to Hong Kong was reported to Deng Xiaoping, who had just returned to the leadership team, and Deng's judgment was: "it is a problem with our economic policy." What was the problem then? Domestic productivity was backward, and there was too much labor but a severe shortage of capital; there was plenty of overseas capital, but it could not be fully used because China's door was tightly closed. This compelled China to come up with a new method: We should not let average persons run off to Hong Kong for work, but we should let capitalists from Hong Kong come here to set up factories and recruit people from the mainland. This was the origin of special economic zones.

Under the original system, to bring in foreign capital would inevitably bump into frictions and conflicts. China's original institutional model was the Soviet model, whereby everything was wholly publicly owned, all economic activities were carried out by the state, and the resources were allocated and production, supply, and sales were organized by commands and plans. The problem with this was that foreign investments were completely outside the plan, so they had to find opportunities from the market. As a result, the monolithic planned economy was no more the entire world. In the beginning, the market opened up just a little. As the government accumulated experience and all parties had some experience, the opening was expanded; the portion of mandatory planning gradually shrunk, and the scope of market allocation of resources gradually expanded. Obviously, it was not a straight path forward; things often went back and forth as China moved forward.

As foreign-invested enterprises came, they needed land, but this requirement couldn't be supported by the original land system. Previously, all institutions were state-owned; whoever needed land just submitted a report, and land would simply be allotted to them. But the land could not be allotted to foreign investment. They were not state-owned enterprises, and it was justifiable and reliable for them to buy the to-be-invested factors. But the problem here was that the previous laws strictly forbid the buying, selling, and transfer of land. This hurdle was later resolved through distinguishing the differences between ownership rights and usage rights by keeping the ownership rights and circulating the usage rights. To resolve the problem, the Constitution, the Civil Law, and the Land Administration Law were all amended, and a groundbreaking land auction market was set up. Looking back, if the institutional costs for land transfer had remained high, foreign capital and domestic private enterprises would have had no place for landing, and there would have been no "China Miracle" at all.

Entering the Global Market After Opening-Up

After the rise of China's manufacturing capabilities, the new question became where the markets is. As a result, China's opening-up had a new version, which was not only limited to attracting investment and technology but also sought to develop the global market share. Initially, no one had expected that China's products would be able to enter the world market on a large scale; so in the late 1980s, the strategy was to first open up the coastal areas, to import raw materials and energy and export the products to achieve large volumes for import and export. After seeing the positive effects, China opened up itself entirely. This was later called export-oriented or export-guided strategy. In the "export-guided" system, exactly who or what is the guide? Only the market system is the reliable guide. In the past, the old concept was that "nourishing water should not flow to the farmland of others," and it was believed that to have two Chinese companies competing and cutting the prices in the international market would give the advantage to foreigners; therefore, foreign trade was monopolized and all China's export products had to be exported by state-owned foreign trade companies. Later, China realized that the monopoly primarily hurt itself, and so the foreign trade system was reformed to allow the customs office of different regions to compete and to also allow all sorts of trading companies from all sorts of places to compete with each other. The foreign exchange system was also reformed. Previously the

RMB exchange rate was set by the government; the more severe the shortfall of foreign exchange, the more overvaluation there was for the local currency. But the more the overvaluation of the local currency became, the harder it would hit export and foreign exchange earnings. How should this be changed? The reform was started by first adopting a dual-track exchange rate system and then consolidating the two tracks at the right timing. The merging of the official exchange rate and the market exchange rate automatically solved the stubborn overvaluation of the local currency. The decrease of institutional costs relating to this aspect soon saw effects; the long-existing low-cost labor advantage was unleashed and shaped China into the world's factory. If the system is wrong, the population and the labor force are just both burdens; and it is not a good long-term solution to control the population through birth control.

The Real Mystery of China Miracle

In 1980, China formulated its Sixth Five-Year Plan. The annual ensured growth target was set at 4% with a stretch target of 5%. Why was the target set only at "ensuring for 4% and striving for 5%?" Was it because China's population was not large enough, or the percentage of working population was too low, or the cost of production was not low? The reason was none of these. The reason why China's economy was unable to exert its comparative advantages in the international arena was very straightforward: despite the low production costs, the institutional operation costs was not low. The reform and opening-up and the emancipation of ideas was a must to lead to the removal of all sorts of institutional arrangements and general policies that severely hampered the productivity. So the significant reduction of institutional costs helped shape the rise of China on the global stage.

Ever since the beginning of the Seventh Five-Year Plan, China's economic growth has started to gain momentum. Over the next thirty years, the average growth rate reached as high as 10%, which was not imaginable at the time the plan was formulated. Looking back, the general underestimation of China's potential for economic growth was, in essence, a general underestimation of its previous institutional costs. The practice of the opening-up and reform lowered the institutional costs and unlocked the economic potential, so the world could not help but look at China's economy with different eyes.

In summary, China's economy relies on comprehensive cost advantages to gain a global foothold. First, although China's long-lasting poverty and extremely large labor force were a burden under closed conditions, once the door was open they became an obvious advantage in production costs. Second, the opening-up and reform has significantly reduced the national economy's organizational costs and system operations costs. Third, Chinese people are willing to learn. Families, local governments, and the state all pay attention to investments into human capital, so the learning curve improves. It is precisely the comprehensive comparative cost advantage synthesized by these three major points that forged China's miracle of rapid growth in globalization.

(C) Re-Increase of Institutional Costs

In 2008, China's economic growth was at its apex; but why then did the ship became heavier and heavier and sail slower and slower? Still looking at the institutional costs, we will find that after this the cost curve has come back and started to rise again along with the high growth rate after experiencing a historically significant decline. This question was widely discussed in 2008 in some events to commemorate the thirtieth anniversary of the opening-up and reform. I was also a participant and I wrote an article titled "What Did Deng Xiaoping Do Right?" In short, the gradual reform had left behind quite a few hard-to-swallow pills and some halfway-completed reform projects, and at the same time the rapid growth continuously sparked new problems. These combined together to cause the institutional costs to rise after the bottom-out, and the curve in the chart was like the contour of a bowl looked at from the side.

Rising Statutory Costs and Increased Corporate Burden

The first item is statutory costs. In market competition, some of the enterprises' costs are determined by the supply and demand competition. For example, if everyone wants to have more land, the bidding process in the auction will raise the price of land and also increase the cost of land for enterprises. If everyone is hiring people, the price of labor will inevitably go up; if everyone fights for raw materials, the raw materials price will go up and the costs will also go up. However, in the real world, there is another type of cost that must be paid according to law; this costs are compulsory, and if you don't pay, it will be against the law. I have checked the statistical yearbook, from 1995 to 2012, China's nominal GDP grew by a factor of 8.6. During the same period, its total wages increased by a factor of 8.8 times, which was slightly higher than the total nominal GDP growth, and this is basically formed by the market. But the rise of statutory costs was very steep: During the same period, the country's total tax income grew by a factor of 16.7 times; this is almost twice the speed of the total labor wage growth. Apart from taxes, other types of government income increased by 18.8 times. The payment of social security, which is another statutory cost, grew by 28.7 times between 1995 and 2012. It is not a problem that the statutory social security payments are drawn from the income of workers and enterprises. But the question is, is the statutory payment rate appropriate? China's social security payment rate is actually higher than many developed countries. There is a historical reason for this: in the past, the system was to rely on young workers from each enterprise to provide for its old workers, and there was no unified social security fund. Once the state-owned enterprises lose money (or even go bankrupt) or go into liquidation, there is no way to take care of the old (retired) workers. By the 1990s, many state-owned enterprises went bankrupt, and massive numbers of workers were laid off, so China rushed to establish a social security system. Because there was too much debt from the history, the social security payment rate had to be set high. At that time and afterwards, scholars did some research and have long provided policy recommendations, recommending to allocate some of the state-owned capital into the social security fund and to use the state-owned capital accumulated over many years as social security fund so as to ease the social security payment burden for current enterprises. But a recommendation is a recommendation; thus far still too few state-owned assets have been allocated to social security, and the social security payment burden on enterprises is still too heavy.

The item with the fastest increase in statutory costs was land transfer fees. The 1988 Amendment to the Constitution clearly put down in black and white that "land usage rights can be transferred according to the law"; it never says that only urban, state-owned land can be transferred and that rural collective construction land cannot be transferred. However, in point of fact, specific laws and regulations have been promulgated on the transfer of only urban state-owned land, and there has, so far, been no nationwide regulation on the transfer of rural collective land. The only way for rural land circulation is to be expropriated and then transferred to the market by the government in the name of state-owned land, and from this the government collects the land transfer fee. From 1995 to 2012, how much did the national land transfer fee increase by? A factor of sixty-four times! From the market perspective, the "land transfer fee" is a usage fee that must be paid by enterprises and individuals to acquire land, and it constitutes the production and living costs. The growth rate of the total of this expense was more than seven times faster than the nominal GDP. These statistics indicate that, even though China's economy has advanced quickly to become the world's second largest economy, in this process the early decentralization and interest concessions have shifted toward a re-increase of statutory costs.

Statutory costs are different from the costs created by supply and demand competition. The latter moves down along with downward economy and presents some elasticity, whereas the former is much more troublesome to be adjusted because it takes multiple levels of reporting, appealing, and all sorts of meetings, and in come cases it also involves amending laws and regulations. To decrease the cost is among the "de-capacitying, de-inventorying, and de-leveraging and cost reduction" tasks for the economic work of 2016 as deployed by the central government. Many places have enumerated which cost items must be brought down, yet many of these items cannot be resolved by the provinces so they have to be reported to the central government. But even at the central government, amendments to legislation cannot take place so immediately as people hope for.

Cost of Market Access

The level of difficulty in accessing the market is not entirely determined by the market itself but depends also on corresponding systems and policies. In China the market is gradually opened up. In each step when the market access is opened, a fierce competition will quickly be formed, sometimes even resulting in oversupply; so it becomes necessary to open up new market to find new access. However, the barriers to open many potential markets are excessively high, as outdated concepts and vested interests will join forces at the gate to prevent the competition mechanisms from playing their role.

If we observe the economic phenomena, we will see that although there is lots of downward pressure and it seems there is no business to do, at the same time serious supply shortfalls exist in many fields. Plainly, there are market opportunities, but people are not able to respond to those opportunities. These artificial frictions and obstacles are also a type of institutional cost. Take medical services as an example: For many years, the "medical reform" has been implemented, but people still have to wait in a long queue at good hospitals in big cities. The new round of medical reform was instigated in 2007. The country has invested billions of RMB, but the improvement in medical services is by far not proportional to the invested resources and the supply still cannot meet the demand. We cannot say that there is oversupply in this aspect; what is the bottleneck then? The problem is with the access to medical services and the improper price control.

In recent years, the shortage of pediatricians has become big news. It's not that there is no reserve, because there are enough medical graduates every year to fulfill the need. However, the full use of reserve resources to form an effective supply needs to be guided by relative price signals. The crux of the problem is that it is extremely difficult to see a pediatric doctor, yet this is not at all reflected in the relative price. Without the market price signal, how can we effectively allocate resources including reserve resources? The only thing we are doing every day is to cry out slogans, and cry them out for so many years even if it does not work and even if nobody listens. Experience proves that access and price mechanism are of decisive significance for efficient resource allocation; as a result, it is necessary to continue to expand access and liberate prices.

The mobility difficulty has been a stubborn disease for big cities for years. The rise of mobile internet has made ride sharing service possible. However, "technologically feasible" is not equal to "economically feasible." First and foremost is the impact on the traditional taxi industry because the previous potential supply has become a real competitor. Next, transportation management also faces new problems. But the convenience of getting a ride is an undisputed fact; we should not stop eating for fear of choking, so to speak. A more general problem is that innovation can be a very vogue slogan, but when the real innovation comes it must touch on incumbent operators and cause new management issues. If the problem comes, we should try to solve the problem rather than kill the new thing with one stroke. Otherwise, there will be no innovation even if the slogan is deafening.

The Problem with Land Supply

Under the current land system, local governments have become the sole supplier of industrial and commercial land. As mentioned earlier, the characteristics of local governments is that they have geographical limits; namely, each individual local government can only be responsible for matters within its own administrative jurisdiction, and they can not go beyond the boundary. However, the flow of population, labor, economic resources, and investment projects has been permitted for decades after the opening and the reform, and the scope of this flow goes beyond the administrative boundaries of counties, cities, and provinces. The destinations of people, money, and projects are not determined by administrative hierarchy. Under such circumstances as these, if the land is supplied by each local government, it is definitely difficult to have a good match between supply and demand. The real estate control has been there for so many years, but have we achieved the target of control at any time? Probably we are actually drifting increasingly further away from the goals. When land supply is tightened across the whole country, housing prices in popular cities immediately go up;

when the government looses land supply, "empty cities" and "haunted cities" start to expand, and "housing oversupply" becomes more severe. This goes back and forth for many rounds, but the land supply side reform has never been put on the agenda.

To add one point: Urban land use is not just about the land surface, it also involves land usage density, namely "plot ratio." Under the current system, the plot ratio of urban land has always been determined by the administrative power. There is a whole set of urban planning laws and regulations, and another whole set of approval procedures. With the additional help of theorists, the advocacy of the so-called "no freedom for urban architectures" has totally ignored the basic fact that the average building height of cities with global influence has always been growing under the combined pressures from population, economy, technology, and management. And along with the reasonably increased height and density, a great deal of worthy learning experience has been accumulated for the "urban planning and control reform." If we allow the "surface land concept" and its relevant policy arrangements to take the upper hand, it is not only difficult to prevent the lingering corruption caused by the excessive control but also severely hinders urban land supply to make agile responses to the demand.

Cost of Moving or Exiting: Not Allowed to Enter in the Past, but not Allowed to Leave Nowadays

Another cost is the cost to move or to exit. Early on, the problem was market separation; some local governments prohibited or restricted the entry of products from elsewhere to protect local industries. This seldom happens today. But now comes a new problem: Once a local company wants to move its headquarter to another city after it has grown bigger and stronger, the local government will not let it do so. This also constitutes a part of "local competition"; many localities work proactively on investment promotions, and once the project comes the locality does not allow the investor to leave. The government's organizational characteristic is the division of administrative jurisdictions; however, the development of enterprises and industries must follow the market. "Local competition" driven by the political achievement of tax income and GDP has both advantages and disadvantages. However, the more developed the market relationships, the more the previously working investment promotion strategies become an obstacle to continued development. Why we are always calling for structural adjustment? From the micro perspective, this is because there is too much friction in the system for enterprises to come and to quit. The optimal layout for a locality and the optimal layout for a large market are not necessarily the same thing.

Currently, agricultural development has encountered a bottleneck; the crucial issue is that agriculture has no competitiveness. Avoiding structural reform and relying on subsidies cannot solve this fundamental difficulty. As a result, when the production is stimulated by financial subsidies, the grains do not at all sell well in the market, so they all end up staying in the national grain depot. The problem is in the structure: The proportion of agriculture out of the total output is 9%, and less than 9% if the subsidies are taken away. But what about the proportion of rural labor force? If it is also 9%, then agriculture labor gets the average income. However, if it is 16%, then the agricultural income is only half of the average income. Year in and year out, the government says that it is important to increase farmers' income; the real sticking point is that we need to enable farmers with a lower-than-average income to exit from agriculture. To do this, we first need to do some investigative research to see what the factors are to prevent these farmers from leaving farming. That is to say, we need to study the role of tax exemptions, of price subsidies, and of land contracting relationships as well as the role of the household registration (*hukou*) and homestead policies. Then we can determine the policies based on the study. In the 1980s, policy research offices at provincial, municipal, and county level did many studies and investigations into local conditions; nowadays, they seldom do this. But what are they busy with? The answer is speech scripts. I really don't understand why we need so many speeches.

Cost of Revising Legal Policies: One Provision Encumbers the Whole Picture

The cost of amending the law is also not low. Even if some laws and regulations have already been found to be inappropriate, amending them is difficult and time consuming. A few years ago, a policy notice was issued: "Urban residents may not go to suburban or rural areas to purchase properties on rural homesteads." This one sentence created big trouble for investment into landscaping, industry, and homestay in the suburbs of all cities. If the intended site cannot be bought, or if the long-term reliable land use right cannot be acquired, how could people make decisions about investment, design, or techniques? Nowadays, the income of urban residents has improved and the car ownership rate has also increased rapidly; the economic development of the suburb is actually an important part of the whole city's economy. We are hoping to boost domestic demand every day, but when it comes, there is no way to make flexible responses.

Yet, after the sentence gets written in the document, it becomes extremely difficult to remove it. In point of fact, ever since the Land Reform in 1950, rural housing sites have consistently been farmers' private property and never been brought under public ownership; so why can't they directly enter the market, and why can't their owners sign the contract in the market according to their own will? The 1987 Amendment to the Constitution states that "land usage rights can be transferred according to the law," and it does not limit the circulation of use rights to only state-owned land which could be transferred. However, the Constitution just could not govern the laws and regulations that can supposedly only conform to constitutional principles.

(D) Institutional Costs Determine the Future of the Economy

It must be seen that the global competition landscape has changed. When China was first opened up, it was at a different sea level with developed countries; at that time, there were some countries even poorer than us, but they had no products for export. Today's global situation is something rather like a sandwich. The developed economies are growing slowly, but they still enjoy advantages in originality and innovation as they often come up with unique new technologies, new products, and new industries to lead the trend. Looking down, we can see that a number of developing countries, such as Vietnam and India, have become emerging market economies, and their cost advantage is even more significant than ours because they opened up later than China. China is caught in the middle of this global sandwich, with no unique advantages but much loss in its cost advantages.

The competition pattern determines the two breakthrough directions for China's economy. The first is to reverse the cost curve, especially the bad trend of the too-steep rise of institutional costs, and strive to bring it down significantly by deepening the reform so as to maintain the comparative advantage for China's economy to participate in the global competition. The second is to encourage innovation and foster unique advantages of China's economy. Both of these two aspects are inseparable from the deepening of reform.

To summarize, China's economy has experienced the process of "ensuring for 4% and striving for 5%," high growth, an apex in 2008, and then the downward pressure. One of the logics throughout this is that changes in institutional costs affect economic performance. Institutional costs not only determined the past but also will determine the future of China's economy.

Is the Rapid Growth Sustainable?

China's economy has risen, but new problems follow. Everyone cares about what China's economy will look like in the next twenty years. My opinion is that the answer to this question depends on whether or not China can face and resolve the current problems with its economy. Different solutions will lead to different futures. Failing to make a decision by procrastinating will lead to yet another type of ending.

Ergo, it is fundamental that we continue to deepen the reform. First of all, we need to have a frame of reference. As to what exactly is "deepening the reform," the answer will certainly be different if the reference standards are different. Next let us talk about some issues that may have significant impacts.

First, China relies on the opening-up to unlock its comparative advantage. When the door is closed, there is no comparative advantage to speak of. It was only after the opening-up that we discovered China was in poverty for so many years and that poverty could be one kind of cost advantage. Closed for such a long time, China was lagging far behind the world's advanced the level, and the gap was huge. In terms of labor costs, the figure for developed countries was dozens of times higher than that for China. The gap was so large, yet China did not open the door to do the comparison. When the door was suddenly opened, of course the tremendous potential would be unleashed. The capital, technology, management, and business models from developed countries came in, and the inexpensive products manufactured in China went out. This explains the rapid growth of China's economy. At the beginning it was difficult to see this point because our labor costs were cheap, but the products we were able to make were limited. But the learning curve will eventually come into play. Chinese people learned by doing; in particular, the opening-up brought about a substantial reduction in learning costs. This is a very important pivot for the "China Miracle," and it also brings about changes in the global economic landscape.

Capital in the Twenty-First Century (Chinese version published by CITIC Press in September 2014) by French economist Thomas Piketty is very eye-catching. However, this economist, who seldom leaves France, seems to have overlooked an important constraint—the labor force of several billion people from the latecomer developing economies has entered globalization. Hence, worldwide competition among labor forces has been intensified. In particular, the compensation has become unprecedented between emerging markets and advanced economies with respect to unskilled and skilled workers, and even some white-collars and golden-collars. The capital is becoming relatively more scarce across the globe; capital flows from developed countries into emerging markets to make money, but their workers experience the aggravation of global competition. This is also the root cause for the widening income gap within developed countries. However, from the perspective of global distribution, the "polarization" has also narrowed the income gap between China and the developed countries.

What are the problems with China's economy itself? Ever since the start of the opening-up, our cost advantage has continuously been released, the income of low-income people with migrant workers as the representative has been growing quite quickly, and this is a good phenomenon. Yet a closer examination has also revealed that there are many nonmarket factors among the drivers that constantly push up China's competition cost, such as the even more rapid increase in the prices of electricity, land, financial services, and telecommunication, as well as the taxes and fees collected by the government for providing administrative service. People have noticed that nowadays quite a number of Chinese goods are more expensive than similar products in the international market. The reason is not fully because China's labor is expensive but rather because other statutory costs are even more expensive. If this problem is not resolved, China's global competitive advantage is bound to be weakened. If the comprehensive low cost advantage is quickly lost, and the "unique advantage" (i.e., the innovation advantage) remains yet to be established, it will be a problem for the "China Miracle" to sustain, which may affect the relative global position of China's economy in the future.

Second is the urban–rural relationship. This is the most important domestic problem in which the greatest structural potential resides. When China was just opened up, the basic national condition was "one billion population and 800 million farmers." Today the situation has changed a lot after more than thirty years of opening and reform, but the change in the basic urban–rural pattern is not enough. At present, China's agricultural output is less than 10% of the GDP, but the registered rural population by *hukou* is as high as 65%, the resident rural population still accounts for more than 45%, and the farming labor force accounts for about 30%. Under this structure, the income from farming is forever far below the national average. Isn't this a huge imbalance? The lesson from the early years of national industrialization is that farmers accounting for the ultimate majority of the population were very poor and didn't have much power; therefore, there was no domestic market to digest although the industrialization was carried out here and there. There was no choice but the self circulation of the heavy industry, yet eventually this road could not be widened. For the current urbanization, we need also be mindful that the majority of people might be unable to be integrated into the city. Today, some 240 million farmers have already moved into cities, but only a very small number of them have moved into the commodity housing in cities and towns. Of tens of trillions of RMB of the total land transfer fee, probably the government has not taken out even 100 million RMB to build urban housing that is affordable by farmers. After moving to cities, where do most farmers live? They live in basements, villages-within-cities, and para-urban areas mostly in the properties of suburban farmers. This is, to a certain extent, still the continuation of the same logic from the early years of national industrialization. Why is the real estate in tier 2 and tier 3 cities not selling well? It is not because farmers entering cities do not need housing but rather because they cannot at all afford it. If this urban–rural imbalance is not resolved, China's urbanization cannot be thick and strong, and its economic growth has to be highly dependent on external demand; when external demand fluctuates, the domestic economy will drop immediately.

Third, there is the quality of goods and services. Currently, food safety has been elevated in China to the level of governing capacity. But, it's not just food that has quality problems; to satisfy existing domestic demand, low quality is a common problem. For example, what is the average service life of housing? After an apartment is fitted out, how many years will the fittings last? How long does a light bulb last before it needs to be changed? As for services, the problem with quality seems to be even more severe. The meaning of this kind of high growth is greatly discounted. As we can see, for the light bulb to be changed every five years or every half year, the GDP growth rates are different—the inferior product quality has a higher economic growth, but the enjoyment by the population is not high, plus there will be additional environmental cost. If quality is not placed to the first position in a timely manner, no matter how high the growth is, it is difficult for the people to have a sense of happiness. It is humiliating to see mainlanders go to Hong Kong for the milk powder shopping rush. Diving deep, the issue of quality involves so many aspects. Conversely, if quality cannot be improved the economy has to rely on rapid growth; otherwise, if there is nothing to replace when the light bulb is not working, it will be very dark. It has long been proposed that the "good" should be placed before "fast," but this slogan has not penetrated into the micro behavior of industries and enterprises. It must be acknowledged that in terms of product and service quality, there is still a gap between China's rapid growth and Japan's rapid growth. When Japan was in rapid economic growth, their product quality also improved rapidly.

Fourth, the relationship between the government and businesses. I am of the opinion that neither economists nor any other social science researchers should skip the "Physical Examination Report" of China's society because the anti-corruption requirements were laid down by the Eighteenth National Congress of CPC. No matter how much emphasis is put on rapid growth and speed first, it only takes a few stories about outrageous corruption to shake people's confidence in China's own model. In today's world, even though it is a common rule that "power corrupts" in civilized countries, it is still heart-tightening to hear that the search of a civil servant's home found over 100 million RMB of cash, which even burned some currency counting machines. This reveals that there is a terrifying ailment in the society. Whatever is the case, as a Chinese citizen, or to study China's economy, we have to face this kind of ugliness. As we see, with the promulgation of the Eight Point Regulations on Fighting Corruption, the price of famous wines and luxuries went down significantly; doesn't this tell us something? This is no trivial matter; it affects whether or not people can feel the minimum justice within the country. Fighting corruption has made some achievements on the symptoms, but to eliminate the root cause cannot be done in one day. Also, it seems that ordinary people's "tolerance" for corruption is quite high. Certain enterprise owners send money whenever they see officials, even if they are not asking them to do any favor, and it is said that they "have got used to this way of doing things." This is the sign of septemia of the society. This problem must be cured for China's growth to continue.

In short, the future trajectory of China's economy depends on whether or not it can face up to the real problems after a big success and on whether or not these problems can be addressed in a targeted manner. Global competition has always been ruthless. Many of my friends travelling overseas come back to say there are not as many Japanese tourists as before in many places of attractions. Just in a matter of ten or twenty years, no matter how good a country's growth rate was, it only took a few missteps to see some changes. This indicates that the future is not fatalistic but rather dependent on the choices and actions of today.

Don't Ask Where the Hero Comes From—Wealth Must Have Rightful Sources

On the evening of June 27, 2016, when my flight back to China from a business trip of more than half a month landed, I learned the news over the mobile phone about Wang Shi's apology at Vanke's shareholder meeting. I didn't listen to more than a few sentences before feeling that he absolutely ought to be apologizing. As the chairman of a large, well-known, publicly listed company such as Vanke, and entrusted with the responsibility of diligence by all the shareholders, of course he should not have made such malicious remarks. Even if there is a "hostile takeover" by others, that is a normal arrangement in the market system; otherwise how could there be good corporate governance under the restrictions from market discipline?

In more recent years, as a heroic entrepreneur in my mind, Wang Shi did have some new situations in implementing corporate responsibilities. More time was spent on mountain climbing, study tours, and media interviews, and less effort was made to communicate with shareholders, both large and small. No one denies that Vanke is an excellent company, but it does have weaknesses in its shareholding structure. Why didn't they set out to solve the problem earlier? The company is now trapped in such a big vortex; as the founding entrepreneur, doesn't he need to reflect on some things?

Since the end of 2015, Wang Shi's situation has once again been improving. As everyone has long seen, although he abandoned his shares many years ago and defined himself as a "professional manager," actually his relationship with Vanke was by no means as simple as a clerk who should "do whatever he is told to, or leave the company." He is, after all, the founder.

This time, I think Wang Shi owes a thank you to Yao Zhenhua (Chairman of Baoneng, which tried to take over Vanke) and related parties for rekindling the sense of duty and spirit of responsibility which he has towards Vanke.

The Card Playing of China Resources Is Difficult to Understand

Let us come back to the topic and talk about the matter itself. First and foremost, we need to ask, in such a large, publicly listed company, why were the stakeholders (shareholders) fighting so badly that the skyscraper almost collapsed? The answer is that the company's foundation was not solid. Needless to say, in the absence of a controlling shareholder, Vanke's foundation was that a super large central government–controlled enterprise holds a relatively large number of shares, and it gives full trust and ultimate support to the founding entrepreneur to lead an excellent operations team to manage the company. So far all the brilliant successes of Vanke have been built on such a foundation.

This foundation is good, but it is not solid. The crucial issue is that the individual who takes the helm of its big shareholder, the state-owned enterprise is not the permanent owner of the asset but rather a "professional manager" appointed by the government. Early on, when Wang Shi was choosing the foundation for Vanke, China Resources was headed by Ning Gaoning. Wang Shi made the correct choice, but it was also by good luck, because Ning Gaoning himself was an outstanding entrepreneur within the system of central government–controlled enterprises. As heroes cherish heroes, and doers generally appreciate and trust doers, so this shapes up the much-told story of Vanke where "the state-owned shareholder gives ultimate support to the founding entrepreneur." And even more luckily, Ning Gaoning's tenure at China Resources was quite long and his successors also followed the same principle in dealing with Vanke. As a result, the "Vanke Model" stood erect like a mountain. The problem is this model has no institutional assurance; if another government-appointed leader comes in, there is no guarantee that the previous prescription will be followed or the previous medicines taken. Once the situation changes, the foundation of Vanke will be shaken. What's more fatal is that people believe habits make things natural; however, things do not go that way in actuality.

In this incident, the part that is most difficult to understand is the cards played by China Resources. From a business strategy perspective, Ning Gaoning decided that China Resources play the role of a financial investor in Vanke, and the precondition for this was to place trust on the management and leverage the strength of the super large central government–controlled enterprise as the back to prevent other forces from coveting the controlling position at Vanke. If the new leader of China Resources wanted to change the rules of the game, he could withdraw the capital and shift the investment into other projects that he believed to be more promising or he could increase the amount of capital until reaching control and replace the company's management which no longer had his trust. He did neither of these; instead, he followed the same old rules; and when strangers—do not say that they are barbarians—came knocking at the door, China Resources dilly-dallied and made no responses. In the beginning, it might be said it was a result of carelessness: How could a new insurance company established only a few years ago be able to challenge the giant enterprise owned by the central government? When the determination of the other party went obvious and it easily became Vanke's largest shareholder, China Resources surprisingly was willing to be the second largest shareholder.

It doesn't matter whether the new leadership at China Resources decided not to increase its holding to support Vanke, but it should allow Vanke to bring other strategic investors on board. Wang Shi and Yu Liang said they had specifically asked China Resources in advance and got its approval before they found

Shenzhen Metro. But, when they came, China Resources resolutely disagreed. No withdraw, no fighting, plus not allowing Vanke to fight; such a move obviously shows that it was ready to see Baoneng's ambition come true. No wonder Shenzhen Stock Exchange issued an attention letter asking whether or not China Resources and Baoneng were persons acting in concert. Why did they ask? Because they certainly looked like acting in concert. But both parties replied no. Interesting, the gentle and cultivated acquaintances!

Perhaps some people will say that a teacher has no right to gossip about the decisions and behaviors of deputy minister-level top leader of the central government–controlled enterprise. This is not a fair statement. I have read the Law of the People's Republic of China on the Assets of State-owned Enterprises, and I understand that all state-owned assets, including for central government–controlled enterprises, belong to "the entire people." Because it belongs the entire people, and I am a member of the entire people, why can't I ask questions when I don't understand? To restate an old point: All state-owned enterprises and state-owned assets, owned by the entire people, should publicly disclose the information and accept the supervision of the entire people. It is best to bring them under the National Social Security Fund to assure the welfare of the entire people. Yet the current information disclosure by state-owned enterprises is far from satisfactory as compared with the requirement for listed companies; shouldn't this be changed? Let's start with the Vanke case to ask more questions and make more changes.

The Hero's Money Should Have Rightful Sources

Regarding Baoneng, for a private enterprise to do a banner acquisition in the capital market and compete with the central government–controlled enterprise for the largest shareholder of Vanke and make it, my belief is that this demonstrates that substantial progress has been made in China's market economy system. I also do not believe that Wang Shi honestly does not understand the principle of "heroes are heroes wherever they come from," because he himself is a hero rising out of the wave of marketization, and he first started with animal feed, which was not so much different from vegetable selling. I have never met Yao Zhenhua, but I learned from the internet that he graduated from the South China University of Technology, which is also where the "Three Color TV Tycoons of Southern China" graduated, and the alma mater of many other entrepreneurs that I have visited across the Pearl River Delta. The aforesaid "vegetable selling" comment was actually a part of the Shenzhen Municipal Government's vegetable basket project. But even if one peddles vegetables on the street and later become a hero, he is still a hero regardless of the background.

However, I also believe that a hero is a hero regardless of the origin, but the money he makes should have rightful sources. In particular, the source of money used to buy shares of large listed companies must be clearly explained. Why? Because there is different logic for one's own money, money borrowed, and money borrowed in different ways. Yes, money is a wonderful thing, and it can be spent in the same way, but different sources have different connotations.

Let us take financed share purchases as an example. At the first glance, the money earned from selling financial products—insurance, savings deposits, wealth management, securities, and the like—is the same as the money made from selling rice, clothing, and mobile phones. But there is a difference, because the essence of whatever financial product is sold is a "commitment." For example, when we pay for wealth management products, the money leaves our hands, but what we have bought is nothing less than a set of promises that there will be such and such benefits in the future. The problem is it takes time for the "future" to arrive, and situations may occur in between; so can the initial promises be delivered? Not always. We say "finance always has risks" because of this uncertainty.

If the "promise" of a financial product is not attractive enough, people will not go to the market, the finance will fail, the society's idle money cannot get used, and economic growth will be hindered. Conversely, if the promise made by a financial product is too tempting and too irresistible, it may get the buyers trapped because the promise can never be delivered. This phenomenon is called "you want his high interest and he wants your principal." It's hard to believe that it has been quite difficult to grasp these kind of matters of weighing the pros and cons in the long human history. People often take care of only one end and forget about the other, and many old tragedies have been repeated generation after generation.

To capture the benefits and avoid the harm, the behaviors of financial markets has to be subject to more restrictions. Simply put, the supervision over financial activities from all three parties is indispensable. The supervision from the first party is the self supervision of the behavior doer, which should have ethics and self-discipline, and should not the subjective intention of making excessive promises and getting people into the trap. This is difficult to be observed, so there should be credit records made available for verification by other parties. The supervision from the second party is the buyer's supervision. When buyers exercise their rights, shouldn't they be more alert and ask how on earth the too-good-to-be-rejected "commitments" can be fulfilled? And of course, the more important one is the supervision by the third-party, especially the authoritative third party; namely, the third party which is backed by legal coercive force and has the right to challenge, to warn, and to punish as necessary within the scope of laws and regulations. The idea that a market economy can be maintained solely by self-discipline and the discipline from buyers is probably a Utopia that never exists in the real world.

By referencing daily life experience, the above analysis is not difficult to understand. Drinking alcohol is a freedom of the general public; then why are citizens checked for drinking and driving? Because the self-control of the person in question will drop if he or she gets drunk, and the self discipline is not adequate to ensure that there will be no harm to the life and property of others. To rely on the discipline from the second party—everyone to shy away from drunk drivers—also cannot prevent tragedies. So the authoritative third-party comes in for mandatory checks and enforcement. Obviously, the control was only limited to necessary links—the drunk guy is not prohibited from walking; at most he himself needs to be careful when crossing the road. But to drink and drive the vehicle is not permitted, let alone to fly the plane, drive the bullet train, or operate the crane.

Where did Baoneng's money for the purchases of large volumes of shares come from? Of course this question must be asked. If it is the money earned from many years of successful business, there's not much risk—they can purchase as much as they like. According to what is gathered so far, the majority of the money used by Baoneng for stock purchase—not just the one listed company of Vanke—came from financing. In other words, it was through the promise of financial products that they raised the funds to buy shares and became Vanke's largest shareholder. To make it clear, under the current legal framework financed share purchase is not something impossible. However, the embedded risks should be clearly disclosed to the market and all potentially relevant public investors. For example, the types of financial commitments, and the obligations to honor, should be made known to all relevant parties so that they can judge what kind of future returns must be met for the capital injected into Vanke's capital structure to deliver those yet-to-be-delivered but must-be-delivered obligations.

This matter cannot be vague because it is critical to both Baoneng itself and all relevant parties, including the stability of several financial markets. My view on this matter is still that the self discipline by the first party and the discipline by the second party are not enough, and that effective third party supervision must be put in place. Putting everything else aside, who are able to fulfill the obligation of disclosing adequate information and to make judgment on compliance with existing laws and regulations? Without the specialized supervision by the third party, who is able to figure out what is happening in the dazzling and confusing financial products and financing agreements, and in the financial markets under separate supervisions? Would it be hopeless to count on self-discipline of the first party? As we all have seen, as soon as becoming Vanke's largest shareholder with less than 25% of the stake, Baoneng made the motion to replace all the directors and supervisors; were they drunk? To have a third party act as the supervision body is, first of all, good for the safety of Baoneng; and sure enough, it is the unshirkable responsibility of regulators to ensure the safety of all other parties and the market as a whole.

Therefore, my view is that we do not need to ask about the origin of the hero, but the money must have rightful sources. It is a minimum requirement that the information should be clearly disclosed for the large amounts financed money used for share purchase. As to whether or not it contradicts existing laws and regulations, this requires authoritative determination by market regulatory agencies; if there is disagreement from the parties in question, the case may be brought to the court. This is not Baoneng's responsibility, nor is it an obligation that they are capable to undertake. The current situation is such that actions cannot be put on hold until the entire financial regulatory framework has been improved to be a sound system. In the unfortunate case, if another financial crisis comes, or the crisis happens every year, who could take up the huge responsibility? This time the behavior of Shenzhen Stock Exchange is worth learning; because it expressed the concerns publicly, some information was disclosed to answer at least partially the concerns of the public in the market, such that they would not be blindly misled by all sorts of rumors.

Do Not Repeat Kelon's Mistakes

To sum up, Vanke's case has progressed to where it is today because the foundation of the company, which has been successful for many years, is not solid enough, and all the relevant parties had deficiencies during their interaction under the new situation. The current question is, because none of the parties is individually sound, can they follow the corporate contract framework, renegotiate, and strive for a win–win instead of a lose–lose outcome?

These past few years, I've researched the cases of some companies such as Kelon, Jianlibao, and Hongtashan. The stories of these companies borne out of transformation are sorrowful. They all achieved dazzling success in the market; customers, consumers, and the market did not eliminate them. But they all had problems with equity and governance structure, and there were often conflicts between major shareholders and the founding entrepreneurs, resulting in the misery of these entrepreneurs as individuals and the vanishing of the huge corporate success.

This leads me to focus on a conceptual question. What on earth is capital? My view is that capital is all the resources that bring about future income, which is to be discounted to today. To put it plainly, capital is more than just money. Money must be combined with human talent before it is possible to create potential future income. To create an enterprise, the investors' money cannot become capital until it is combined with the entrepreneur's ability based on a corporate contract. Try an experiment and things will become clear: Pile up the money and leave it there, there will never be value addition no matter how long you wait. If left unattended, the money will definitely be decreasing.

Currently, we have lots of money, and even more floating money. "Financial investment technologies" are becoming ever more popular, but the number of good companies remains limited. The worst of the worst is that some people mistake money as the capital and as the "king" regardless of the source of the money. They do not know to respect human capital, and to respect the human capital devoted to technology, product development, and management; neither do they understand that wealth can be truly created only when the financial capital is combined with the human capital. Conversely, human capital also must respect financial capital. Entrepreneurs are business people with ambitions. To achieve any cause in the ambitious goals, they always find themselves short of resources, and the financial capital is even more indispensable. Therefore, neither side is separable from the side, and neither side can be headstrong; the only way is to look for ways of combination within the framework of contracts.

After the Kelon case, I wrote an article entitled "Kelon: What a Pity," and I hope I do not need to write another one entitled "Vanke: What a Pity." In the recent couple of days, things were turning for the better for the case of Vanke: Wang Shi apologized at the shareholders meeting. China Resources has also followed the attitude of the State-owned Assets Supervision and Administration Commission (SASAC; it will support whatever is good for Shenzhen and for Vanke), and declared together with Baoneng that they are not persons acting in concert; Baoneng also said that it did not nominate the candidates for new directors and new supervisors because they still place hope on the management. Well, that's good. After enough fighting, they should sit down on the table and try to find a good cooperative solution.

Breakout Through Reform and Through Innovation: China's Economy in 2017[19]

External Demand Shrinks; Anti-Globalization Trend Shows Up

In term of growth rate, China's economy peaked in 2007 and 2008. Although there have been some fluctuations afterwards, the general trend has been downward. Compared against the peak in 2007, the annual growth rate for 2015 and 2016 for this world's second largest economy has declined from 14.2% to 6.7%. The amount of decline is already more than half, and this is no small change.

Economies will always have ups and downs, but it is still a big challenge to go downwards from a high level. If we have skied, we will know that there will be lots of inertia to go downhill from a high position; sudden deceleration means that the expectations of enterprises, markets, and localities and all other aspects need to be quickly adjusted otherwise the economy will stall out of control.

Then, where exactly did this downward trend come from? The financial crisis erupted in the United States in 2007, which happens to be the apex of China's rapid economic growth since the opening and reform. In the following year, namely 2008, China's growth dropped to 9.8%, still reaching the average for the period from 1979 to 2008. China became the world's second largest economy in 2009, the world's largest exporter in 2010, and the world's largest trader in 2013. And as per the purchasing power parity (PPP) calculation method of IMF (International Monetary Fund), China became the world's largest economy in 2014.

However, this can not stop the big dip in China's growth rate. Initially the government thought that it might be able to work out some ways to prop the economy and even bring it back to previous growth levels. But eventually it turns out that China's economy, which was victorious in the globalization, could not move away from the basic trend of the global economy.

The first thing to discuss is, why is China's economy shifting from rapid growth to about 6% to 7% growth rate? In my view, if this question is to be answered, it is not enough to look only at China by itself. This is because China's rapid growth was achieved through opening-up and was an integral part of the landscape of globalization.

19 This section is adopted from the speech by the author on January 18, 2017, at the Shenzhen Innovation and Development Institute.—Editor's note.

It is complicated to talk about the global economy. One way to understand it is to simplify and reduce it into a very simplified scenario, where we can assume that there are two economic entities, one being wealthy and the other, poor. Here "wealthy" means having abundant capital and high per-capita income, and "poor" means having little capital, a large population, and low per-capita income.

If these two economies are isolated by a wall and each lives its own life, what will be the result? The impoverished country does not have capital and thereby has no means to improve productivity, so the economic growth will be slow. The wealthy country has adequate capital, which can be translated into even higher productivity. Therefore, the gap will continue to widen if these two economies are segregated.

What will happen if these two economies get connected? Let us assume that the wealthy economy has 100,000 RMB of capital and 300 workers with a per-capita output of 100 RMB, and the poor economy has only 10 RMB of capital but 3,000 workers with a per-capita output of 1 RMB. Now comes the question: If these two economies get connected to each other, what changes will take place to the aforementioned parameters?

After the connection, the math should be done by putting the two economies together. Then the total capital becomes 100,010 RMB, and the total number of workers becomes 3,300. As a result, the relative ratio of the factors will change, which is actually a change in the competition landscape. So what will be the changes after all? Probably the following aspects:

First, the wealthy country originally had a capital of 100,000 RMB and 300 people; now the capital is increased by 10 RMB and the work force is expanded by 3,000 people, so there will be a total of 3,300 people competing for the 100,010 RMB of capital. It is obvious that the scarcity of capital has increased. This is also why, after globalization, Wall Street can make lots and lots of money; the shining performance of the financial industry is attributable to more relative scarcity of global capital.

Second, owing to long-term accumulation, the wealthy country has science and technology and large numbers of patents, and the scarcity of these has also seen significant increases because previously there were only 300 workers as users, but now all the 3,300 people want to equip themselves with the better technology.

Third, the original 300 workers of the wealthy country now need to participate in the competition among the 3,300 workers from across the globe, because globalization has led to a significant increase in the number of workers participating in the competition. Of this, blue collars and lower-level white collars of the wealthy country face the biggest pressure because they directly face the impact of competition from massive numbers of inexpensive labor (with a per capita income of 1 RMB). Then, as the workers from the poor country improve their ability to learn, more laborers from the wealthy country will face greater competitive pressure.

Fourth, income differentiation within the wealthy country will accelerate. The wealthy country's olive-shaped income distribution structure, which has been there for a long time since the end of the war, starts to come back towards the shape of a pyramid. At the top are Wall Street and top technology elites of the Silicon Valley, as their scarcity soars up in the globalization, so they virtually can get anything they want. But at the bottom of the population pyramid, more and more blue collars and white collars are facing the pressure of lower income as affected by the open poor country.

This "silent majority" also get certain benefits from globalization. A large number of high-quality, low-price products made in China have been exported to the United States to reduce their cost of living and increase their real income. The problem is that they are experiencing a bigger competition pressure. What's more, income is always about relative income. Compared with Wall Street and Silicon Valley elites who have made big money from globalization, the manufacturing workers and the class of grassroots white collars in the United States cannot help but feel a great sense of loss.

Fifth, after the opening-up, the poor country's massive labor force will have opportunities to combine with the technology and capital from the developed country. Technology and capital cannot be moved in a simply way, and they require improvement in the learning curve. But as long as the learning curve can be improved, the poor country's comparative cost advantages will come into play, so the income level improves rapidly along with the improvement in productivity.

Sixth, the income gap also gets widened within the poor country; this is because of the different conditions to acquire foreign technology and capital, and even more because of the different degrees of improvement in the learning curve.

Taken together, when the rich and poor countries become connected with the removal of the barrier, the global average income growth will be accelerated as a result of globalization. The average income growth rate for the poor country with a faster rising learning curve is even faster than for the rich country. Income differentiation within the rich country will take place, with sectors benefiting from globalization getting richer and richer, but the income-impacted sectors will become stagnant or even decline. Additionally, income differentiation within the poor country will also occur.

This kind of world map has a simple logic, but the results are a bit complicated. A couple of years ago, a French economist by the name of Thomas Piketty wrote a book called *Capital in the Twenty-First Century*. The book primarily pays attention to how globalization leads to severe income polarization in developed countries. He proves that the Gini coefficient for income distribution in the United States and major Western European developed economies dropped significantly after the end of World War II; however, since the beginning of the 1980s, especially after the 1990s, the Gini coefficient for developed countries has reversed and come back to the historic high point. Piketty believes that the income is too high from capital and too low from labor in developed countries, and the situation is similar to the historical background in the nineteenth century for Karl Marx to write *Das Kapital*, namely that the Industrial Revolution led to aggravation of the conflict between labor and capital in the United Kingdom. Piketty proposes that the only way out is to restrain the capital (impose high tax on capital gains), otherwise there will be a social revolution.

I have read Piketty's resume; he has always been teaching in France except that he spent two or three years as a visiting scholar in Boston. He has never really been to any other places, and he never visited China or India before this book was published. He is talking about developed countries from their own perspective, and he seems to assume that the developed countries are the entire world economy. However, in point of fact, in today's world, both developed and developing countries are involved in globalization. From a global point of view, the income distribution is improving—the developed countries' average income growth is moving closer to the developing countries' average income growth. Piketty has put the trend chart in his book, but it seems that he himself does not quite understand what it means.

It is relatively easy for Chinese people to understand. The time was 1980, when Deng Xiaoping proposed that the China's economy should double twice; and back then China's per capita GDP was only USD 200. After the opening-up, our per capita GDP is now USD 7,000 to 8,000. The per capita GDP for the United States in the early 1980s was more than USD 10,000; currently it is just USD 50,000. Taking China and the United States as examples, the average "global" income distribution has of course improved a lot; this is also why it is worthwhile to uphold globalization.

The problem is that it is another story if developed countries are looked at alone. Piketty did not even bother to take a look at how much money China's farmers and migrant workers could make before and now. He only sees that the proportion of income of ordinary people in developed countries has decreased as compared with their own country's capital and science and technology elites.

This also indicates that globalization has not managed to achieve—neither is it able to achieve—a situation with equal benefit to every person, every social class, and every economic sector. There are always highs and lows, and gains and losses; therefore, there will always be social conflicts. China also has this problem. The excessively large domestic income gap is a problem which it has tried to resolve for many years but has not resolved yet. With our domestic income gap, those who are close to technology and capital or whose learning curve improves more rapidly have quicker income improvements, otherwise the income growth is slow. Additionally, because transformation is far from in place, rent-seeking from corrupt power is also a source of abnormally high income for some people.

Therefore, from a global perspective, every country has its respective problems. However, on the whole, globalization has greatly liberated human productivity and increased the possibility of income convergence between different countries of the world. The layout is a complicated one, although the embedded economic logic is quite simple.

China's Economy is Closely Linked to its Opening-Up

Now, let's discuss China's economy. In terms of cognitive methods, we must avoid such limitations as with the case of Piketty, who only sees the tree but not the forest. China's economy is one moving towards openness and closely linked to globalization; therefore, we cannot move away from globalization and look at it in an isolated way.

For example, why has China achieved decades of rapid growth? In terms of economics theory, it all comes down to the role of comparative advantage. Comparative advantage is a theory proposed by the classic political economist David Ricardo. Before Ricardo, people were accustomed to the theory of absolute advantage, which says as long as Country A is more advanced in producing something than Country B, there is no need for Country B to produce it any more. Ricardo says this is not necessarily the case; even if Country B is not as advanced as Country A, that does not mean that the best strategy for Country B is to produce nothing. Among all the backward industries of Country B, there must be some things with relatively high productivity. If Country B focuses on producing products with its comparative cost advantage, and exchanges with Country A—and the latter also focuses on producing products with its comparative advantage—then the total output of both countries will be even greater.

The first and most important part of the theory of comparative advantage is "comparison," and the premise is to open up the market and implement free trade. Since the birth of this theory, most economists support the theory of free trade because, theoretically, free and open trade leads to more optimal economic growth.

However, as the world changes, theories also get updated accordingly. Around 2003 or 2004, American economist Paul Samuelson, winner of the 1970 Nobel Prize for Economics, started to cast some doubts on the theory of comparative advantage. In one of his articles, he proposed a question on dynamic comparative advantage. For example, originally the United States has a comparative advantage in manufacturing aircrafts whereas China has a comparative advantage in manufacturing labor-intensive products such as socks. According to Ricardo, if the United States manufactures aircrafts and China manufactures socks and the two countries conduct free trade, this will be most optimum for both economies. Samuelson has no objections to this viewpoint.

The problem is that China will not always be content with producing socks. For an economy to produce a certain product all the time, both the cost and the income will change on the margin.

We have a popular slogan here in China: "Industrial Upgrading." This means we should not be content with always producing socks with low margins; although this was the right move in the early years, owing to changes in costs the profit will go down to zero if the same socks are made all the time. So can we produce something else? And the industry needs to be upgraded. And because of the rapid growth, we are required to "accelerate the upgrade." In fact, the upgrading of China's manufacturing has been quite impressive. From some period of producing bicycles to manufacturing motorcycles, from assembling auto parts to assembling whole automobiles and then to making automobiles, and next China moved to aircraft manufacturing. Why not? China also has the conditions; China's market is very large, so we can "exchange the market for technology." Buying so many aircrafts from others, China could always have some negotiation chips. What China could do is to add one condition for each batch of aircraft purchasing, for example, having the rear wing produced in China. If this works out fine, then add another condition for the next batch, say, to have the wings manufactured in China. Moreover, Chinese people are also able to make innovations from the introduced technologies and make hybrid innovations or application innovation in the process of imitation. As this goes on and on, China started to make our own commercial aircrafts.

But, Samuelson asks, what should the United States do? China originally manufactured bicycles, now it has upgraded to make airplanes. Then what should the United States, who made airplanes to exchange with China, make in the future? Indeed, the U.S. industry can also be upgraded, but the problem is that the two countries might upgrade at a different pace. China enjoys the latecomer's advantages; after making bicycles, it looks at the leader and move on with airplane manufacturing. What products will the United States make? This requires groundbreaking and innovative explorations, because there is no forerunner to reference. More importantly, in the global supply chain growing out of globalization, whoever make a virgin creation, regardless of its type, during mass production, the principle of comparative advantage would be followed when all countries are open. Take Apple, for example; the original creation of course comes from Steve Jobs. But to supply across the globe, it seems to be more optimum to have its production in China. Samuelson's judgment is this: If the pace of upgrade of the comparative advantage of one party (i.e., the United States) is constantly slower than the other party (i.e., China or India), then it may suffer from "permanent damage."

With all the compelling stuff, the result might not necessarily lead to Ricardo's optimistic conclusion. If no cooperative solution could be found, trade friction, trade war, or even global political and military tension could follow. In any case, the long-term trade imbalance cannot be sustained. As for China, the previous high growth maintained by high volumes of trade surplus cannot sustain.

In the past, China's economic aggregate was quite small, and a little bit of trade surplus could not be noticeably felt. But when it became the world's second largest economy, maintaining a too-high surplus will definitely spark a big change in the global situation. In point of fact, there has long been some early signs. Before the 2008 financial crisis, who would have expected that fast globalization would see the outbreak of problems first from Wall Street of the United States? One of the factors for this was that the dollar reserve accumulated from China's surplus could not be put in China; instead, it needed to be invested back into the United States; and where to invest, though? A very big portion is to buy U.S. treasury bonds. The American government has no fiscal surplus, and it has been running a deficit ever since the Iraq War. However, from globalization many countries, including China, India, Russia, and the oil-producing countries, have earned lots of dollars to buy the U.S. national debt. So, because the American government "has lots of money," it generously provided housing loans to low-income families even without a down payment. But these families were really unable to keep their houses bought with low interest loans, and they had to return the houses to the bank. However, the bank loans had already been packaged into fairly complicated financial products, and that was how the fire of the financial crisis was ignited.

Therefore, it is impossible for globalization to have only positive benefits, the challenges it brings about will strike in unexpected places. Ever since the financial crisis, external demand on the part of developed countries has declined, and we have found our exports going down from the original high annual growth rate of 20% to 30% to –20%. With this shock wave, China's economy encounters unprecedented challenges.

The Challenge of Descending from a High Level

Therefore, the first factor in China's economic downturn is the worldwide contraction of external demand. The main driver of China's rapid growth is export, which is highly dependent on external demand, so when external demand shrinks, China becomes the first to bear the brunt.

Domestically, tremendous changes have also taken place; the most obvious one is the change in cost advantage. Originally, we relied on comparative cost advantage to participate in global competition and make big strides. In the simplified model described above, the per capita output is only 1 RMB for the poor country and 100 RMB for the rich country. Actually when the income gets converted it becomes production costs—the poor country's labor is 99% cheaper than the rich country. For sure, if the poor country does not know at all how to produce the products that the rich country is able to produce, nothing will happen no matter how cheap the labor is. However, as long as the poor country is also able to make some of the products that the rich country makes, then the former will have a strong competitive strength in the world market. This indicates that the poor country will be staying poor for many years for no good reasons if it does not open up. Only with the opening-up can people find that poverty is also a competitive advantage. Poverty means nothing more than low salary, and low salary means low cost. For the same product, low cost means low price; is there any buyer in the world who does not like low price and good quality? To put it straight, there is no secret about it. Comparative advantage is comparative cost advantage, and the premise is to open up and make the comparison possible.

The problem is that the cost changes. When the poor country has not yet opened, the per-capita output is 1 RMB. After years of rapid growth, it is impossible for it to stay at 1 RMB. Along with the rapid growth, the prices for all factor such as labor costs, land, and energy will change rapidly.

China's experience shows that the most important change is the change in institutional costs. What are institutional costs? Institutional costs are the costs outside the production and required by the operation of the economic system. The original concept was proposed by Ronald Coase, who in 1937 said that the produced product needs to change hands before it is consumed, but the process of changing hands is not free—it takes what he defines as "transaction costs." Because of this discovery, he was awarded the Nobel Prize for Economics in 1991. To further the understanding, the system operation still needs to spend capital even in places where market transactions are prohibited. In the 1940s in China, there was a Mr. Zhang Peigang, who studied China's economy during the War Against Japanese Aggression. For example, if the coastal areas were occupied, what would happen to the inland cities' food supply? At that time, many coastal parts of China ate rice from Thailand. The farmers of Jiangxi and Hunan were very poor, and their grain production cost was extremely low; why didn't Ningbo, Hangzhou, and Shanghai eat rice from Hunan? Through his investigations, Zhang Peigang came to the same conclusion as Coase; namely, even though the cost of producing rice in Jiangxi and Hunan was very low, the local separation forces charged arbitrary fees during the process of transportation, which pushed up the price. At that time, Zhang Peigang defined this as a "pure commercial cost" and believed that as long as the commercial organization is improved, the pure commercial cost can be reduced.

This understanding is still very helpful for analyzing China's economy today. The reason why China's economy is able to develop, if strictly examined, is not just the low labor cost owing to poverty. Before the opening-up, was our labor cost high? It was even lower. But at that time there was no miracle of rapid growth in China. Therefore, it cannot be said that low labor cost will definitely be converted into competitive strength. For factors to be translated into a competitive strength, they must first be converted into products; and the factors must be organized to be converted into products, and they need to operate within a system.

The real secret behind the "China Miracle" is to change the original closed poverty to openness and at the same time instigate the institutional reform. Without the household contracting responsibility system, the rural workers would not have been liberated. When I arrived in Beijing for university, I always heard the phrase "one billion population and 800 million farmers." Deng Xiaoping once said: "we have 800 million farmers in farming, but there is not enough to eat." The main reason was that the system was inappropriate, and—for a very long time—changes were not allowed, so the farmer's enthusiasm for production could not be fully leveraged. Without the household contract responsibility system to solve the grain problem, where could the many laborers who later worked in the Pearl River Delta have come from? When there is not enough grain and there is no foreign exchange to import grain, it simply is not possible to develop the industry or develop cities.

In China, each round of reforms serves to liberate a wave of productivity. The liberation of rural labor force posed a problem: how could they find jobs? It was impossible for state-owned enterprises to recruit several hundred million farmers? The results is that the private economy was forced out. Walking with both legs, especially labor intensive private enterprises got quite developed. Initially people looked down on the private sector as nothing more than a supplement and no big deal. Previously, all industrial sectors were state-owned and built under the instructions of U.S.S.R. experts and China's ministries, and the access threshold was very high. Later on it was found that the non-government sector, including farmers, also had a great learning curve. Under open conditions, and with the right system, over time China's manufacturing capabilities were built.

The manufacturing capacity was formed, but where were the markets? It was not enough to have just the domestic market because the per-capita purchasing power was still low. Starting from the strategy of opening-up the coastal regions in the 1980s to the WTO accession in 2002, China finally opened the gate to the global markets. Originally, China saw exports as very important, but it was also afraid that its enterprises would slash each other's prices so the "nutritious water would flow into other people's fields." Afterwards it was found that sufficient competition was more helpful for China's enterprises to enter the global market. This is because only competition could stimulate the potential of China's producers and entrepreneurs and enable them to understand the depth and breadth of the global marketplace.

China's reform was gradual and its competitive advantages were released step by step. Without the opening-up and reform, no matter how low the production costs are, they won't be able to become competitive strength. China's reform has sharply reduced its institutional costs, and its opening-up has enabled itself to take big strides into the global competition. The opening and reform has significantly moved down the extremely high institutional cost curve.

In the past, many things related to economic development simply couldn't be done. A man in Guangdong named Chen Zhixiong contracted a fish pond and hired several dozen people to do fish farming after he discovered that people liked to eat fresh fish but there was no supply from the market. This led to a huge controversy and the debate spread from Guangdong to Beijing. In the earlier concept, a person who hired more than seven people was considered to be a capitalist.

Now that Chen hired more than 20 people, was he not a "capitalist roader"? Fortunately, the Secretary of CPC Guangdong Provincial Committee and a team of central government leaders disagreed to put such a hat on the people; also fortunately, the Third Plenary Session of the Eleventh CPC Central Committee had set the ideological line that practice is the sole criterion for testing truth. Evidently, this episode shows that the productive forces were freed by reducing the institutional costs. With decreased institutional costs, it became easy for the cheap factors cost to be combined to produce products; this, coupled with learning curve improvements, has shaped up China's economic miracle.

For many years I have been talking about "the two sea levels"; one is the high sea level comprising developed economies, and the other is the low seal level comprising developing economies such as China and India. There was originally no connection between the two sea levels, so each side lived their life separately. But once they are connected as a result of opening-up, capital and technology will fall from the high seal level to the low sea level. Then the cheap factors of the low sea level are effectively organized through institutional reform, and many products with comparative advantages get exported. This is the China story.

Seizing Comparative Cost Advantage as the Key

What is the new problem? The new problem is that the cost curve is forever changing. In economics, the cost curve always goes down and then up; it will just go up again after hitting the lowest point. Therefore, the re-rise again of the cost curve is something that must be eventually faced by any individual, any household, any enterprise, any region, and any national economy. The logic is exactly the same as that every individual life will eventually die and physical structures will eventually disintegrate.

Now let us look at how specifically the cost of China's economy went down and then up. Decentralization of power in the early years did achieve China's objective of activating the economy first through "running the water into the pond to raise fish." But gradually, in the midst of rapid growth, the system operations cost started to rise again. Currently, many people conclude that China's cost advantage has disappeared as they start with labor and the higher salaries. This problem does exist. However, after checking the statistics between 1995 and 2012, namely China's highest economic growth period, I have discovered that during this period China's nominal GDP grew by 8.6 times, and the gross pay grew by 8.8 times, but the tax grew by 16.7 times, non-tax government revenues grew by 18.8 times, the social security contributions grew by 28.7 times, and the land transfer fees shot up by 64 times! These items are all statutory costs, namely costs with enforcement behind them. Indeed, the tax revenue will grow as the economy grows. However, China's taxation rate still has not been decided by law, and many tax items are directly determined by administrative departments without NPC (National People's Congress) review and approval; therefore, it is quite easy to charge too much tax.

What's more, the early years of opening-up and invigoration gradually got rid of the improper original concepts, policies, and systems based on the result of tests by practice. However, some improper controls gradually crept back. For example, the government of this term focuses on streamlining the administration and delegating power, and so many administrative approvals have been canceled. A closer look will find that these canceled items were not left over from the planned economy period but rather added during rapid growth. During rapid growth, it seems to not matter that much to add things hither and thither; but in the face of economic downturn, if those improper controls are not removed and still must be followed, then the friction coefficient for economic operations will be too high. It is not that anyone is deliberately making things difficult; rather, it is an institutional issue. So much ado just ends up with nothing more than creating trouble for yourself. Nowadays, the "'big hat" of capitalism is gone, but there are many small ropes; this is not allowed and that needs approval, and when things add up the friction coefficient becomes quite large.

Innovation also faces institutional costs. Because innovation is new, it often causes misunderstanding in the mindset, and plus there is the incumbent economic interest, therefore there will be frictions. For example, online ride-hailing service went through all sorts of twists and turns from the emergence to legalization. I have checked the history of taxis, which were born in New York City in 1907. Previously the common practice for hackney carriages was bargaining. An overcharged passenger was very annoyed so he invented the "taxi," which fee was "metered" by distance and the price was published; this approach became popular in the market and eliminated the haggling.

However, 100 years of development for the taxi industry also formed a fixed and ossified model whereby the law prevents the access of other competitors and the administrative authorities manage both the price and the volume. In recent years, passengers in metropolises have put lots of criticism on taxi services and complained about the difficulty of taking taxis. The online hailing-cars gave a huge shock to the traditional taxi model and provided an opportunity to solve the difficulty of mobility through mobile internet technology. The problem is, even though we call for innovation every day, when the innovation truly comes sometimes we find ourselves afraid of too much change in the existing order, which will "affect the stability."

Let us move on to urbanization. It only takes a few years to astound foreigners if they have not come back to China to see the cities. However, there are also many problems accompanying their astonishment. The common problem is that even though population and resources are all flowing and people have choices, the administrative-led urbanization still imposes strict geographical confinement, and whoever runs the country wants his county to be the "center." The problem is that the administrative rank is not high enough, and people might not necessarily choose to come to your location. Therefore, there are two sides of the coin. The job is well done for urban construction, but still with mind-boggling waste; so many desolate infrastructures and housings have been built, so much steel and cement have been consumed, and so much emission from the steel and cement has eventually come back to the lungs of adults and children. Looking at the overall picture, isn't there anything that needs to be changed? We should invest more into places where people want to go; actually, the investment into central cities is still far from enough. And where people do not want to stay, we should return the farmland back into forest, pastureland, and environment to have clear waters and green mountains. Two places of the same rank on the administrative hierarchy could have completely different urbanization prospects, and resources should be allocated along this logic rather than by the administrative hierarchy.

All in all, along with the rapid economic growth, the institutional cost fell first and then rose again.

Meanwhile, the global situation also changed. China's experience obtained through its opening-up also affects other countries. The lesson is nothing more than converting the poverty into competitive strength, and changing the domestic system for this goal. This can be done by China, and equally by India, Vietnam, all southeast Asian countries, and Africa, too.

Therefore, now the previous "two sea levels" becomes a "sandwich," with China squeezed in the middle: the cost is not the lowest, but at the same time we also do not have in hand very many unique or competitive products. As pointed out by Ronald Coase, to actually stand out from the crowd in the global competition, you need to either lead by cost or by being unique.

It is true that thirty years of opening-up and reform has created China's rapid growth, but today China's economy gets caught in the middle from a global perspective. Down below, the cost of India and Vietnam is even lower and their investment promotion is even more vigorous than the then China. And above

China, there is still the ceiling comprising of the United States, Europe, and Japan, who continuously introduce unique products in spite of the low growth rate.

This means that, from a global megatrend perspective, China's economy is about to have a stage-wise change. False flames are currently blazing, and money comes easily through all sorts of speculations; this actually erodes entrepreneurial spirit and it cannot mobilize more energy to be aligned to products and services. It's not for any individual to blame, because the difference in money is simply too huge—the income from speculation on housing is even higher than many years of managing the real economy. Under the backdrop of external demand contraction, this is the second force to drag China downwards.

The third is the dynamic comparative cost, especially the institutional cost within it. This cost cannot be reduced just by relying on the strength of the people, because it is a statutory burden; whoever reduces it is violating the law. So this matter still depends on strong leadership by the CPC Central Committee and the State Council to deepen the reform, otherwise it will be difficult to for the institutional cost to go down. Things like tax cuts, reducing social security payments, and transforming the land system involve a wide spectrum of aspects, and one move will affect the whole system; therefore, they cannot be achieved without a systematic reform.

Recently, Cao Dewang, Chairman of Fuyao Group, said that the tax rate for China's enterprises is too high, and he is right. He is not incorrect in saying this. In 2016 autumn, I visited a factory opened by a Taizhou-based manufacturing company in Pennsylvania, United States. When asked why the factory was opened there, they told me that the energy is cheaper, the land is cheaper, the social security burden is not as high, and there are also tax holidays in the investment incentives. The absolute labor cost is higher than in China, but the productivity is also higher. After the comparison was made, it was economically justifiable to set the production right there for products mainly sold to the United States.

In all forms of competition, the first move is to control costs. If an enterprise wants to gain a foothold, it would be best to have the Sunday punch, but still the costs needs to be managed. As for highly competitive products, the survival in the "red ocean market" (with very fierce competition) depends precisely on cost control. When the 2016 Central Economic Work Conference put forward the idea of "cost reduction," it was by no means a trivial matter. Cost reduction ought to be achieved through joint efforts between the government and enterprises. We should try as much as possible to extend the period of having the comparative cost advantage, because it is impossible to acquire a unique advantage all of a sudden.

Relying on Reform and Innovation to Break the Siege

In 2017, the most important thing is to tenaciously advance the reform and to break the siege through the reform. A gradual reform has the benefit of less shock, but its difficulty lies in the perseverance. Experience proves that if institutional costs are reduced, the economy will develop well; if institutional costs suddenly comes back to rise again, the national economy will be dragged down.

Therefore, to deep the reform as determined by the decision of the Third Plenary Session of the Eighteenth CPC Central Committee, what are the difficulties? I will list three points:

First, previously the reform was driven by crisis. Life was too hard, there was not enough food, and so the system had to be changed. Should the household contracting system be implemented? Deng Xiaoping said, stop arguing and let us solve the food problem first. Should China open itself to the outside world? Many laborers escaped to work in Hong Kong, Xi Zhongxun proposed to allow capital from Hong Kong to set up factories in the mainland, and this was how China started to have special economic zones. China was forced to perform the reforms in the early years.

Today, China's economic aggregate is No. 2 in the world and has attracted much of the world's attention; even with the slowdown, it is still a very large economy with a medium to high growth rate. This seems to make people fail to see the size of the danger. Therefore, with very little keenly felt pain today, it is very difficult to reach the consensus on the reform.

Second, in the past we pushed the reform forward with the opening-up, but some of the policies adopted by many developed economies are very bad. When these policies get transmitted into China, many people would say they are all doing this, why should we change? During the discussion on online hailing, some people say it is forbidden in France, and in certain cities in the United States, so why don't we put a ban? The problem is, we need to choose whatever is good. Currently it seems that the opening-up cannot push the reform forward. Hence we need a new logic of learning, and we truly need to start from our own actual situation and choose which things should be changed and to what extent they should be changed.

Third, reforms cause relative changes to interests; some will benefit, others will suffer. Today's math on gains and losses is different from the 1980s. Back then the reform was basically incremental; everyone did not have enough to eat, most people were happy to have more grains with the implementation of the household contracting system, and at the most the production team leader was a little unhappy because previously he had the authority to ring the bell and give commands and now nobody would listen to him. But the vested interest here was very small because he would soon hurry up to farm his own land. However, today, the reforms of many fields need to touch very large amounts of interests in stock. This is why the reform becomes difficult as it moves into deep water. Not only is it difficult to see the targets clearly, but also it is difficult to apply strength in the deep water. In the deep water area, one single punch doesn't have much strength. The punch might look nice from the distance, but the strength is not enough to solve the problem.

As the reform moves deep, the distinction between right and wrong is no more so obvious. To truly solve a problem, it has become a big challenge to find the new balance point. In the autumn of 2016, I visited New York City, and the time of this visit coincided with the centennial anniversary of the city's urban planning legislation. The regulatory changes throughout its history have left lots of enlightenment, which might be helpful in dealing with the balance between complex interests.

New York City passed its first urban planning legislation in 1916, with the main content being "zoning and height restriction." The backdrop for the legislation was that the land rights from the agricultural society were no longer suitable for urban development. In the traditional land rights configuration, everything from the center of the earth up to the top of the sky belongs to the land owner. However, the city is a dense society, and so tall buildings would block other people. In the early twentieth century, the American economy entered the fast lane of rapid growth, and companies making lots of money all rushed to build skyscrapers. In 1915, the Equitable Life Building was completed in lower Manhattan. With 39 stories, it was the world's tallest building of that time, and the size was so large that its shadow covered seven acres of blocks, leaving no sunlight for its neighbors and pedestrians. The aggrieved parties cried out that a height limit be put for building in residential zones, industrial zones, and commercial zones. If the limit is exceeded, the building should "setback," or shrink inwards at the upper part of the building to allow the sunlight to shine down onto the streets and let fresh air to flow. After this law was adopted, many famous landmark buildings were built in New York, such as the Empire State Building and the Chrysler Building; and, without exception, they all have a pinnacle.

But new problems followed on the heels of this development. Because Manhattan was so attractive that people, resources, and projects continued to aggregate into this small peninsula, the height limit set by the 1916 legislation became a constraint for the city's further development. In addition, the construction technology was advancing; advances in metallurgy, elevators, ventilation, and glass actually allowed for taller buildings to be built. But of course, the previous regulation remained an obstacle.

By the mid 1950s, the situation started to cleared up. The Seagram Building was to be built on Park Avenue in the Midtown area, and the designer was the famous German architect Mr. Ludwig Mies van der Rohe. His architectural philosophy was functionalism, with a special focus on simple rectilinear and planar shapes, so he could never accept the inward tapering. But because it was against the law for tall buildings not to taper, there ensued a deadlock. In the end, the project got Phyllis Lambert on board. Not an architect herself, she found a comprise between the architect and New York City government. The solution was that there will be no setback at the top of Seagram Building, but the owner should relinquish a large piece of land to build a small plaza that would be fully open to citizens so as to allow the building to be tall and rectangular.

This experience inspired New York City government, which revised its urban planning legislation in 1961 to introduce the new concept of "incentive control." From that time onwards, developers had the option of openly "discussing figures" with the city government—to relinquish how much ground space to New York's public in exchange for increased plot ratio for the skyscrapers. And further still, other practices containing market logic such as "plot ratio transfer" and "air rights trading" were incorporated into New York City's "elastic control" framework. The city not only grew even taller but also had more diverse architectural forms, while giving more considerations to the balance between individuality and public interest.

This also enlightening to our reform. If there is no control from the government, the competing interests in the market may find themselves in conflict. But once control is added, the system might become ossified. Here in China, we often talk about the government and the market, and it seems that if the government is there the market should absent, and vice versa. But New York's urban planning reform successfully identified a meeting point from seemingly irreconcilable positions.

This leads to the second direction of breakthrough which I want to talk about today; namely, to break the deadlock through innovation. Economics already has this tradition of analysis from the past. Joseph Schumpeter says the only way to break out of the repeated cycle of mediocre economic growth is to rely on innovation, or to introduce new products, or to improve quality, or to use new production processes, open up new markets, and acquire new sources for raw materials and semi-finished products, or to create new economic organizations. Only continuous innovation can bring about sustained economic growth.

To add one further point, innovation is important and it is great, but its occurrence is not necessarily guaranteed. Otherwise, how could there be so much overcapacity, so many zombie enterprises, so many "chicken rib businesses," so many critically ill enterprises, and even stagnant economies?

Innovation requires certain conditions. In fact, this is also related to the question of how innovation takes place: Innovation always starts with an "idea." But the question is worth careful examination as to under which conditions this "idea" will become intensified, polished, translated into actions, converted into an invention, consolidated into a product, and then grow into an industry. Next I would like to share some of the experiences that I have seen.

In 2015, I got quite irritated during a trip to Israel. Israel's land area is even smaller than Beijing municipality at only 12,000 km^2 (about 20,000 km^2 under its actual control), and it has only eight million people. The natural resources conditions are not so good. It is said to be a land of milk and honey, but in fact half of the country is desert, and one-third of its land area has an annual total rainfall of only 50 mm, so it does not seem to be a nice place to live. But this country lives on human capital and technological innovation. Every single plant we saw in Israel adopted drip irrigation—that's an Israeli-invented technology, and it has built Israel into "Europe's Vegetable and Fruit Kitchen," which exports not only fruits and vegetables but also fresh water and desalination technologies. The number of people fed by Israel's agriculture has increased by 100 times since its founding through innovation. Israel has 7,000 startups and the highest number of NASDAQ-listed companies only next to the United States and China. And its per-capita amount of venture capital is even higher than the United States and Europe. These startups are densely distributed throughout Tel Aviv and Haifa, and many of the most critical technologies for amazing products from Silicon Valley are developed here. Every major Silicon Valley company has an R&D center in Tel Aviv. Israel does not have a very large domestic market, nor does it have the capacity to easily manufacture large volumes of products for export; so they focus on technology. Their high-tech sector contributes to 50% of Israeli exports and 10% of Israel's jobs; in 2014, Israel's per-capita output was USD 35,000. What's achieved by such a resource-poor country is nothing short of amazing.

To develop science and technology, what does Israel rely on? They rely on valuing education. Actually we Chinese people also always value education. But the focus in their way of valuing education is different. The Jewish Bible writes that they "are the people found by the God to wrestle with the God," so they come to this world to also wrestle with the God rather than only worship the God. At the age of 5, Jewish children need to study the Old Testament and the Talmud. However, they do not stop merely at reciting the words of the sages; they are encouraged to ask questions, to discuss and debate, and to interrogate. When children come home from school, Jewish mothers do not ask "did you do well in the exam." Instead, they ask: "Did you ask questions at school today?" and "Did you ask good questions?" This is the fountainhead of their productivity.

Aaron Ciechanover was the first Israeli winner of the Nobel Prize for Chemistry. He delivered a speech, which taught us quite a lot. He said that when he was a little boy his mother told him: "When you walk into a river, you may go downstream or upstream, but you must always and forever go upstream." Going downstream is easy and going upstream is difficult; for his whole life he was going upstream, stopping doing things when they have been figured out and picking the next most challenging one. After becoming a tenured professor in the United States, he returned to Israel where he eventually won the Nobel Prize for Chemistry. There is a sentence in the Talmud, "difficult things are easy to accomplish." This saying is very much in line with the principle of economics. Other people do not dare to do difficult things; the competition becomes less fierce, so it is easier to get success.

In June 2016, several of us teachers and alumni took a trip together to the United States to see Silicon Valley and Boston. These two places are centered around universities. For universities, scientific discoveries are the core. However, they have formed a system which allows the universities to grant all of its inventive patents to private individuals, including professors and their teams, who could launch a start-up just by paying a licensing fee. As a result, the channels between scientific discovery and technological invention, and between science and industry, become open and connected. At both Silicon Valley and Boston, if you read the map you will find tens of thousands of start-ups densely situated around universities. Here in China universities also have relationships with scientific innovation enterprises. But the main form is to provide them with graduates; then enterprises come to the university for partnership if they encounter technology problems, plus some government entrusted projects. However, the form of connection is still wide apart between university R&D and industrial market, which are not closed integrated together.

The U.S. targets big markets, and it is the same case for China. But Americans have wild thinking when dealing with problems, and this is their obvious advantage. In a small desert town more than 100 kilometers east of Los Angeles, we saw dozens of engineers and managers persevering for eleven years just to develop an engine to be used on the spaceship that is able to make a round trip to Mars. Put the level of science and technology aside, we were all shocked by this type of thinking alone; and they do not see spaceship and space technology naturally as the country's business. These dozens of people have been committed to this job in the desert after they found venture capital. This is truly the integration of wild thinking and down-to-earth doing.

Another example is the ultra-high-speed train. Maglev train technology suspends the train to reduce the frictional resistance, but the resistance from the air is still there. The ultra-high-speed train takes the idea further; it builds a large tube, pumps out all the air, allowing the train to move in the vacuum environment. We did not know whether the project can succeed or not, but we are touched by the enterprising spirit. The project was launched with several dozen million USD of venture capital raising and has been going for several years; no one took it as something that should only be considered by the country.

We also went to see the "electric popsicle," a product designed to help the blind to "see" the world. In point of fact, blind people's inability to see the world is solely a problem with their eyes as an information channel, which fails to transmit the perceptual image information to the brain for image formation. Blind people only have a problem with their eyes; their brains still have the image formation function, and as long as another channel can be found to transmit the image into their brains they will be able to "see." It is to follow this principle that the company has already spent more than ten years in research, and their second-generation of products has just been launched. They found the transmission channel under the tongue, then designed the "electronic popsicle," which is connected to a camera in the front; the signal is transmitted from underneath the tongue to the brain, so the blind person is able to "see the world."

I brought a book to read on this survey trip, *The Essence of Technology* (published by Zhejiang People's Press in April 2014). The book says, "technology uses new or different principles to solves problems targeted by the current purpose." This truly combines the "principle" as the result of scientific discovery, the "current purpose" namely the real demand from the real world, and a way of using the principle namely the "technology" into an entirety.

Now not just Silicon Valley and Boston, the United States also has a number of emerging small "brain belts," namely brain-dependent scientific innovation industry belts or industry clusters as opposed to the name of "the Rust Belt." Take Austin, the state capital of Texas, as an example. I went there more than twenty years ago, when the largest employer was the government, followed by the university, and there were basically no other industries. Now, however, the University of Texas at Austin is surrounded by 55,000 science and technology start-ups, in a way very similar to how Silicon Valley surrounds Stanford and Berkeley. And this area has also got a good nickname as the "Silicon Hill." To trace back to the origin and history of this area: In the 1960s, Russian descendant George Kozmetsky started his venture business as a new graduate at the fledging Silicon Valley, and after the success he sold the business. According to his own experience he felt that it was critical to establish the connection between fundamental scientific research and the industry market, so he founded IC^2 Institute to specialize in the research of how to bridge the barriers between science, technology, industry, and markets.

These are also the same as in China's experience. For example, innovation is a phenomenon which happens in a highly aggregated environment: gathering of talents, meeting of minds, and brainstorming of ideas; everyone sticks together to encourage exploration and tolerate failure, with the addition of financial and legal support. Although we have the slogan of building an innovative country, as we examine carefully we will see that innovation does not happen all over the places. Currently speaking, the main sites are Zhongguancun in the north and Shenzhen in the south.

On this visit to Shenzhen, I have visited a number of companies and gained some perceptions. Last week, I exchanged some views with Tencent Research Institute, and the topic was "Innovation Upstream and Downstream." To go from principle discovery, technology invention to products and industries is to go downstream; conversely, to start with industry and product to look for technology and explore the principle is to go upstream. Innovation always combines the upstream and the downstream. Shenzhen's starting point was to go upstream, or, as Gao Yunfeng, Chairman of Han's Laser Technology puts it, reverse innovation. Gao himself is not the scientist to invent the principle of lasers, nor did he own any laser patent in the beginning. Instead, he started with laser application, opened up a market, and then went back to upgrade the technology by seeking support from universities, research institutes, scientists, and academicians; in this way, he built an industry. Most companies in Shenzhen, including Huawei and Tencent, followed the same route; it's just that the self-initiative and self-consciousness of different enterprises innovation into the upstream are different. Excellent companies have a strong impulse to go upward and persevere in taking the difficult path, and with accumulation they become strong innovation companies. After growing stronger, they have the ability and the strength to go downstream from the principles. For instance, Huawei started quite early on to invest into such fundamental research as algorithm, and it has also accumulated many patents and demonstrated its advantage in long-lasting competitiveness.

On this trip to Shenzhen, I also visited several companies working downstream from principles, which means making scientific discoveries first and then developing technology and producing products. BGI had the dissertation first, and so did Royole, Huaxun, and Kuang-Chi Institute of Advanced Technologies; DJI's Wang Tao also first wrote down his "idea" in his graduation thesis before he converted it into an industry. This kind of downward route is very much in line with the type of innovations at Silicon Valley and Boston; although quite risky, this approach has vast development prospects. The greatest thing about humans lies precisely in discovery and exploration.

As things currently are, it is necessary to connect the upstream and the downstream for China as a large country to gain a foothold in the world stage of innovation. In the past, the main method was to go upwards because we were constrained by the initial conditions at departure, and it also turned out to be the correct choice. However, as the economic strength builds up, with such a large population and so many smart people, China should have the opportunity to make contribution corresponding to its scale of population in terms of finding new principles. Sure enough, to go from principles to products, previous experiences accumulated from reverse innovation should be summarized and can serve as a good reference.

Coming to this point, our comprehension of innovation can be summed up in the following keywords: the first keyword is "concentration." That is to say, the distribution of innovation is extremely imbalanced, and the innovators need to gather together for things to happen. Such qualities as being discontent with the status quo, daring to dream, and having ideas are unwelcomed in many places and will sink into laughingstock among others if the concentration is not enough. So these people need to flock together to encourage each other, appreciate each other, motivate each other, and refine each other. It is a hard-earned fruit for Shenzhen to become a hot land of China's innovation; innovation land can not be shaped up as easily as claimed.

The second is "density." Density takes "concentration" and projects it into a specific space. Shenzhen is not large in area, and Nanshan District is even smaller; however, it has a sufficient density of innovation enterprises, talents, and all sorts of services. It seems to make good sense, and we should not spread out too wide to dilute the concentration. The third is "frequent interactions." It is necessary to strive to bring all resources together such as scientists, universities, research institutes, governments, defense demand, local development, start-ups, and venture capital so as to form an atmosphere conducive to innovation. When I visited Royole the other day, they said they spent several years at Stanford and felt that the best thing about Silicon Valley was the atmosphere, which could not only add more to knowledge but also more importantly change and influence their attitude towards life. No matter how immature the idea you bring up is, the first sentence from others' response is always "that's very interesting," and this is an encouragement. I have also interviewed an entrepreneur who came to Shenzhen from elsewhere to do R&D on the Tencent Open Platform. Asked why he set up his research and development center in such an expensive place, he told me that nothing make sense there in his former site; whenever a new idea is brought up, the response would be "No, no, that not work." Therefore, the atmosphere is a priceless treasure.

In the post–rapid growth era, China faces new challenges in comparative cost advantage. To grow through reform and innovation is something that China cannot shy away from. Currently, the black swan could be anywhere, but I do see no uncertainty for this basic option. It is absolutely certain that only reform is able to sustain China's comparative cost advantages, and that only innovation is able to generate higher added value at the higher income level and establish a foothold on the global stage. Shenzhen has a lot of experience in this area, which is well worth learning.

Question and Answer Session

Q: Not that long ago, Shenzhen and Hong Kong signed a cooperative agreement on building an innovation park in the Hetao area. I would like to ask how do you see prospects for the innovation cooperation between Shenzhen and Hong Kong, and what kind of influence will it bring to the future development of these two cities?

A: Hong Kong plays a big role in China's opening and reform. At the international level, when the reforms are compared between China and the Soviet Union, one of the points is that because China has Hong Kong, and so it is closer to international market, finance, and commerce and the information is lower. This point has been written into history. In the early years, the first investors to invest in the mainland were also from Hong Kong.

However, Hong Kong's economy also has problems. I once heard a professor at the Massachusetts Institute of Technology (MIT) answer a question from a Chinese student: "How is the American economy different from the economies of Europe and Japan?" The professor replied, "All of today's strongest American companies were not heard of twenty years ago, but if look at the strong companies in Europe and Japan, they were already strong a long time ago." If we use this enlightening viewpoint to look at China's Hong Kong, the situation seems to be similar to Europe and Japan. The strong companies remain the same several old strong companies, and we seldom see newcomers. On the flipside, if we look at Shenzhen, many of today's strong companies are rising stars. Therefore, in terms of joint innovation, probably Shenzhen will give more help to Hong Kong.

Q: I am quite interested in the topic of innovation, and I'd like to focus and ask one question: From the perspective of economics, the main player of innovation should be enterprises; what kind of role should the government play here? The United States does not have the Ministry of Science and Technology, but they do very well in science and technology. They also do not have the Ministry of Education, but their education does a pretty good job. While China is pushing forward innovation, what should the government do to play a good role?

A: In abstract terms, what are the differences between governments and enterprises? Actually, if you look at an enterprise's CEO, the chief executive officer, he is also an "officer." From the perspective of organizational structure, governments are very similar to companies, especially large companies. They have a structural framework and also need someone to give orders and make decisions. But there is one point which make the governments different. That is, governments have in their hands what we call "legal coercive force," which enterprises generally do not have. Most enterprises need to convince consumers in the market to buy their products, and there is no enforcement. They also need to convince investors to invest into them with performance.

Therefore, probably your question can be rephrased as: "What role does legal coercive force play in innovation?" I think it is still indispensable.

First, it helps maintain market order. For example, the protection of intellectual property rights cannot rely on the protections by enterprises and inventors themselves. If it were just themselves, there might be a big fight and eventually it would take an army to do protect the intellectual property rights (IPR). This is not completely impossible, but it is not economical either. It is just better to have the government to exercise the legal coercive force to take up this job. Without this legal coercive force, there will be no innovation to speak of.

Second, transform the social atmosphere or the ethos. China is still undergoing transformation. According to my experience, changing the social atmosphere or mindset can also be done by people without the government taking the lead, it is just much more difficult. For example, the opening-up and reform, emphasis on science, supporting talents, encouraging innovation, etc.; the cost of changing the habits and customs can be reduced significantly if the government takes the lead.

Third, government procurement, especially defense contracts, is a very important "buyer" of big country's innovations. It is true that the United States does not have a Department or Ministry of Science and Technology, but they have a very strong Defense Advanced Research Products Agency (DARPA). Their military purchase orders play an irreplaceable role in the development of Silicon Valley, Boston, and other places. If you have read *Abundance: The Future Is Better Than You Think,* you will know that the four drivers for innovation are curiosity, wealth, fear, and the search for the meaning of life. Why is "fear" included on this list? Just think about how atomic bombs were invented. Indeed, scientists' curiosity about the laws of nature is a critical part; but writing the research paper does not equate to having the Manhattan Project. According to intelligence, Hitler was working on atomic bomb development. If the Americans had not sped up the process of research and development, the outcome of World War II might have been very different. This is the role of national fear, and it is completely different from wealth-stimulated innovation. The market logic is that he who has new things first becomes developed first. With regard to national fear, on the other hand, the idea is that if the enemy has something but I do not, then the game is over. Therefore, the focus of innovation demanded from national defense is exceptionally different. The internet originated from a method to maintain the communications system in times of war, and it was not invented for you and me to use WeChat. However, some military technologies, after being invented, can also be converted for civil purposes. I learned in Israel that the "Iron Dome" (anti-rocket system) technology developed by their Ministry of Defense was later used to break up thrombi in human blood vessels. For the next step, China has a great potential for integrated military and civil innovations; this is also, in the broad sense, the role of the government in innovation.

Of course, the government is an exclusive organization. Its competition pressure is more indirect, and it is quite easy to have bureaucratization and even corruption of power within the organization; so it must pay special attention to avoiding the shortcomings when playing a role in innovation. Currently, the more controversial question is whether or not the government needs to give subsidies to support scientific innovation. The attitude from my research is that we should make the judgment based on specific actual conditions. For example, what kind of subsidies are given, what is the effect? Which items of subsidies have achieved the intended purposes, and which ones have been distorted or even gone into the opposite direction? During this survey, we have also discussed these topics. For example, Take Tencent Open Platform as the example: Nanshan District Science & Technology Innovation Bureau also gave support to the project, the government support fund was given the open platform, and the enterprise partners are selected by Tencent; this is better than having government officials directly pick support targets.

Q: As you mentioned just now, Shenzhen has its unique advantage as a hot land for innovation; but we all know that Shenzhen's higher education is relatively weak in the country. We don't need to compare with Beijing, it is even quite behind Guangzhou. So, I'd like to ask, is this fact a shortcoming which will negatively affect the development of innovations in Shenzhen?

A: That's a good question. To go from the discovery of a principle to the invention of a technology and then the creation of a product, the discovery of the principle is the original source. Therefore, lack of universities and research institutes is a weakness, and definitely a shortcoming. However, the Silicon Valley was also once backward. There were no Ivy League–quality schools in Silicon Valley; Stanford University was founded quite late. Latecomers could come from behind and become the leader, but that needs to be viewed in a time frame of 100 years.

Currently Shenzhen has brought in many universities, including Peking University, which has set up a branch in Shenzhen, and at the same time Shenzhen is building its own university. The method is like walking with both legs, which are both worth exploring. Let me say, if I may, Shenzhen needs to see building its own university as a fundamental task with centuries of significance. After all, universities have inextricable cultural links to their "place of birth." For example, no one has heard of a Harvard campus in California, or the Oxford University Scotland Branch, or Humboldt University Stuttgart Institute. Why not? There is always a reason behind this. Of course, the pace will be slower to build Shenzhen's own universities, but this is the root. It is better to put the majority of investment on Shenzhen University and Southern University of Science and Technology, and then try to look for best professors from around the world. Shenzhen University has only been around for a short time, but there are already good signs. Didn't Pony Ma (Chairman and CEO of Tencent) graduate from Shenzhen University? After Chen Shiyi became its President, Southern University of Science and Technology has been joined by seven academicians; this is the same experience as what Stanford did, keeping the brand to yourself and hunting for people from all over the world. And certainly, I also can't forget to mention Hai Wen[20] of Peking University is also doing a good job in education here and making important contributions to Shenzhen.

Q: Just now you mentioned about Cao Dewang, "the King of Glass," and it seems you agree with him; but the view on tax system reform is always different between the government and the public.

A: There's not really any difference. The decision to reduce tax burdens was made at the Third Plenary Session of the Eighteenth CPC Central Committee. Tax types need be fair, common, and simplified, and the tax rates need to be reasonably lowered, so the tax burdens of enterprises must be reduced. But obviously, tax cuts are not easy. Especially with recent years of economic downturn, many local governments experience lower tax revenue, so they have increased the tax. Here is another calculation method: If businesses and enterprises are crushed, wouldn't the local governments' burden become even heavier? Therefore, when enterprises and the governments both face difficulties, they must work jointly to overcome these hardships. Tax system reform is complicated because it involves legislation; it is very difficult to proceed without top-level design and a strong top-down guidance. Therefore, it must be put into the scheme of the top-level reform.

Moderator[21]: I'd like to add something. Just now, we were talking about the "killer tax rate" problem as brought up by Mr. Cao Dewang, the "Glass King." There is no such thing as "killer tax rate" in our country. I think what Mr. Cao referred to is totally different from what we are talking about. He was talking about not only the taxes but also all sorts of enterprise burdens brought about by the enterprise's system costs, whereas the taxes we are talking about do not include other things, so the basis for comparison is different. What Mr. Cao was saying is that the enterprise's system costs are much larger than the taxes. It is universally acknowledged that the burden of enterprises is much too heavy, the proportion of government revenue is much too high, and and the public is not sharing the benefits. This is a consensus for all of us and also the direction for the future reform.

Q: Although China's economy is currently undergoing a downturn, Shenzhen has a primary characteristic in that the city's economy and fiscal revenues have always

20 Hai Wen served as the Dean of Peking University Shenzhen Graduate School from 2008 to 2013, and Dean of the HSBC Business School.—Editor's note.

21 The Moderator is Zhang Enping, former member of the Standing Committee of CPC Shenzhen Municipal Committee and Director of the United Front Work Department.—Editor's note.

been maintained at a high level. In 2016, Shenzhen's total revenue was more than RMB 700 billion, and the local fiscal revenue was more than RMB 300 billion. When a city has such a high amount of wealth, there may be no incentive to make changes. So, when the resources are abundant, how can the government and the society maintain the impetus for reform and innovation? Additionally, rapid growth in itself will create a certain degree of unfairness. When the development reaches a certain level, how can the society continue with next steps of innovation in a more fair or more shared manner?

Just now, you touched on institutional costs. Our country has been fighting corruption, which, to you, will reduce the system costs. But will the system costs increase during the process of fighting corruption? How do you see this?

A: This is a problem reported by many places. My personal take is that this is in line with logic from a methodological point of view, because there will always be a series of new problems triggered by solving problems. Leave the problem there unresolved, you only have the one problem going back and forth. And it really must be resolved. To resolve it, one new problem will pop up after another; so we need to follow the rhythm and move forward. Corruption must be attacked, I think everyone agrees to this, yes? The atmosphere of corruption and extravagance a few years ago, has—by any measure—weakened China's competitiveness. If all the efforts are put on clinging to powerful persons and creating personal relationships, how can people be dedicated to products or innovation? Fighting corruption definitively brings about new problems: The previous norms of behavior and the unclear way of life were there for so long, now all of a sudden they do not work; certainly people will not be used to this. Putting everything else aside, just the simple question of extravagant eating with public fund is very difficult to manage; people get used to it and feel unhappy when it is banned. This is also why we need to discuss how to move forward in the next step. We cannot move backwards; we cannot allow for corruption to come back because of inaction by officials or change the "Eight Points of Anti-Corruption" into seven or five points. None of us will agree, right? Then how can we move forward in the next step? After the atmosphere has been curbed, we might still change the structure, simplify and cut out the unreasonable steps so that it does not matter whether officials are proactive or not. We do not need so many approvals. When the approval system is changed into a registration and archiving system, it does not matter at all whether the officials are active or not, this is a best choice.

But no country can be without a government. There must always be necessary administrative agencies. How can they be both effective and clean? It is indeed difficult. But for many things, we need to have the faith and persistence after the goals have been determined. Hong Kong originally had a very bad corruption problem.

When the Independent Commission Against Corruption (ICAC) was established in the 1970s, people were also not used to it, and there was inaction. Some 5,000 police besieged ICAC and wanted to maintain the vested interest. In the end, the authorities decided to forgive small previous mistakes, but still deal with the big cases, and to follow the new rules for everything in the future. Coming back to the reform, we need to hold on and build a policy system; things will become easier as we form the habit.

3 Urban–Rural Bottleneck

Next Journey of Urbanization

If we are to say that a city is a living organism, then it should have different stages of growth and development. Over the past twenty-odd years, China has been rapidly urbanizing. This can be seen in the large numbers of people moving into towns and cities, the enormous investment and development in infrastructure, and the expansion of the physical size of cities. China's cities seem to have entered their puberty; their skeletal structures are growing and are ready for fast body growth.

With the national economy shifting into moderate to rapid growth, and the constraints from debts and environment, China's urbanization will inevitably face transformation. To begin thinking now about the next journey of urbanization is perhaps to fix the roof before it starts to rain.

Let us first come back to common sense. The reason why cities become cities is because they accommodate large numbers of diverse, complex, and colorful economic and cultural activities in their limited space. Viewed this way, cities inevitably need to be defined by density. As for why population and resources come together to shape into a high-density spatial form, the answer is that aggregation improves division of labor, and improved division of labor increases productivity and thus significantly improves the income of urban residents.

Usually no one will disagree that cities have a higher density than rural areas. How high, then, can the city's density be, and what density level can it reach while still maintaining the capability of organizing a vibrant economic and cultural life in a normal and effective way? I do not believe that my imagination is good enough to give an answer, so I need to move myself around to observe and feel the life in cities with the "highest density." Once I visited Columbia University for more than a month and stayed in upper Manhattan, providing me with the opportunity to remember the density of this global city: Each square kilometer had 27,000 residents—this is only the number of people living here during the night; if you include commuters from neighboring areas and around the world, business travelers, tourists, and audiences who come to Broadway for the shows, the figure is several times this. In terms of economic density, Manhattan's annual GDP per square kilometer is 1.6 billion U.S. dollars (USD). Manhattan is, of course, the very heart of New York City. Looking at New York City as a whole, each square kilometer has on the average 16,500 residents producing a GDP of 1.128 billion USD.

After returning to China, I checked the density of our cities and found a very large gap. The population and economic aggregate of Beijing, Shanghai, and Guangzhou are world-renowned. However, the number of residents and the economic value per unit land area are still embarrassing. China's densest city is Shenzhen. In 2014, each square kilometer had a total of 3,809 residents and a GDP of Ren Min Bi (RMB) 820 million, or about USD 137 million.

This difference is very interesting. China's total economic aggregate is very impressive, but it still lags behind in the per-capita figure. The same is true for China's cities; the total economy is leading but the density is quite low. So is there any reason behind this similar pattern?

One reason is that China's "cities" refer to the entire administrative jurisdiction in the broad sense, which encompasses not only the urban area but also the suburbs and sometimes even a big rural area and a number of outlying villages. Putting counties under cities, changing counties into cities, and the vague urban–rural integration have been practiced in China for many years; this makes the concept of a city here different from the popular ideas of the rest of the world, so there is no comparability. Can the observations be comparable if we focus on the "urban area" of cities?

After hard searching I found that Shanghai's Jing'an District has a land area of 7.62 square kilometers and a resident population of 243,000 (as per the Sixth

Population Census in 2010), with 31,000 people per square kilometer; its GDP in 2013 was RMB 66 billion, which translates to USD 1.4 billion per square kilometer. The population density is higher than Manhattan, and the economic density is also close! But, it needs to be noted that Jing'an District is just one district of the greater Shanghai, and its land area only accounts for 1.2 thousandths of Shanghai's total. By doing the math, only forty Jing'an Districts will exceed Shanghai's total economy. But how big is the area of forty Jing'an Districts? Just 5% of the total of Shanghai.

It seems worthwhile in the transformation of the urbanization to put the work on the agenda to focus on "the urban area" and come up with criteria and boundaries for the urban areas of China's several hundred cities. We need to understand that if the urban area as the core of a city is insufficiently dense, the city's agglomeration energy will be insufficient, and so it will definitely be difficult to leverage the radiation and guide the growth of the national economy. Can't we see that the so-called global cities are defined by influence and radiation power rather than total economy and land area?

In physics, water will overflow only after the glass is full. During the previous journey, China's urbanization expanded at an astonishing rate. However, for no few cities the situation is like putting many glasses on a big table, but none of the glasses is full and all the glasses are half filled or almost empty. This being the case, if we still continue to expand the city in the way of pancake making, the cake is going to be thinner and thinner and the city will look neither like a city nor like the countryside; how could there be overflow, radiation, or influence?

Starting from the actual and present facts, the next journey of China's urbanization needs to pay more attention to density, aggregation, convenience, and the broader overall quality of urban life. Obviously, the problems left over from the previously journey must also be resolved, and it is very worthwhile to summarize the lessons and experiences. However, what's more important is to face the future and take a problem-oriented attitude towards promoting the healthy and sustainable development of urbanization. To use a vivid analogy, we need to let muscles grow on the stretched skeletal structure and let the city organism develop; this is the focus for the next journey of urbanization.

To this end, it is necessary to renew the mindset. In international ideological trends on urban theory, there is a proposal called "compact city." After reflecting on the inconveniences and environmental unfriendliness brought about by the urban sprawl, this school of theorists do the exact opposite; they advocate to better use modern technology and management to achieve high-quality and sustainable growth for urban economy and society through rationally increasing rather than decreasing the urban density.

Let us take Tokyo as an example. Occupying only 3.4% of Japan's land area but gathering 28% of its population and more than 30% of its GDP, the greater Tokyo area is currently one of the world's densest cosmopolitans. However, when you go deep into the city, it is not difficult to find even in the core of the city center lots of areas and buildings which are functionally poorly planned, inconvenient, and environmental unfriendly, and they become the barriers for hosting higher-quality city events. In 1986, the Mori Building, a private enterprise, proposed to adopt the new concept of "three-dimensional city garden" to renovate some of the locations in the heart of the city. After more than ten years of explanation, communication (including with the government, with urban planning departments, and administrative departments) and perseverance, they successively completed landmark urban heart renewal projects such as ARK Hills and Roppongi Hills, which serve as a blueprint for "cosmopolitans in the new century" which is experienceable to all parties.

Roppongi Hills in particular is very exciting. I have visited it twice by taking the advantage of the opportunities of going to Tokyo for conferences. As an outsider I went there not to see the design secrets but for fun and to satisfy my craving. Imagine the land area is 11 hectors, and a total floor space of 760,000 m^2 has been built, and it includes all sorts of architectures to integrate all sorts of urban functions that you can think of, ranging from residences, offices, shopping, catering, social networking, arts display, library, school, hotel, media, all the way to transport hub. Within this area of walking distance, 800 households comprising about 2,000 people live here, 20,000 people work every day here on different industries, and some forty million consumers or tourists come here every year. Leaving everything else to be experienced by dear readers yourselves, I will just tell you know that on the fifty-four-meter-tall roof of the performing hall, unexpectedly the scenery is idyllic with trees and flowers, and even some paddy field! What is it like to become urbanized but still be able to see the mountain, to see the water, and to remember the nostalgia? You will know if you come to the site.

This shows that the therapy for the "Big City Disease" can be diverse. Apart from the easy method of not letting people in or evacuating them away, increasing the urban density under the condition of more rational city investment, construction, and management might also be a solution.

For small cities and towns, there are even more possibilities of increasing the density. Also in Japan, there is a city called Toyama in the Hokuriku area of Honshu Island. Toyama has a population of fewer than 420,000, and its population is decreasing as a result of pressure from aging. How to maintain the city's vitality and build a higher quality of life? Toyama's strategy is to "build a compact city." We went to the site and asked how to make the city compact. The answer from the locals is to first improve the tram public transport, then activate the inhabitation circles along the line especially around the stations, and the final target is to attract senior people to live within the circle of 500 meters from the station. At the sight of the beautiful landscape from the tramcar on the streets of city, we visitors were interested to know where the investment came from. The Mayor of Toyama explained: the rail lines are invested by the government, the tramcar research and development are sponsored by the government, the new tramcars are bought by the operating company using money raised from the market, and the money to build the stations comes from the donations from citizens—including legal persons and natural persons. Yes, that's true; on the wall of each station looking like a scenic spot and on the folded seats for waiting passengers, there is an inlaid copper plate with the name of the donor.

The question of rationally increasing the density is also valid for rural areas. The change in the economic structure, the decrease of farming population, plus improvements in transport and communication are creating conditions to choose the opportunity to change the extremely scattered pattern of production and inhabitation in rural areas. Around 2003, Shanghai's suburb became the first to propose the idea of "three concentrations" (to concentrate the industry into industrial parks, to concentrate farmers into small towns, and to concentrate the farmland into farming specialists); this model was later spread to many places and got upgraded into higher versions, such as Chengdu, Changsha, and Jiangsu. In Dujiangyan, there's a village called Chaping, which we have visited many times. The majority of the farmers' houses collapsed in the 2008 earthquake. During the post-disaster reconstruction, special attention was paid to building a compact village. Many scattered people previously living in the mountain ridges with many inconveniences were relocated to the foot of the mountain, and a suburban village with tourism and resort value was built through raising money via the surplus land quota. Now the local villagers have a better place to live, and many elderly people from Chengdu are attracted here to escape from the summer heat. The project brings benefit to both urban and rural areas; why not?

It must be understood that China's urbanization has come to a turning point. From any dimension, large-scale demolition and construction and even mandatory requisition and demolition purely to serve the purpose of urban area expansion will definitely be unsustainable. For the next journey, the urbanization must be transformed. And the direction of transformation is worth the thinking of the decision makers, managers, and builders of cities. If "people-centric urbanization" is not just a slogan, then there must be a clear answer as to how to implement the principle and which is the direction to move in.

A realistic option is to shift the focus of city investment and construction toward aggregation and reasonable density increase within the scope of the already-stretched urban skeleton. For example, many localities have built grand theaters; we can ask them: do they have performances, how often, and what level of performances? Barcelona has only two million people; the world-renowned Palau de la Música Catalana, built more than a 100 years ago with 1,000 seats, has more than 300 performances every year. The musicals at Broadway of New York and the West End of London are indispensable elements of the long-lasting glamour of these two global cities. In contrast, China has built no few grand theaters in recent years, with hardware good enough to challenge anywhere in the world; the challenge is how to organize the performance programs. Indeed, there are also some good signs. Take the concert hall at the Tianjin Grand Theatre as an example. They had sharp eyes and recruited Qian Cheng, a graduate from Peking University National School of Development, as the general manager. In two and a half years, he has led the theater in staging 800 performances, as if this music hall has become a center for music in China. This indicates that once the city's "skeletal framework," such as facilities and hardware, has rolled out, the key has shifted to whether or not there is a team of "urban careerists" to organize a more active and vibrant urban life. Cities are people's cities, so it should provide conveniences to people, and popularity is everything. In the previous journey of China's urbanization, it seems what gets compared is who requisitions more land, whose new district is further away from the main city with wider roads, and whose buildings are more high end and gorgeous. Now, it is a different season for the game; it is time to compete with new capabilities to see which city, which block, or which building cluster is more popular, more active, has better quality economic and cultural activities, makes people's life more convenient, and is more business-friendly and more livable.

During this process, the institutional mechanism deserves attention because it restrains human behavior. If the restraints are improper, the resulting behaviors will often go against the original intent. The journey of urbanization should be centered on improving the quality of urban life, and it badly needs a team of "urban careerists," who might be the mayor, entrepreneurs, artists, or ordinary citizens. But their common role is to make full use of the city facilities built with large investments, organize more lively, better quality, and more environmental friendly economic and cultural activities, and use them to nurture urban civilization and drive the sustainable development of the national economy.

Integrated Considerations on Farmers' Moving to Cities and Rural Land Reform

Background and Issues

The rapid growth of the national economy is accompanied by corresponding structural changes. The share of agriculture drops, the share of industry and commerce rises, the regional layout gets constantly adjusted in line with the global industry shift; tremendous amounts of rural population have moved into cities or towns, and some resident population are flowing and shifting between different cities. All these are easily visible phenomena in China's economy.

The use methods of the land bearing the weight of the aforementioned changes are bound to change drastically. Of this, the most prominent is the steep rise of the market prices of lands for certain purposes and at certain locations as compared with lands for other purposes and at other locations.

None of the Economic entities of all sorts, inclusive of farmers, enterprises, and governments, will stay indifferent to this situation. The basic trend is that people will scramble for land with increasing scarcities, and the competition for land is becoming more intense than ever before.

However, competition must be consistently constrained by mindsets, habits, systems, and policies. It must be seen that with more than thirty years of opening and reform, China's land mindsets, systems, and policies have undergone some adaptive changes and adjustments, but they are still lagging far behind.

With regard to the mindset, the dominant thinking takes the land as a physical fringe benefit; all sorts of prevailing ideas claim land to be very special and refuse to admit that land is also an ordinary economic resource, the effective use and fair distribution of which can also be achieved through appropriate property rights and market system. Some logically or empirically untested "land myths" and "land fears" are restraining the decision mindsets, preventing them from making realistic judgment to the question and the situation.

With regard to the land system, there are institutional inequalities and inconsistencies in multiple types of land rights between urban and rural areas and within their respective self. Out of all urban and rural land resources, only urban commercial and residential land, which accounts for a small portion, is included into the scope of the market; the large volumes of other lands are ruled out from the market principle, such as industrial land, land used by the government and social causes, the self-used land of farmers, and rural areas. The only lawful channel to convert agricultural and rural land into higher income nonagricultural and urban usage is the mandatory requisition by the government.

With regard to land policies, it is a very common practice to replace property rights and markets with administrative control. As a result, many land policies get repetitive and complicated, the implementation cost becomes very high, and the effect is very poor, and from time to time this sparks workarounds and unspoken rules and leads to a wider range of extralegal activities. Plus there are too many violations against laws and regulations to be punished or prohibited, and it this provides a hotbed for corruption.

This shows that it is very necessary to continue to renew the land mindsets, to reform the land system, and to adjust the relevant policies. Avoiding or delaying the reform not only means that it will be impossible to provide a reliable foundation for sound and high-quality urbanization, industrialization, and agricultural modernization, but also the current government will probably have difficulties handling the social problems focused on land and keep themselves too busy with the random outbreak of land-related incidents.

Starting Point and Goals

To continue to deepen the reform, the starting point is the existing land system. Therefore it is necessary to properly look at the pros and cons of the existing system and study the conditions that need to be satisfied in order to advance the reform further.

China's current land system was formed through an initial reform to the previous land system under the planned economy. It has three main features: (1) the household contract responsibility system for farmland; (2) the usage right of urban state-owned land may be transferred to the market; (3) usage control of urban and rural land.

Regarding feature (1), practice has proven that the household contract responsibility system for agricultural land is a good system as it meets the requirements form the development of productivity and gains deep support from farmers. In particular, with the addition of such provisions as "the system will be unchanged for the long term" and "autonomous transfer of contracting is permitted," the system is also able to satisfy the needs of circulation and reorganization within a bigger scope.

A further reform should focus on improving the household contract responsibility system so that the land resource can be effectively used within a bigger scope under the backdrop of urbanization.

First, for the household contracting system to truly realize the goal of "unchanged over the long term," it is necessary to implement the idea of "land will not increase or decrease with the population change," and to establish a reliable boundary for land contracting rights of the rural households. This is the foundation for nurturing the transfer rights for the farmland, and it has a vitally positive impact on the large-scale farming operations, continuous shift of agricultural labor, and giving farmers more income opportunities through urbanization.

Second, based on the transfer right of the farmer's contracted land, diverse market contracts may be developed to form new forms of economic organizations. The government's responsibility is to safeguard the rights of all parties and ensure equity of contracts; to prevent tort, and prevent personal subjective preference and "supporting" certain contracts and organizations while suppressing other contracts and organizations.

Third, apart from farmland, rural areas also have large amounts of construction land which has always been used by farmers, and so far there has been no clear definition of the power and function of property rights for the acquisition, use, income, collateralizing, and transfer of such land. It is recommended to draw experience from the farmland system reform, to first define the usage rights and then make the transfer rights clear until the market fully covers the utilization of all the land resources.

Regarding feature (2), the usage rights for state-owned land is transferred to the market via leasehold, which has demonstrated the enormous potential of land capitalization and opened up a new path for financing the infrastructure construction required by China's urbanization and industrialization; this contribution should not be left unrecognized. However, the disadvantages of this approach are also becoming increasingly prominent. The most terrible of these is that many local governments are stimulated by land finance and have become more motivated to requisition more land from rural areas, and taken the "halfway marketized" path characterized by the abnormal combination of forced requisition and rushed sales, which puts the governments in the unrighteous position of contending for benefits and land with civilians.

In light of future development in the awareness of rights in the society, the troubles from evading the land requisition reform will only grow greater with each passing day. In this regard, the line of thinking for the further reform should not only be limited to reducing the scale of land requisition because for the future the land requisitioned by the government will be restricted to public welfare only. Therefore, under the premise of "separating the government and the land," the government-monopolized land capitalization should be changed into non-governmental land capitalization with competitions from multiple sources.

There is no reason to worry that the reform "will endanger the urbanization," because the land stock controlled by the government, in terms of the total volume, is already sufficient to satisfy the public land required by intensive urbanization. Also, there should not be too much worry that putting an end to the "land finance model" will detonate the risks of local debts because the fact is just the opposite: only proactively initiating the transformation of local finance can help balance the local fiscal system, eradicate local debt risks, and improve the quality of bank assets.

Regarding feature (3), the goal for China in adopting land usage control is to protect the resource of arable land, which has a relative lower price, and to prevent too much of it from being converted into other usages. There is nothing quite wrong with this policy goal; however, in the implementation, full consideration should be given to the differences between China and the industrialized and highly urbanized developed economies. Improper control ignoring these differences will damage the normal development of urbanization and industrialization and make it hard to sustain the control itself.

To this end, land usage control needs to be both upheld and adjusted. The focus includes two aspects. First, appropriate compensation should be given when the government restricts the land from being shifted to a higher-yield activity. Second, on the premise of ensuring that the farmland resources are not "reduced in area or quality," "location swap" should be permitted. These two adjustments will help to effectively implement the usage control under China's conditions.

The near-term goal for the reform is to remove the parts that need to be removed most urgently and are removable and to improve the parts that need to be improved most urgently and are improvable so as to provide the institutional assurance to the healthy advancement of the urbanization. The long-term goal is to form a land system with long-term peace and stability and make it an integral part of the institutional civilization in the socialism with Chinese characteristics.

Four Key Reforms

(A) Establishing Rights for Rural Land

It is proposed to no more put a limit on the term of contracting on the right to use and operate the collective land contracted by households and to adopt a "no change over the long term" policy.

The meaning of land rights establishment is to delineate the behavioral boundaries for the use and transfer of land by farmers and to enable their land rights to have a formal legal expression. The registration can be done with the property rights administration department of the people's government at or above the county level, and the land usage certificate can be issued by the people's government at or above the county level.

The confirmation of rural land rights is first to establish usage and operation right of rural land and then establish the farmers' transfer right after the usage right is clarified.

While the rights are established for farmland, the scope of rights confirmation can take some steps to encompass mountain forests, grasslands, water surfaces, and all sorts of rural construction lands and rural residences.

The confirmation of rural land rights should be done down to the household level; for jointly used collective land, the transferable equity rights (ownership) should be established for households.

The land rights confirmation can be completed through such procedures as registration, public notice, community mediation and verification, public notice by the government, and government certification; if problems are encountered for historical reasons or if boundaries of rights cannot be made clear for the moment, it is advised to first register and record all relevant information and then gradually complete the rights confirmation.

The government should provide perennial service for rights establishment for immovable properties in rural areas and responsively handle such requests from farmers as registration, rights confirmation, and renaming. Qualified rights confirmation services from the government are a prerequisite for the government to levy the land tax or the real estate tax.

We need to do some publicity to make everybody know that rights confirmation is the precondition for lawful circulation and transfer of rural land resources and the relevant contract signing

(B) Nurturing Urban and Rural Land Markets

It is proposed to establish a new constitutional principle that "the usage right and transfer right of collective land are both the property rights of farmers, which is protected by the law of the state."

Follow the above-mentioned principle to tidy up existing laws, regulations, and policy documents, and abolish or revise the clauses prohibiting or restricting the transfer of rural land.

The transfer of rural land rights can be freely carried out between people (without government intervention), after which the changes in registration or owner name shall be applied with the property rights department. Depending on the scale, the transfer can also take place in a centralized way under the legal principle that "the government shall not exercise the requisition right on land not for public welfare," which also strictly limits the scope, procedure, and compensation standards for land requisition by the government.

Because the land for public welfare does not enter the market, it can therefore be announced that the government will withdraw from the land market to achieve the "separation between government and land," and the government only performs function as the land market regulator.

It is also proposed to abrogate the legal provision that "urban land belongs to the state," and change it into: "For the original rural collective land included into the scope or the built-up area of the city, as long as the usage is for commercial utilization, the rights establishment should first be done to confirm the usage right and the transfer right to the members of the former rural collective, and then the collective ownership can be changed to state ownership."

Break the government's monopoly of the primary market for urban land, and make the land market universally and equally open to state-owned institutions, collectives, as well as to individuals, family farms, cooperatives, and companies which have the right to the use or transfer the state-owned or collective land.

(C) Introducing the Mechanisms of "Farm Land Protection Compensation" and "Location Swap" into Land Use Control

It is proposed to continue to adhere to land use control, but to cope with the requirement from China's situation and its stage of economic development, two new mechanisms can be brought on board: (1) A mechanism for arable land protection compensation; and (2) a mechanism by location swap between lands with different purposes.

(D) Dealing with Problems Left over from History (Omitted)

Urbanization and Reform

China's current urbanization rate, namely the proportion of urban population out of the total population, is slightly higher than the world average. The worldwide average urbanization rate is 50%, whereas China's figure is 52% to 53%. Compared with its past, China has made a great deal of progress. In 1978, the urbanization in China was only 18%; therefore, the progress made in the past several decades is extremely obvious.

However, it must be seen that China's urbanization rate still does not match with the development of its national economy. Agriculture currently accounts for only 10% of China's GDP, but 65% of the population's household registration (*hukou*) is still in the countryside. Just imagine, if 65% of the total population only accounts for 10% of the total national income and only produce 10% of output, the imbalance in the national economy is very serious. Thanks to the policy allowing population and labor flow, the number of people with a rural *hukou* but stay long term (more than six months per year) in the city to make a living accounts for 47% to 48% of the total rural population; however, the number of people living in rural areas still exceeds 50%. And also thanks to the fact that not all people living in rural areas live on agriculture, some people are commuters who work in a nearby city or town during the day and come back to the village for the night. For example, many people living in Shanghai's suburbs work in Kunshan, Suzhou, or downtown Shanghai on a daily or weekly basis. After the number of people working in urban areas but living in rural areas is deducted, there is still approximately 20% to 30% of the population living on agriculture in the rural areas.

Looking at urban and rural income from this perspective, we will understand why disposable income of urban residents is at least two times higher than that of rural residents. The problem is with the structure where more than 20% of the population only create 10% of the output. It all comes down to the fact that still too many people live on agriculture. Additionally, it is not a very economical configuration to live in rural areas but engage in industry, commerce, or services; this is because these economic activities are very different from agriculture, for which staying close to the farmland and scattered inhabitation is a must. Industry, commerce, and services can and should aggregate in space such that the demand could come together to stimulate the division of labor.

The urban–rural income gap with at least a factor of two is also one of the main driving forces for continued urbanization. As the old Chinese saying goes, "people always move towards higher places"; they always move to places with the possibility of earning higher income. From the perspective of trends, reallocating the layout of population and labor across urban and rural areas can continuously release the potential of China's economy. This is a judgment to the basic trend.

To make a simple revisit to the origin of this trend, it is not difficult to see that the reform is a decisive factor. In 1978, China's urbanization rate was only18%, and this figure was even lower than in 1959. The movement to "go up to the mountains and down to the countryside" for people of my generation was, in point of fact, a reverse shift of labor from the cities to the countryside. Being dispatched to the countryside did give the educated youth different degrees of exercise, especially the experience of the real life of China's farmers, but it probably did no good to the development of the national economy; it equated to moving population from high-productivity sectors to low-productivity sectors, hence the growth of per-capita income was dragged. The reform opened up the door between urban and rural areas. Previously, children from rural households had no opportunity to move into cities unless they were admitted into university or joined the army as a soldier. After joining they needed to be promoted to be an officer, otherwise they had to go back to their village after the term of service was over. The reform first allowed the rural population to move to cities and towns; second, the labor force were also allowed to flow between different cities. Many people adventured into Shenzhen and Hainan or drifted to Beijing; most of them were from other cities. In the past, grains were supplied by quota; therefore, when farmers were first allowed to enter cities, there was a particular sentence in the Central Government's Document No.1[22] in 1983, which says: "farmers will be allowed to enter cities and towns to work or do business if the can bring their own grain rations." This limitation was later resolved by the marketization of grain and agricultural products. The next thing was about housing; rental was permitted plus buying and selling was also permitted in many places. This helped the rural migrants to settle down first and then gradually fit themselves into the city. All of these are opportunities for citizens created by the reform, with the basic logic being to use the law to safeguard citizens' freedom to seek higher income opportunities.

22 Refers to *Several Questions on Current Rural Economic Policies* promulgated in January 1983.—Editor's note.

Experience has proven that, as long as economic freedom is increased, the pace of urbanization will be accelerated. Because urban aggregation brings about higher incomes, it will attract more people to move into and gather in towns and cities. Today's several billion passenger trips during the Chinese New Year rush every year are a record in human history. The question is, should the population always flow like this? As soon as Chinese New Year approaches, Beijing, Shanghai, and big cities empty out, and the small towns and villages become lively; then after Lunar January 15, their situation gets reversed. Will we Chinese people live like this forever? The answer seems to be no. Aggregation has already occurred in the flow of population. It is like after the water flows, the stone and sand will precipitate. Then we would be interested to know, how many people out of the flowing population will precipitate, and where will they probably precipitate?

According to census data, in 2011, nearly 79% of China's migrant population went to the eastern parts of China; of this number, 80% to medium-sized and large cities, and 44.1% to provincial capitals, municipalities with independent planning status, and the four municipalities directly under the central government. Looking at the changes over the past ten years, the resident population of Beijing, Shanghai, and Tianjin has increased by 37% to 40%, but the national average resident urban population growth rate for the same period is only 5.8%. This suggests that big cities are more attractive in terms of "recruiting people." Putting the whole country together, 65% of the migrant population gets absorbed by big cities with a population of more than one million, and 29% is absorbed by megacities with populations of more than five million. At the same time, the absolute resident population for hundreds of counties, county-level cities, and prefecture-level cities has decreased and they have a net population outflow. Where does the outflow go? To other cities and towns.

How should we understand the above changing trends in population migration? I believe the simplest dynamic mechanism is the income gap. Why do big cities attract people? This is ultimately because higher income can be earned in big cities. The income gap between China's urban and rural residents is about three times, but the gap is even greater when the comparison is made between metropolises and the rural areas of backward provinces or autonomous regions. For example, the disposable income of a Shanghai urban resident is about 8.8 times that of a villager in Guizhou. The gap is so large that people would certainly like to come to Shanghai. In the past it was permitted; after the opening-up some people were too old to come, but young people from the rural areas were able to come to Shanghai. The cost of living index is high in Shanghai and low in rural areas of Guizhou, But even after this factor is taken into account, the net income of rural people entering big cities is significantly increased. If this is not the case, it will probably be unable to attract the villagers to leave their hometowns for cities.

Why is the income higher in large cities? The first reason is that the aggregation of population and the convergence of demand lead to substantial increases in productivity. As we all see, the division of labor is intensive in cities while it is quite coarse in the countryside. Generally, you do not see people selling breakfast in a village; is this because rural people skip breakfast? No, that is not the case; they do take breakfast but they need to prepare it themselves, because villages are too small to have a breakfast business split out as the result of division of labor—with only a few people buying, whoever is selling breakfast will lose money. However, in the cities, selling breakfast is a big business. It is population aggregation that leads to detailed division of labor, and the detailed division of labor is the fountainhead for productivity improvement. This has been a longstanding and clearly articulated law in classical economics, and it still works here today.

The urban–rural income gap is, in essence, the difference in productivity. On top of this, the resource redistribution pattern further widens the gap. For such discussed things as good schools, good hospitals, and good cultural facilities, which places have more of them? The answer is big cities; certainly this also involves the preference for cities in resource distribution. However, please also allow me to comment, where should the country's best doctors be placed, in remote villages or in Beijing and Shanghai? I would take the risk of being attacked and say that the better place for them is Beijing and Shanghai. The reason is that their transport is convenient, and it will be easy for patients from all over the country to find them if they need to. To place them in distant villages is a damage to patients from cross the country. Of course, the more good doctors, the better, and if we have much more than enough good doctors, the ideal situation would be nondifferentiated urban and rural hospital configuration.

However, the ideal is the ideal, and the reality is the reality. When the urban–rural income gap continues to be evident, allowing people to make active responses to the lingering gap is still a workable way to narrow the gap. It is particularly important to allow a low-income rural labor force to move to higher-income cities to work or do business, to gradually integrate themselves into the city and become urban residents. In this way, with the decreasing rural population as the denominator, and the increasing urban income earned from the urban areas as the numerator, over time the per-capita income will gradually come closer to eliminate the too-exaggerated urban–rural income gap, and this should be the proper meaning of urban and rural development.

The problem is, even though the opening-up and reform has already been there for several decades, the friction coefficient that hinders the flow of population, labor, and resources between urban and rural areas according to the principle of economics continues to be too high. The biggest problem is that the property rights of urban and rural residents have not yet achieved equality before the law. As everyone knows, urban residents' housing can be bought and sold, and so they more or less can share the opportunity from urban land appreciation. Urban residents' housing can also be collateralized to get financial service. But the houses and land of rural residents can neither be lawfully transferred nor used as pledge. The central government's policies have long said that it is necessary to increase the property income of both urban and rural residents; however, without the removal of the legal obstacles to obstruct the change of hand for rural residents' properties, how can we talk about property income?

Another source of the urban–rural income gap is the too-large discrepancy in public service levels. Quite a few items of public service made available to urban residents since their birth are beyond the reach of rural residents throughout their lifetime. This problem was formed by history and cannot be resolved overnight. But if the delay is prolonged and the topic is not put on the agenda after several decades of rapid growth, to shift to domestic demand-driven growth will an empty talk. Now there are also some signs of change to the situation: On the one hand, some rural population move into cities and enjoy the urban public service; on the other hand, some villages with outflow of population have expanded the aggregation scale of rural communities through rationally concentrated inhabitation, which will help with the improvement of public service. However, a more fundamental solution would require the fiscal and tax system reform to make overall considerations across urban and rural areas; otherwise, the so-called "equalization of urban–rural public services" will be unachievable, just like cooking a meal without rice.

In short, the big topic of urbanization must contain lots of content from the further reform. From the perspective of my field of research, there is no way to evade the deepening of the reform in the following three points.

The first point is the land system, where the status quo comprises three circles. The first circle is agricultural land, which was previously owned and cultivated by the collective. After the implementation of the household contracting system, the operation contracting rights were made clear to belong to the rural households, and a set of quite complete laws and policies have been put in place except for a "small tail," namely whether or not it is necessary to adjust the amount of contracted farmland according to the changing household population. The paradox here is that, if the land is adjusted with the population change, then the idea of "unchanging the contracting for the long term or permanently" does not get truly implemented. If the land is not adjusted, no few people will see it as unfair. The direction for a solution is to safeguard the long term unchanging contracting relationship through the establishment of rights, expand farmland circulation, put an end to the outdated system of using population as the chips for land redistribution, and let market norms and market mechanisms play a decisive role in the obtaining, use, and operation of farmland.

The second circle is the land for urban use. The old system was free of charge allotment; it has been now switched to a new system of market bidding. However, it is still necessary to continue and resolve a series of new problems brought about by the administrative monopoly as the sole source of land supply. The direction is to let the market mechanism play its role within a greater scope, especially to work on how to form a unified urban and rural land market cross different administrative jurisdictions. Among this, the design of the tenure for the transfer of the usage right of urban land should match up with the upcoming real estate tax policy. And more efforts should be made to accelerate the nurturing of the secondhand urban land market along with the progress of urban renovations.

The third circle is the biggest problem. The land area taken up by cities was originally quite small, and in the suburbs and outside cities all land was rural land. But cities expand; what kind of system should be used to incorporate this land originally belonging to rural farmers into the urban land category? The status quo is that the only way is the land requisition system. The provision in the Constitution limits that "the state may requisition land from rural area for the purpose of public interest," but what actually happens is that lots of land for commercial purposes is also obtained by land requisition. Many conflicts and group incidents have occurred, and the social cost for the requisition has also risen to make it difficult to sustain. The next step of the reform is to follow the deployment of the decision to deepen the reform across the board made by the Third Plenary Session of the Eighteenth CPC Central Committee, gradually shrink the scope of land requisition, and gradually admit rural construction land into the market.

The second point is the urban and rural public services. In principle, no one opposes the equalization of public services across urban and rural areas. This is because even if there is any objection, it is unspeakable. The dual system of urbanites and country cousins should be ended in the hands of this generation. However, to truly change it, the vested interests involved are also substantial. The conflict is already huge in the single move of starting to allow students to take the college entrance examination across different places. Because of historical reasons, quality education resources are concentrated in big cities. The opportunity space for people from smaller places and villages is very small, and it is very difficult for them to be admitted to good universities in Beijing and Shanghai. Back then I was admitted into a university in Beijing from Heilongjiang and later I found the admission score in Beijing was lower than elsewhere. How could this be described as equality? Additionally, the financial burden for compulsory education is also localized. Anhui takes care of the children in Anhui and Guizhou takes care of the children in Guizhou. The strengths of local financial resources are different, and the difference in the quality of compulsory education is also quite substantial. What steps can be taken one after another to ensure that all these problems are solved? To turn the largely different urban and rural public service across different areas into an integrated service system with roughly comparable and acceptable level; is something related to the universal identity of all the people towards the country; therefore, it is a significant modern revolution.

And the third point is to reform the urban management system. Traditionally, China has had a long experience in managing its territory with an agricultural civilization, and cities were historically the primary nodes of the administrative network. In the modern era, more and more cities have been built with the rise of industry and commerce, but the urban management system is still highly administrative or administratively-led. Up till now, we still emphasize the administrative ranking of cities; is it at the county level, prefecture level, provincial capital level, or municipalities directly under the central government, all of this is decided by administrative approval, with no consideration at all to the city's aggregation energy or its radiation towards or influence on other cities. Currently, a very big practical problem is that China's urbanization rate has just exceeded 50%, but a contradictory phenomenon has popped up: Most of the cities that people are willing to go are overloaded and control of population inflow is required. At the same time, there are a lot of "empty cities" or even "haunted cities," with many houses built and reasonably nice infrastructures but no residents and the popularity is very low. This constitutes a twofold waste of resources. The crux of the problem is that the city's administrative cost or rank has a big conflict with the flowing population and economic resources, which seek optimum allocation within a bigger scope. If the market economy is to play a decisive role in resources allocation, it is necessary to chase down and ask: Does this allocation also include urban and rural space resources? If the answer is yes, then our city management system needs a major overhaul.

An Irreversible Transformation[23]

During China's land reform in the 1960s, the country's land was divided into the binary system: collective ownership in the rural areas and state ownership in cities. These two types of land have different prices and different rights. State-owned land in cities and towns can be freely transferred through bidding and auction, and it also can be collateralized. On the other hand, the only way for collective land to become transferable is to be converted into state-owned land through requisition (In recent years some local areas have carried out the experiment on the circulation of collective land, but still point one the total scale is very small, and point two there are still all sorts of restrictions such as the prohibition on homestead transfer to people with an urban household registration or *hukou*). However, this sole and only path has become the blasting fuse to spark instability. According to statistics from the State Administration of Petition, there are about four million disputes each year arising out of land requisition, and more than half of the group incidents are caused by land acquisition or demolition.

The increasingly ossified land system has been heavily impacted by economic development and the urbanization process since the opening and reform. Under the reality that it is more and more difficult for urban state-owned land to satisfy the needs from economic development, on the one hand, all sorts of "underground" circulation, driven by the strong interests, have popped up one after another, such as the acquiesced "rural workshop buildings" and the repeatedly forbidden but recurring "small property right housing"; on the other hand, the central and local governments are conducting various experiments including the increase-decrease link-up within the framework of the existing system in the hope of finding a breakthrough for the reform.

In 2013, the central government laid down the "rights establishment" for rural land into Document No.1.[24] At the local level, Guangdong has already issued documents to expand the scope of circulation of rural houses and homesteads from within the same village to within the same town or township, and Wenzhou is trying to expand it from within the same township to within the same

23 The interviewer is *Southern Weekend* reporter Wang Xiaoqiao, and the original article, "An Irreversible and Unstoppable Reform: The Bait and Root of the Land Reform," was published in *Southern Weekend* on October 24, 2013.—Editor's note.

24 Refers to *Opinions of CPC Central Committee and the State Council on Accelerating the Development of Modern Agriculture and Further Enhancing the Vitality of Rural Development*.—Editor's note.

county. However, because this reform involves significant long-term impacts, and it is hotly disputed, the pace will probably be what was originally expected by the market.

How were the two different land systems formed in China for its cities and rural areas? How did the land belonging to farmers in the early days of the founding of new China become collective owned? What are the key points and dynamic mechanisms for the current reform? Will the next step of reform irreversibly go to the direction of "equal price and equal right for equal land," or will it stagnate due to certain distortions? The *Southern Weekend* reporter interviews Professor Qiren Zhou of Peking University National School of Development on these topics, because he has followed the land reform for many, many years.

There Is No Law to Prohibit Urbanites from Buying Rural Houses

Why can farmers grow cabbages and sell them to urban residents, but they cannot sell their houses? Both items are equally the property of farmers. Since rural land is collective owned, it should be decided by the collective. Hence the first step of the reform should be to remove the state's control over collective land.

Southern Weekend: The Third Plenary Session of the Eighteenth CPC Central Committee is near at hand. In terms of land reform, it seems that there is more room for reform in rural land than urban land. In reality, rural land is also the focus of many regional pilot programs; this is especially the case in 2013. In August, *the Guangdong Provincial Administrative Measures on Rural Homesteads (for Review Draft)* was published for public comments and suggestions, and the document permits the circulation of rural houses and homesteads between rural *hukou* holders within the same town. Then, in September, Wenzhou tried to expand the scope of rural house transactions from within the same village or town to within the same county, but this aroused too much attention from the public opinion, so the formulation of the detailed implementation measures was temporarily suspended. Can this be seen as a small breakthrough in the reform of the rural land system? However, for a very long time now, the freedom of buying and selling urban housing has been permitted, but buying a farmer's house by someone not from the same village is not protected by law; these pilot programs have not seen a breakthrough on this point.

Qiren Zhou: The first question is, why can't urban residents buy rural houses? The Property Law only states that the existing laws should be followed, yet there is no clear provisions in the existing law. In 2007, the *Notice of the General Office of the State Council on Strictly Implementing the Laws and Policies on Rural Collective*

Construction Land has made it clear that urban residents cannot go to rural areas to buy homesteads, rural houses, or "small property right housing."

To me, property rights as the basic rights of citizens should be spelled out by law rather than being laid out in a policy notice from any government department at any level. Are they worried that the transfer will damage the rights and interests of farmers? Isn't this too paternalistic?

In reality, the *Sixty Provisions on the People's Commune* of 1962 (namely the *Regulations on the Work of Rural People's Communes*) recognizes the farmers' houses as their private property, which can be bought, sold, or transferred in various ways; at that time, there was no provision that the transferee would be subject to *hukou* or geographical restrictions.

Cross-village buying and selling of farmer houses has existed in reality for a long time. This reflects that when the relative price of any resource changes, the resource will always flow towards the direction of the subject who feels that the resource is worth more, namely towards the hands bidding with a higher price. This is an unstoppable economic law, and it does good to the society. If we do prohibit or restrict it, then the real world will find bypasses and there will be violations everywhere. The *de facto* existence of "small property right housing" and its growth in spite of the prohibitions also follow this same logic.

Southern Weekend: Even if the restrictions on the buyer's *hukou* are removed, only the sale of farmhouses has been opened up; the homestead beneath the house still belongs to the collective. Once this truncated property rights is greeted with the question of compensation for demolition and resettlement, wouldn't it stimulate new conflicts?

Qiren Zhou: Again, the *Sixty Provisions on the People's Commune* also states that the land belongs to the collective and cannot be sold, leased, or transferred. This results in the separation of the house and the land and artificially creates disputes and conflicts. If the house can be transferred, but the land beneath cannot, then what to do? Suspend the house in the air for the transaction?

The collective ownership in rural areas is not a more loose system as we have imagined; it is still in fact under the full control of the state. In the past, the unified purchase and unified marketing of products and the prevention of urban–rural migration actually made the state the controller of collective ownership. The collective ownership is not the entire people's ownership or state ownership; the real difference between the two is that the state dominates and controls the former, but it does not assume the direct financial responsibility for the consequences of its control.

The first step of the reform needs to remove all sorts of control by the state over collective land, such as not allowing rural house and land to be freely sold to urban residents. Why can farmers grow cabbages and sell them to people in the city but cannot sell to them their idled houses and land? Both are equally the property of farmers. Therefore, both should be transferable.

Because the ownership is collective, then the first step should be to delegate the decision rights to the collective, which will decide whether the transfer is permitted or not. Otherwise the collective ownership system is empty and fake.

How Did the State Create the Collective System?

After the 1950s, the state power went deep—all the way down to the village level—which was never achieved at any time in China's traditional past.

Southern Weekend: Where did the collective ownership of rural land come from? In the early years after the establishment of the New China, farmers enjoyed complete property rights over the land; it was only later that the land became collectively owned. Under what backdrop was this dual system for urban and rural land formed?

Qiren Zhou: After the 1950s, China's administrative organization reached all the way down to the village level; this was something never achieved before at any time in its historical past. This was closely related to the goal of national industrialization, and one of the most important targets after the founding of New China.

Generally speaking, the capital accumulation for industrialization originates primarily from the country's agricultural surplus. But back then, the land rent in rural areas—along with the Land Reform—was evenly divided by the entire rural population; except for agricultural taxes, more agricultural products stayed in the hands of farmers themselves and became their private consumption or investment. Beginning from 1953, farmers became reluctant to sell grain and agricultural products, making it difficult for the state to purchase agricultural products. In essence, this was a conflict between the small peasant economy formed after the even distribution of land and the ambitious goal of national industrialization.

The country also tried to levy more tax, but several attempts for higher taxes in the 1950s led to farmers' collective protests. Because this was a result of equal land distribution to farmers, the re-concentration of land was to fundamentally transform the private ownership system of smallholders.

Initially, farmers were given more restrictions such as setting food and cotton production targets for each household and shutting down the market trading. Later, the collectivization further eliminated the farmers' mutilated private ownership. The mutual aid movement put the farmers' production activities together; the primary cooperatives consolidated their main assets; the advanced cooperatives eliminated dividends from land and livestock; and the people's communes implemented public ownership over a wider scope. And at this point, the state had taken down the ownership fence of the rural society and entered the countryside on full scale.

Why did the farmers accept such a change? Because their previous land ownership was not fully from inheritance or bought but rather obtained via land distribution in a political movement (i.e., the Land Reform). Now that the country called for collectivization, did the farmer have other choices than following the instructions? This was the property rights foundation for China to make the collective system.

Southern Weekend: China's villages have their own traditions. Under such a backdrop, how did the sudden birth of the collective system affect the rural areas and the economy? Also, how will it evolve?

Qiren Zhou: The tradition of China's civilization is to evenly divide the land to all sons of the family; this is a problem from the tradition. With the equal distribution within the small family, no son is willing to leave the hometown, because whoever leaves suffers a loss. This is a path of small peasant economy. The reason why Britain was able to rapidly urbanize and industrialize is because they had a tradition of primogeniture; under that system, all sons other than the eldest son had to leave the land.

But, back then, our tradition was only equal land distribution within the family; it was not possible to get some land from other families because you had a child.

The collective system was going from bad to worse. After the tradition of even distribution within the small family, the "village community" system was introduced from the Soviet Union. In this kind of "village community socialism," the main idea was to continuously redistribute land as the population changes. The Soviet Union had a small population and lots of land, so the system probably worked for them; however, China's situation is the exact opposite, we have lots of people and limited land.

For all the wrong reasons, China duplicated the system from the Soviet Union, and its villages also actually became village communities. First, the members were not allowed to flow freely, and they couldn't move to cities. Second, as the population changed, the land was continuously adjusted and redistributed.

The limited amount of land was continuously subdivided and redivided among China's massive population, and the several hundred million farmers added to the population after the founding of New China were all shackled onto the land. This was actually the root cause of rural poverty. Farmers were confined within a specific frame, and they were unable to move; so they had nothing to do with industrialization, urbanization, or modern civilization.

Rights Establishment Forces Collective System Reform

The establishment of rights is not a formation but rather the termination of a relationship. And, it is forcing the termination of the collective system. The practice of "increasing land with births and decreasing land with deaths" is affecting rights establishment, thus influencing rural land circulation.

Southern Weekend: In 2013, at the central government level, what was emphasized most for rural land reform is the "rural land rights establishment," which was put into the Document No. 1. In fact, this work of establishing the rights has already been practiced for five years in Chengdu as an important place for "land reform experiment," so why did it take so long to start to roll out across the country? And, the then-Minister of Agriculture, Han Changfu, also admitted that the establishment of rights would take at least five years. It seems that the task is still difficulty. What are the difficulties in the confirmation of the rights?

Qiren Zhou: Based on my observations, it would be amazing if we can complete the rights confirmation of all rural land of the country within five years, because the land includes the contracted farmland, homesteads, and collective construction land.

The establishment of farmland contracting rights and issuing certificates is a very good point to watch for. As far back as the 1980s, a total of five No. 1 Documents proposed to issue land contracting certificates to farmers; however—up till now—the land contracting in most of China's villages is just a slip of stamped paper from the village. China lacks the administrative traditions of respecting property rights or attaching importance to property registration. As a matter of fact, clarification of property ownership is probably the government's most important task after national defense and public security. Property registration is the most important link to maintain peace and stability in the society. We have skipped this link, and all the changes made over the years have made the clarification even more and more difficult.

In rural areas, the circulation of contracted land was opened up as early as in the 1980s, but the scale always stayed small, not because no one was willing to take over the contracting but because the property rights relationship was too complicated for people to rashly enter the business.

In many rural areas, after a child is born, a piece of contracted land will be distributed to the baby, and when an old person dies, the contracted land will be taken back; this is called "land increase with births and decrease with deaths," and it is also the result of learning the "village community socialism" from the Soviet Union. If the arable land taken today via circulation or transfer might be changed tomorrow because of the birth of one child or of a group of children, how can the "contract" still be reliable?

Southern Weekend: Are there any adjustments made to the practice of "land increase with births and decrease with deaths"? We have learned through interviews that the practices has been stopped for about ten years in the rural areas of developed regions such as Jiangsu and Zhejiang.

Qiren Zhou: The People's Republic of China Rural Land Contracting Law (hereinafter referred to below as *The Contracting Law*) came out in 2002. It has made some adjustments to this practice of "land increase with births and decrease with deaths" and specifies that during the contracting period, only the reserved land accounting for a small proportion of the total land, newly reclaimed land, or land returned by farmers who have moved into the city can be contracted to the incremental population. At the same time, however, China's villages also implemented autonomous governance by the villagers. So when there is a problem with the allocation of the contracted land, a decision can be made by voting where the minority is subordinate to the majority.

That is why the paces on this practice are different across the country. Some places follow *The Contracting Law* and the decisions of other places are made by autonomous voting. In the first place, land property relationship should not be easily reinvented through voting, but at the village level the government and the land are still not separated, so the complicated relationships cannot be cut off and are still chaotic.

Southern Weekend: Is this one of the primary reasons why rights confirmation is so difficult?

Qiren Zhou: What our research team has observed in Chengdu is that rights establishment does takes lots of time and effort; this is because as soon as the farmers realize that formal land certificates will be issued after the rights confirmation, they will naturally believe that "there will be no change after the confirmation," so they will ask that all population change factors since the start of the contracting be accounted for, and even directly request a redistribution; the process is extremely complicated.

This is not a bad thing, because the establishment of rights is not a formation but rather meant to put an end to a certain relationship; namely, the rights establishment is forcing the collective system to terminate the relationship where the land is constantly distributed according to population.

Figuratively speaking, it is the "increase with births and decrease with deaths" that is affecting the rights establishment, which then influences the circulation of rural land. And fundamentally, if the collective system is not changed in the practice of distributing land by population, the circulation cannot develop. Under the backdrop of industrialization and urbanization, the land needs a new cooperative system with circulation rights included, rather than the geo-based village community system with no flow of population.

Use Circulation to Form New Subject of Interest

Let stakeholders see the possible benefits from the appreciation, and use this as the driver and the bait to move the rights establishment forward—the rights must be established first in order to circulate the land.

Southern Weekend: During the land reform of the past few years, "land circulation" and "increase/decrease link-up" have been discussed most and practiced most, but "rights establishment" sounds like a technical work. How to understand the logic relationship between them and the significance in the land reform?

Qiren Zhou: Logically speaking, rights establishment is both the foundation and the prerequisite. If land does not go through rights establishment or confirmation, the property rights will be vague; so once full-scale circulation is opened up, it will definitely arouse new tort and snatching behaviors, and it will easily lead to new unfairness in the distribution.

However, viewed from another perspective, the purpose of rights establishment is to achieve circulation. If the house is for the farmer's own living, there is no need at all to have the land certificate and the real estate certificate; the simplest way is to keep a dog to keep strangers away. But this does not work for circulation; no rights establishment means no certificate, so the road of circulation cannot reach far.

Southern Weekend: A common worry about rural land reform is that, after the land circulation is opened up, people who have ways to obtain more rural land may be given the opportunities for wealth appreciation and cash-out, causing new unfairness. Rights establishment is restraint to this problem, but it takes time, effort, and money to do it. How can local governments be encouraged to do this and do it well? How to get proactive cooperation from the farmers? And where does the driving mechanism for the reform come from?

Qiren Zhou: Circulation is the driving mechanism. The experiments of land circulation and "increase–decrease link-up" will eventually produce incremental value, enabling stakeholders to see the potential income from the incremental value and use this as the driver and bait to push the rights confirmation forward.

It might be possible that farmers would not cooperate because they feel it is too troublesome. But there is no need to worry about this point. For example, if the buying and selling of farmhouses is opened up, both farmers and urban residents will proactively ask for rights establishment. This is because the farmers themselves want to know how many square meters they can sell and urban residents will worry that a neighbor might come up to create trouble after they buy the house.

For the local governments, it is quite easy to understand the incremental yield from the circulation of arable land contracting rights. The "increase–decrease link-up" pilots need—on the surface—to give a portion of the incremental yield from the newly added construction land to farmers and also bear the cost for their residence concentration, so it looks like not as economically justified as land requisition. However, local governments who truly understand the situation will discover that the total volume of usable land has increased, and so has the total land yield. This is a new vested interest formed during the reform, and the force to push the reform; the reform cannot rely on just talking.

As for local governments, we can enable them to see the incremental yield brought about by the circulation and then place rights establishment into the precondition. If you want to have circulation, establish the rights first. This is the advantage of systematic reform. Without thorough and complete rights confirmation, one cannot develop real estate, do post-disaster reconstruction work, and collateralize the house. This being the case, even if rural cadres are not active, the farmers themselves will block the gates of the government building and demand rights establishment.

After resources are circulated, they bring amazing benefits to the whole society. For the government, the tax alone is a huge fiscal revenue, but many people have not seen this point. Year ago, before the reform to "change public housing into private ownership," public housing was a huge burden; however, after the reform a huge market was formed. What did the government do then? It just issued the real estate certificate, opened a market, and eventually obtained financial revenue through taxation.

Southern Weekend: Currently speaking, as the earliest city of land reform pilot, Chengdu is also leading the way in rights establishment. How do the vested interests of the reform there push forward the reform?

Qiren Zhou: Chengdu's land reform was neither without difficulties nor achieved overnight. While conducting the survey in Chengdu, our research team found that many county-level officials have a strong reserved attitude towards the property rights reform and the rights establishment. For example, some officials proposed not to establish the rights for rural land already planned as built-up area (meaning the land will become urban construction land within five years as per the land utilization master plan). After Sun Ping—who was then Executive Deputy Mayor of Chengdu—learned about this, he started to debate with them on the one side to convince them to change the line of thinking, and on the other side he required that the subordinate work units must do a good job on this matter.

Of course, I'm not going to say that the then leadership team of Chengdu are a group of saints or the idealists for the reform. Xiaogang Village in Anhui managed to implement the household contracting system, not because its cadres were born reformists but because everyone had their respective problems; then they discussed together and came up with the idea for the reform.

My summary is as follows: First, after the coordinated urban and rural development is well implemented in Chengdu, it becomes a good card for political promotion. Second, when the card of political promotion comes out, if forceful demolition is used to coordinate the urban–rural development and implement the "three concentrations," the negative rebounds will be quite large but the political requirement is to have no group incidents. Third, the new vested interests have formed, looking at the whole picture, the total amount of land available for urban construction has been increased.

No One Can Stop This Reform

The central government, the local government, and the village's farmers—all of them are integral for the process of this reform. Both consensus and disagreements are indispensable forces for institutional change. What China is most afraid to have is a reform that is universally agreed to as it might easily be driven wild by the people below.

Southern Weekend: Even with the recent years of land reform experiment, still many places are not willing to push forward the rights establishment. Instead they use "increase–decrease link-up" and building the new countryside as the pretext to force farmers into apartment buildings and snatch exorbitant benefits from it. In other words, these local governments are not willing to establish the rights to farmers, but they grab benefit from the circulation. It seems the current still-chaotic state of the reform has become another round of deprivation of the farmers' rights and interests; is this also the state that some local governments and stakeholders are more willing to maintain?

Qiren Zhou: These conflicts, contradictions, and problems will inevitably arise during the process of reform. It does not matter; just let them do things first. There will always be some local governments that see the benefits of circulation and cash it out through administrative means; this will also definitely cause conflicts. But at the same time, the farmers there will also realize where the new interests are and they will also safeguard their rights and interests. Over time, the balance point will come with the adjustment.

China is a large country, it takes time for anything to change. We must believe that China's farmers are not stupid. At most, they will figure things out just a little later than the government. Eventually the farmers will come to understand that rights establishment and circulation will give them more rights and interests than the previously monotonic land requisition model. What the central government needs to do is actually transmit the signal of opening-up the circulation, and at the same time emphasize the protection of the farmers' interests through rights establishment, reduce the information costs for the institutional change, and encourage local governments to learn from advanced role models. The central government, the local government, and the farmers of the village are all integral for the process of the reform. It's just that the process to mobilize each party is different, and the mobilization process is not an ideal one; so we cannot say which one should go first and which one should follow.

Southern Weekend: There is another concern. If more and more social contradictions are caused by the land reform and more and more distortions occur, will it lead to stagnation or even retrogression in the reform? As a matter of fact, in the recent years, the voice has become louder to criticize the "increase–decrease link-up" for "forcing farmers into tall apartment buildings."

Qiren Zhou: During the process of reform, there has to be someone to step on the brake. Otherwise, the evil fire of "tort-type of circulation" ignited by some local governments will go wilder and wilder. What China is most afraid of is the formation of a one-sided reform where people down below would take the advantage and make it a mess. When there is some disagreement at the top, people down below will be discreet. When you look at it this way, you will see that both agreements and differences are indispensable. Indeed, here in China we have a strong tradition of infringing on private property rights, and the slightest lack of care in this respect will lead to repeating the tort. However, if we do not touch anything and continue with the conservative therapy, we still actually cannot keep things intact.

Why was Chengdu's land reform pilot program operated in such a careful and cautious manner? Because there were so many different opinions, the future was unclear, and no one could tell whether it would be a spank or a candy waiting ahead.

If a reform complies with the laws of economics, criticizing or attempting to stop it will be useless. The decisive fact is, industrialization and urbanization have already brought about huge changes to the relative price of rural land. No one can stop this from happening, because the unstoppable economics laws are playing their roles in the background.

During this process, local governments will naturally put circulation as the first and the most important task. At this time, if the resistance against forced administrative snatching is small, the forcible taking will be the dominant method, but the cost of maintaining social stability will definitely rise, and this increase in costs will eventually lead local governments back to the path of rights establishment. This will be a path that no government can escape from.

Southern Weekend: In other words, although there are some rotten practices and criticisms on the reform over the past five years, the current land system reform has entered an irreversible stage? However, six years ago when we started to see the large-scale emergence of "small property right housing," you concluded that "the time has come to change the land system." Yet, up till now, there still seems to be no institutional breakthrough for the "small property right housing." How to understand this?

Qiren Zhou: First and foremost, a door has opened in the institutional space for the legalization of small property right housing. The outcry for prohibition and demolition has been there for many years, but actually not much has been taken down. To the contrary, recent years have seen many local governments using the small property right housing as a way to fill the vacancy of affordable housing. And, the "three old revamps" (revamp the old townships, old factory buildings, and old villages) of Guangdong Province is also actually to explore a lawful channel for rural construction land to enter the market.

Next, as for the timing to change the land system—between "small property right housing" and Chengdu's experiment, no one is able to conclude which one will be the outlet, but the economic strength and institutional motivation behind these two possible outlets are the same. A few years ago, I saw the soaring urban housing prices and concluded that "small property right housing" could be a hopeful breakthrough, but I had not anticipated that now another path was opened up by the "increase–decrease link-up." Reform is not fully the result of design; instead, it can only be formed by guidance of the trend via the aligned force from the whole society.

The road for China's reform is always winding, taking some steps forward and then backward. The then household contracting system also went back and forth for quite some years. One thing we can be sure of is that the rural land reform is already like a flowing river and no one can stop it.

Southern Weekend: How to do a good job in this irreversible reform? In the current stage, where is the most important breakthrough?

Qiren Zhou: I would like to quote a few sentences from Chengdu: "rights establishment is the foundation, circulation is the core, and auxiliary policy is the key." "Circulation can only be achieved through rights establishment"; this principle should be changed into the demand of farmers, the requirement of the central government, and the program of action of local governments. These forces, when combined, will force the land reform onto the right track.

After rights confirmation is completed, and large-scale circulation is achieved, another pathway for land transfer will occur side by side with the land requisition system; then at last discussion can be held on how to consolidate the two of them and achieve a complete reform to the land system.

Therefore, from the perspective of the current stage, three things need to be accelerated. One is rights establishment, which is the foundation; one is to advance the cross-county (it would be better to make it cross-province) land circulation, including for rural lands and homesteads; and still the other one is to speed up the establishment of land exchange so as to post land circulation information and discover the prices.

Past experience has also proven that reducing the cost of information is conducive to the reform. In this aspect, scholars and the media can do many things. Whenever bad signs pop up from the reform, we should criticize them in time and stay constantly alert.

Abuse of Power Leads to the Need for Property Reform[25]

In October 2008, the Third Plenary Session of the Seventeenth CPC Central Committee passed The Decision of the CPC Central Committee on Several Major Issues Regarding Advancing the Rural Reform and Development. The Decision has put forward some much-anticipated deployments for the reform of the rural land system. These deployments include "gradually establishing a unified urban and rural construction land market," "gradually shrinking the scale of land requisition," and "enabling lawfully obtained rural collective construction land for commercial operations to enjoy equal rights and interests with state-owned land." Since then, China's rural land reform has become one of the reforms attracting the most attention. Under the backdrop of strong prices for urban land and extremely uneconomical utilization of urban and rural land stock, this reform is not only related to rural development but is also the key to the healthy advancement of urbanization.

Over the past more than six years, what progress has been made in this reform? What are the constraints? How to overcome these difficulties so as to achieve the objective of the reform? China Newsweek has interviewed Professor Qiren Zhou of Peking University National School of Development.

The Key Point Is to Implement the 1988 Amendment to the Constitution

China Newsweek: Since the Third Plenary Session of the Seventeenth CPC Central Committee up till now, it seems that the rural land reform is progressing on the whole, but the pace is rather slow. How do you see this?

Qiren Zhou: In February 2015, a plan was set to conduct pilots in 33 counties and cities. There are more than 2,000 counties in China, and thirty-three of them were chosen for the pilot. When this pilot is over, it will be only two years from 2020. In the span of two years to roll out from thirty-three counties and cities to the whole country is probably very difficult.

China Newsweek: The name of this document is *The Draft Decision of Authorizing the State Council to Temporarily Adjust the Implementation of Relevant*

25 The original title of this section was "Qiren Zhou: Return the Land Circulation Rights to Farmers," published in *China Newsweek,* March Edition 2015.—Editor's note.

Laws and Regulations in 33 Pilot Counties (Cities, and Districts) Including Daxing District of Beijing. This document has made provisions on the circulation of rural construction land for commercial operations, but it has made no arrangements for the much-discussed homestead circulation.

Qiren Zhou: Probably there is still fear about the circulation of homestead. Recently, I came across a claim: To prevent counter-urbanization, urban residents should not be allowed to purchase rural properties from farmers. Where does this concept come from? If urbanization refers to the increase of the proportion of urban residents out of the total population, then what on earth does this "counter-urbanization" refer to? Does it mean the decrease of the proportion of urban residents out of the total population? Or does it mean that whenever urban residents move to the countryside, the hat of "counter-urbanization" will be put on their heads? Urbanization, as we see it, is a product of the flow of the population; some people move to the city, and some go to the countryside; taken together, as long as the population entering the city is greater and the proportion of urban population is increasing, it is called urbanization. The decrease of the proportion of urban population might happen in the future, but is not at all possible for the current China with just over 50% of urbanization. To coin an ambiguous "jargon" without thinking and fight against the windmill like Don Quixote, then use a big knife stroke to kill the economic requirement for the farmer homestead circulation which has occurred on a large scale in the real world and will continue to occur, will this make any real sense?

In my opinion, the fundamental question is still whether or not "the land usage rights can be circulated according to law." The 1988 *Amendment to the Constitution* clearly states that it may be transferred according to law. Everyone can verify this; no restrictive wording is added. It does not say that only state-owned land can be circulated but collective land cannot. Nor does it say that the land for a certain purpose can be circulated but land for other purposes cannot. There is only one sentence in the constitutional principle: "the usage right of the land of the People's Republic of China may be transferred according to law." Is this not the top-level design for the issue of land?

The problem lies in the implementation of the constitutional principle. After 1988, the transfer of state-owned land was started. Experience proves that, without land usage right transfer, the opening-up, foreign investment, private enterprises, and urbanization would all be a castle in the sky. The "lawful transfer" of state-owned land has not only constitutional basis but also increasingly improved laws and regulations.

However, as for the farmers' collective land, to date the "lawful transfer" only has the constitutional basis, and there is no concrete law or regulation to support its implementation. Even worse, the *Land Administration Law* as revised in 1998 completely goes against the correct statement from the Amendment to the Constitution made ten years ago, stipulating that both state-owned and collective land can be transferred according to the law, and it states that "the transfer of collective land should not be used for non-agricultural purposes" (but with a provision to opening a small hole for the transfer of the land of bankrupt rural enterprises). Let's forget everything else; are there such limitations on the transfer of state-owned land? Some time later, such wording also occurred as "the transfer of construction land for commercial purposes can be tried under the premise of usage control" (this is not universally in China). Let me ask: Is state-owned land transferable only when the usage is for commercial purposes? If this article had been added in those years, could China's first land auction ever take place in Shenzhen? What was the original purpose of that land? It should be noted that before the circulation was allowed, no land could be called land for commercial purposes because all land was distributed or allotted by the state mandatory plan, and no land was used for commercial purposes or business. The 1988 Amendment to the Constitution was to change the mandatory allotment into marketized transfer. Why not start from a reliable experience such as this one in Shenzhen Instead of hiding so many devils is in the details? Such practices seem to have lots of reasons, but the essence is to have lost the basic direction of the reform.

In this way, state-owned land can be transferred but collective land cannot, so a halfway reform project is created. Its crux is that the allocation of land resources has to fall in the hands of the government to be marketized. What about the farmers' collective lands? Sorry, they must be requisitioned into the hands of the government. With regard to the two basic aspects of resource allocation efficiency and fair income distribution, the consequence of this land model is becoming increasingly serious, therefore the system must be changed. Putting everything else aside, why do so many seized corrupt officials have something to do with the land? The institutional rent-seeking space is simply too large for effective prevention.

Therefore, the fundamental problem is about this or that kind of trivial details, but rather the implementation of the constitutional principle, namely "equal rights for equal land in front of the law." As we see, twenty-six years have passed since the amendment was made to the Constitution in 1988. Should practical experience indicate that the constitutional principle expressed by the amendment is not suitable, then we should first revise the Constitution. Otherwise, specific laws, regulations, and policies will fight with the constitutional principle, and the superstructure will fight with the practice; it is not a good idea to allow this to happen.

China Newsweek: And what are the underlying considerations for dividing rural land into several different types?

Qiren Zhou: This shows that there are doubts about the circulation rights. Except for bankrupt rural brick and tile factories (analogy for rural enterprises), no rural construction land is allowed to enter the market. When the farmers' collective land is not allowed to enter the market, how to solve the land for industrialization and urbanization? The approach is to requisition more land, and this method is still the same as in "land finance" (in the end it will actually become land debt). Nothing gets changed; how can we call this a reform?

Also, we need to see that in reality the flow of land resources between urban and rural markets has long exceeded the framework set by the subjective judgment of people. Rural construction land for non-commercial purposes is traded in the suburbs and para-urban areas of each and every metropolis. This is happening everywhere, only that it is not legal. As far as the competent departments are concerned, so long as they announce this as illegal, their administrative responsibility will be relieved. It's like burying their head in the sand (like an ostrich) to hear no evil and see no evil.

Because these are all illegal, we should enforce the law to rectify the mistakes. But we are unable to rectify; at most, we only selectively enforce the law. Consequently, many people are allowed to live in the extralegal space; what is stated in the legal document is something, and what gets done is something else. From the perspective of economics, this does nothing more than increase the system operation costs. People will just play the game of cat and mouse with all sorts of odd tricks, hiding from something today and preventing other things tomorrow.

Give Whatever Rights Belong to the Public Back to the Public and Make Officials' Misbehaviors More Difficult

China Newsweek: So where exactly is rural land reform stuck? Some people say it is out of concerns about stability.

Qiren Zhou: Yes. Reform always has some uncertainty. What will happen cannot be fully predicted in advance by anyone. Therefore, there are no few warnings and reminders, claiming that something will go wrong here and also there. It seems that nothing would go wrong if everything stays unchanged! Is it a wise choice to hold on until it is too late to change?

China Newsweek: Then, is the problem with the decision level, or with local practice?

Qiren Zhou: If you read *The Decision,* it shows the Central Government has the determination to reform; the difficulty lies in how to put it into practice. Do you know what is intestinal obstruction? The progress of changes in the land system ever since 1988 is such a case. Nothing is so easy, sometimes the hero needs to cut off his arm to save his life; but this kind of situation seems to be very typical on the question of land.

Some people think that the farmers' land should never be marketized. After selling their land and houses, where can they live? And some even worry that once the land circulation is opened, the farmers will go and gamble with the money from selling their lands. If this logic stands, then urbanites should not be paid with a salary; instead, they should be given soap, steamed bread, and towels so as to prevent them from squandering the money immediately after they get the salary. All sorts of cases exist in reality; however, for institutional arrangements and policies, should we really need to use a few weird cases as the excuse to take away the legitimate rights of the people whose majority are able to normally exercise their rights?

To me, none of these is the reason to prevent farmers' land from entering the market. The pilots of some localities have also shown that homelessness resulting from land circulation as feared by some people has not become the trend as they have expected. We always need to start from the experience to test whether any concern has a basis. We can't simply make assumptions and see all the farmers and grassroots people as minors as if they were unable to safeguard their interest without us making choices for them.

China Newsweek: Some people also say that the rural land reform is going very slowly because there are some considerations to leave room for low-cost land requisition by local governments.

Qiren Zhou: There is no way to tell. We study human behavior, not the motivation. You can only see what the result is, what effect the result has on economic development, and what kind of effect it has on resource allocation and income distribution. As for the motivation of all the aspect, it is useless to make wild guesses.

China Newsweek: The rural land reform still seems to have big differences of opinions both at the decision level and among the people?

Qiren Zhou: China's reform has always been like this. It's like what Lu Xun says, "If you say the room is too dark and we need to open a window on the wall, people will disapprove. But after all the pressure when someone shouts out 'remove the wall,' somebody will stand out and say 'forget it, let's open a window.'"

Additionally, for land reform and the reform of other key areas, what is really worth worrying about is that as long as power is not properly constrained, any reform could be distorted. Under this type of reality, we have two choices: one is to change nothing, at least this will not increase the opportunities for misbehavior; the other is rightly because of the misconduct of some people, it is even more necessary to pull out the root of the headstrong power. By returning the rights belonging to the public back to the public, the official who want to misbehave will not be able to do so.

Coming back to the topic of land, according to my experience, if we do not give the rights of circulation to farmers, this power will actually be concentrated into the hands the government, departments, and a few officials. Urban and rural areas always need the land circulation; as a result, the circulation rights will be allocated to the administrative power. This is the currently focal point. If for the fear of misbehaviors by power we dare not change the system where the land allocation rights are concentrated into the authorities and individuals, will there any possibility to cure the root cause of the disease?

The correct method, I think, is to prevent the abuse of power, especially to prevent all sorts of distortions that do harm to the people, and at the same time to push the reform forward. We should rectify the distortions and correct the abuse of power by fighting corruption. But still we need to advance the reform, because it is the strategy to remove the root cause. At the beginning of the reform, had the land not been contracted to rural households, there would be many tricks from many people.

Therefore, we should not stop the reforms simply because there are distortions of power. On the contrary, rightly because the soil is there for power distortion, it is even more necessary to advance the reform across the board.

Two Questions on Rural Property Rights Reform: Permanent Unchanging Policy and Convenient Circulation[26]

During the socialist transformation, we hoped to better develop productivity through the public ownership system. But the implementation led to many bad

26 This section is adapted from the author's speech on November 28, 2015, at the

results and triggered three years of famine. The pains will stimulate people to rethink about problems. The earliest origin of the rural property rights reform can be traced back to the central economic policy adjustments after the 1961 famine, namely the restoration of private land plots. The private plots system left some hands-on experience to cooperative members and cadres of some regions; namely, the output could be increased by contracting the land to farmers and giving the farming right to the households. With this as experience, the household contracting was re-initiated in 1978 and then spread across China to become an institution.

The household contracting responsibility system reform was not first proposed by people who wrote the document but was instead the result of explorations from the grassroots. Up till now, this experience is still very important for China's reform. It is quite difficult for things purely coming out of the pen to take root, but things coming from grassroots explorations have exuberant vitality. Not that long ago, Mr. Du Runsheng passed away. During the process of this reform, he has made a significant contribution. His contribution is not the invention of the household contract responsibility system but the legalization of grassroots experience and putting it into the document of the central government so that the reform gets protection from the authorities of the central government.

After the 1990s, China's rural reform basically stopped. Why? Because the dynamic mechanism changed. Why the reform needed to continue after the food problem was resolved; this was a question left from that time. What is the meaning of the rural property rights system reform? Although we did some of the work, a high degree of consensus is still yet to be formed from the ideological and theoretical perspective, still less can it be converted into more conscious behaviors. In addition, after Deng Xiaoping's speech during his southern China tour, industrialization, urbanization, and China's opening-up were making big strides forward, the rural areas became relatively less important, which also led to the lagging in the reform of rural property rights systems. From the perspective of using the market for resources allocation, the ratio of urban resources entering the market is higher, while many rural resources have not formally entered the market, so the rural areas are relatively lagging behind. The key to moderate affluence depends on farmers, and farmers depend on the rural system and on

Annual China Reform Conference, themed as "Comprehensively Deepening Reform and Accelerating Urban-Rural Integration," in Neijiang, Sichuan Province.—Editor's note.

how much decisive role is played by the rural market in resources allocation. And for this market to come into play, the foundational work, namely rights establishment and circulation, must be completed.

For now, after the implementation of the household contracting responsibility system, the framework of the rural property rights system has been established and the basic economic system has been formed. But there are still two pending questions: First, it was said the contracting system will remain "unchanged for the long term," and later the wording was changed to "unchanged permanently," but this promise has not been fully delivered, and some forces are pushing it to change. Second, the resources in the hands of farmers and collectives are not fully circulated; they are not continuously transferred, according to the requirement of the market, to the hands of organizations and individuals with higher utilization efficiency, and the release of the economic potential is therefore hindered.

On the first question, namely whether or not the permanently unchanging policy can be fully put into practice, there is already no obstacle at the superstructure, because no one is mentioning collectivization or eating from the big rice pot, and this theory has long disappeared. Currently, the issue is at the grassroots level. Should the land be adjusted after rural household population change? This question has never been resolved since the start of the household contracting system. If yes, the "permanently unchanging" would be hollowed; if not, many farmers would see it as unfair. So, do we make adjustments or not?

In point of fact, in the mid to late 1980s, Guizhou's Meitan County conducted an experiment with the launch of a local pilot project: The land does not increase or decrease with the increase or decrease in population, and the land contracting right is controlled at the family level. Back then, apart from farmland, Meitan had lots of resources as mountain forests and barren slopes. To keep the farmland boundaries unchanged for the families was helpful for the development of non-farmland resources. After the boundaries of agricultural land were clarified, people were forced to go farther out. If the land were constantly adjusted, people would forever plan everything around the land. For twenty-five years Meitan has adhered to the idea of "no land increase or decrease with the population change" and firmly implemented the permanently unchanging policy. Proven successful by experience, this practice was written in 2002 into the *People's Republic of China Rural Land Contracting Law*, which says that during the contracting period, land cannot be changed, or adjusted, and the rural households have the permanent right to use and operate the farmland contracted to them. However, China also has other laws, such as the autonomy by villagers included in the Constitution. Of the six items of villagers' autonomy, the first point is the determination of forms of land contracting. Therefore, in some places, the land adjustment still needs to be made if the majority of farmers see it as necessary. The global picture for China is the parallel existence of both methods: One is not to increase or decrease the land with the population increase or decrease, the other is to adjust the land after the population changes.

Today we are issuing iron-clad certificates and establishing solid rights to achieve economies of scale and attract capital from the society to sign contracts; but if the land gets adjusted frequently, how can the contract be signed? If boundaries are not clear, the contractual binding force will be unreliable and capital will not dare to come. "Permanently unchanging" was written into central government documents, but it still has not been implemented in all rural areas in all aspects. If this matter is not fully put into practice, it will be very difficult to achieve other things later. Why is the establishment of rights difficult? The reason includes the fact that the farmers at the grassroots level cannot reach consensus on this issue.

As for the second main question, the circulation is even more lagging behind. After 1992, industrialization and urbanization have made rapid progress with big strides, rural labor also have become active, with more than 200 million farmers leaving home for cities. But the problem is, if the people are moved but other resources are not moved accordingly, the people cannot go far away or go for a long time. As we all see, many migrant workers live in basements in cities, but their house back at home is empty and their land is left uncultivated. The resources at both ends are poorly used. It is impractical for the country to buy all the social security for farmers because there is not enough financial resources. The Fifth Plenary Session of the Eighteenth CPC Central Committee has set the target of lifting more than seventy million people out of poverty, including the last twenty million people in poverty into the minimum subsistence assurance program; this is what finance is capable of doing. Many farmers have houses and land back at home, but they cannot enter the market. The country is promoting marketized resources allocation, but the law does not allow rural houses to enter the market, and further the law states that urban residents are not allowed to buy rural properties; I do not think this makes sense. Currently, agriculture accounts for 10% of China's GDP; the figure is below 8% for Jiangsu and 0.5% for Shanghai's suburb, which is at the same level as Britain. The trend is that this share will become smaller and smaller; if the large amounts of labor do not go out and get tied onto the farmland, we will not be able to balance the urban and rural income. Therefore, we must make the flow of rural labor more smooth; and to make it more smooth, other resources in rural areas need to be circulated.

Without this force, it will be unsustainable to rely on finance to subsidize farmers and agriculture, and we are already having fiscal difficulties.

What is the difficulty in allowing rural resources to enter the market? This touches on the current land requisition system, which is a half-way project. The earliest land to enter the market was mostly rural land. When the legislation was made, the Constitution said that land usage rights can be transferred according to law; it does not say that only state-owned land can be transferred. But the departmental legislation, on its formulation, specifies that only state-owned land can be circulated, embarking on a road where the government requisitions land with one hand and sells it with the other.

This road is not a useless one, because it has brought about the nice infrastructure to cities. However, it also has built up conflicts. As the government has directly rushed into the market and become one of players in the market to contend against the people for benefits, the negative cost has grown larger and larger. Not only that, what is easily obtained does not get efficiently used; so our cities become very large, the industrial zones become very wide, all built with lots of debts. However, this is so large a vested interests that it is difficult to move it.

The central government has performed the top-level redesign for the land requisition system reform, with the target to gradually shrink the scale of requisition and explore the way for rural collective construction land to enter the market; this was laid out in a document in 2008. However, the real shrinkage has been inadequate, and not enough efforts have been made to explore the pathway for the market entry. To me, China cannot purely count on the top-level design to solve these problems; we also need to rely on explorations by the grassroots level. All sorts of explorations in these aspects by local governments are very valuable, such as those in Shanghai, Chengdu, and Chongqing.

It is very difficult to advance the reform to the land requisition system, especially when all local governments are heavily indebted today. I do not see how the land requisition system can be completely changed all at once, but a gradual reform is feasible.

Make Good Use of Cities, and Build the Countryside[27]

Today, at this forum we have many friends from villages as well as many friends who have long been working on rural affairs. We all care about a common

27 This section is adapted from the author's speech at Zhejiang Lishui Rural Internet

topic: that is, how to build a better countryside. Taking this opportunity, I would like to ask a question: In the process of developing and building the countryside, and in the program to build beautiful villages, at which position should we place the cities? Or, perhaps I could rephrase the question and ask: How to introduce and grasp the urban elements in rural development?

I will be proposing an idea for your comments and criticism: The more you care about the countryside, the more you should examine and use cities. Why? Because cities are the engine of the national economy, the motor for and the traction force for rural construction. According to this view, to build the new countryside and the beautiful villages, it never means that rural construction should be achieved by closing the door and depending on rural resources in isolation. Instead, we need to open the door, borrow the strengths from cities, make good use of cities, and strive to maximize the urban elements in rural development.

Next I would like to share with you some of my observations, and you can judge whether they support what I have said. A few days ago, I visited several villages in Songyang County. It's already winter, but I saw many persimmon trees still with ripe red fruits hanging on them; it was a nice view. Why didn't the villagers pick down the persimmons and sell them for money instead of keeping them on the trees? Local friends explained to me that they have sold over the Internet a hot topic called "The Persimmons Have Turned Red." The theme shot its fame with all the nice pictures and attracted many visitors, the rural tourism was initiated, and people set up homestay business. Keeping the persimmons on the trees has a more irresistible attraction to people. One of the villages is Yankenglingtou Village of Fengping Township. The small village, with only 300 villagers, has even attracted many teachers and students from the Academy of Fine Arts to come here for sketching and painting. It is said that the village's tourism income in 2014 exceeded RMB 1,000,000. It turns out that persimmons are more valuable when left unpicked.

From this we can see the importance of cities. What kind of people would come here for tourism when they see the unpicked persimmons? It's people from cities. This is worth studying. Now, in the construction of villages, and in the construction of beautiful villages, of course, the first thing we need to do is to improve living environment of the villagers themselves. But, if we are to grow the economic income, we must bring in urban elements. This is also the basis for my argument in today's topic. The more discussion we have on constructing the new

Development Forum in December 2015.—Editor's note.

countryside and the beautiful villages, the less should we talk about the countryside just from its own perspective and the more emphasis should be laid on urban elements and their use. As a matter of fact, when we talk about Taobao Village, or rural e-commerce, already lots of urban elements have long been playing the role of the engine in the development of rural areas. The question is whether or not we can understand our existing experiences more consciously; whether or not we can be more active to upgrade these experiences into strategies, tactics, and more conscious actions so that we can strive for greater breakthroughs in this aspect.

In the interest of time, I will speak about three points and hope to attract your attention.

First, make good use of urban consumption power. In our country, the average disposable income of urban residents is still three times that of rural residents. This is a readily available purchasing power in the market; it would be a pity if we do not leverage it. Obviously, it's also not impossible to sell rural products to rural residents; the problem is that it is not easy to sell them at good prices. Selling rural products to urban residents can increase rural residents' income by quite a lot; I believe this is also one of the basic experiences of Taobao Village. I told the story about the unpicked persimmons just now, and here is another story taking place at the Taobao Village I visited yesterday in Gushi Township of Songyang County. A farmer household raises turtles and sells several million palm-sized turtles every year to all places across the country. I asked them why people buy them, they said they are mainly bought by urban people to release life. If their sales destination is only the countryside, it is impossible to have such a big market. Therefore, if we make good use of the urban–rural income gap and give full play to the comparative advantage of rural areas, it is also possible to increase the farmers' the income and narrow the gap.

Second, make good use of urban brain power. I do not mean that city people are smarter than country people. There are many gifted children inn the countryside, but, according to my experience, their superior brainpower will have a better opportunity to be developed if they have the opportunity to enter cities. Brainpower does not fully equate to intelligence. To flourish, smart people need to get together and meet even smarter people, so that they can polish, challenge, and learn from each other and share their knowledge. Without aggregation and without the right atmosphere, it is hard for the brainpower to be developed. This is also why education, scientific research, academics, and arts are all in separable from aggregations, and they are located in big cities or otherwise in small cities nearby big cities; this is the environment needed by the generation of intelligence. As long as the opportunity is given, rural people will definitely go to school in the city and broaden their horizons. But the knowledge generated in the city can completely be applied to rural areas. Look at things like Alibaba and Taobao; aren't they created by city people? But, as we develop rural areas, we can and definitely must leverage the new technologies, new business models, and new ideas from cities. The first time I came across a Taobao Village was when I heard the story of Shaji Township. All the three founders are from rural families; they entered the city working as migrant workers in telecommunications for many years; after seeing the outside worldand building up the knowledge, they went back home and created Shaji Taobao Village. Therefore, we shouldn't be thinking that a Taobao Village can be built just with the resources of the village. Without urban areas being connected with rural areas, there would be no way for the Taobao Village to be created.

Third, make good use of urban land power. Rural people need to earn money from people and build good infrastructure and nice houses, which takes lost of money. Where does the money come from? Fiscal spending or subsidy might be one of the sources, but no matter how strong the financial strength of a local government is, it is not able to afford the construction of such a vast countryside. So what to do? I did an investigation project at some remote villages in Chongqing. The farmers had many shabby houses taking up a large piece of land, and they were unable to build new houses just by relying on their own financial strength. However, after finding land prices to be very high in Chongqing's city center, people invented "land coupons." This means to demolish the idled desolate houses and reclaim the sites into farmland, and after acceptance the certificates or "land coupons" will be issued. Then the land coupons are taken to Chongqing Land Exchange and get listed. City center land using private enterprises, state-owned enterprises, and development zones will bid for the coupons, and then winners can build their projects in locations with high land prices. The proceeds from the land coupons auction is sent back to the countryside and serves as the capital for the construction of the new countryside. As I see it, this is a good method; to leverage the land power of the city to build the countryside, the essence is for the city and the rural areas to share the high land prices from urbanization. Lishui also has similar experiences in selling your land quota to more developed cities such as Ningbo and Hangzhou so as to finance the construction of local villages here.

In short, we should not separate the city and the countryside when we think about rural development, and still less should we talk about the countryside only from its own perspective. Instead we should jump out of the box and think about the mutually connected urban and rural areas and the integrated urban–rural development. It seems that to leverage the strength of cities and make good use of cities is one of the key conditions for the task of building the countryside, the new countryside, and the beautiful villages.

Indeed, the current urbanization rate of our country is just a little over 53%, and only 36% in terms of *hukou* population. Therefore, when we discuss the construction of the new countryside, we still should not forget to advance the urbanization, especially the "urbanization of the population's *hukou*." In a fifty/fifty urban–rural population structure, the city's traction ability to the countryside remains relatively limited. When the split gets sixty/forty or seventy/thirty with urban population taking up the majority, will there be more better things to watch for in this traction? Recently, there seems to be a new trend of encouraging rural migrant workers to return to their hometowns. This might be okay during an economic downturn, but the long-term trend is still that we need more farmers to move into cities.

4

The Logic of Innovation

How to Get Rid of Mediocre Growth?

Joseph Schumpeter put forward a theory of innovation in the 1930s. He believed the growth of most economies cyclically repeats itself; namely, the total economic output increases with the increase of population but without much increase in the per-capita average. This is a mediocre economy. Only by breaking through this mediocre cyclical economy can we achieve modern economic growth; namely, sustainable increase in the per-capita output and the per-capita income. Why is per-capita income extremely important? This is because only when the per-capita level gets higher can there be a big change in the economic structure. When the per-capita income hovers at a low level, it is difficult to satisfy the need for food and clothing, so there will not at all be room for high value added economic and technological activities as well as cultural enjoyment.

Then how to break through the repeated cyclical mediocre economic growth?

Schumpeter put forward an idea which is still very influential to this day, and that is innovation. He believed that if there is no innovation, it will be very difficult to break through the economic growth; the economy will just grow along with the population increase and there is no way to achieve sustainable growth in the per-capita income. For example, China proudly has a great civilization with 5,000 years of history; but for a very long historical period, its population and total economy growth did not come together with obvious improvement in the per-capital level. According to research by economic historians, roughly from the thirteenth century to the nineteenth century, China's was the world's largest economy, but the per-capita level did not increase much in 600 years. After 1840, the per-capita level dropped, which became a challenge to threaten the survival of the country. Why does the traditional economy present such a trend? The reason, as per Schumpeter, is lack of innovation, or the innovation is not popularized and maintained after some signs of innovations pop up.

The economy of contemporary China has started to realize an improving per-capita level, especially with a rapid growth in per-capita income since the 1980s. Indeed, this fast per-capita income growth also poses new challenges.

One basic question is where will people's consumption demand go after food and clothing is resolved? It seems to be more and more difficult to grasp the answer. The main categories would certainly still be clothing, food, housing, and travelling, plus telecommunication, networking, and entertainment; but no one knows which products will be "hot" and for how long. The market and industry respect consumers and embrace the philosophy that the "consumer is the king," but even consumers themselves often have no idea what they should buy next. For example, in the era of horse-drawn carriages, if we did a survey on consumer needs through a questionnaire, they might say they want the carriages to be faster and more comfortable, and that's it. Would they ask for cars? Probably this idea would have been very difficult. That is to say, to advance from the demand for food and clothing, some non-continuous flight may take place in the continuous change of the demand. Continuous improvement to the horse-drawn carriage may not necessarily lead to the birth of cars, and similarly the continuous improvement to the traditional postal service routes may not necessarily lead to the sudden emergence of trains. However, immediately after the pop up of a car or a train, probably the vast number of consumers will say, "that's what we want"! Here, from the continuous incremental improvements to the non-continuous leaps, do we have the chicken first or the egg first?

In Schumpeter's view, the people who can make the non-continuous flight are precisely those who he defined as "entrepreneurs." Regardless of the actual social identity (be it a boss, engineer, craftsman, literati, or even an ordinary person with an idea like a flight of fantasy), whoever has and sticks to his crazy idea and turns that idea into a product which becomes acknowledged by the market is an entrepreneur in Schumpeter's sense. Therefore, it is logical that Schumpeter's economic development theory regards entrepreneurs as the key to economic growth.

What is truly exciting about the economic growth is the non-continuous leap. Most economic activities are continuous. To have significant transformations in the era of economy, to have something really big, the key to this is to the non-continuous leap. This leap is innovation, including innovations in products, in production methods, in raw material, in business model, or opening up new markets to discover a set of new methods to develop the economy. Without the impact from innovation, the economy will inevitably be mediocre. At most, the population will grow along with the total economic aggregate, but the per-capita level will not improve sustainably.

Schumpeter also has another viewpoint, namely economic growth is a human activity, and it will always have fluctuations. Of course, from today's perspective, the split of long-term fluctuation cycles and the short-term fluctuation cycles seems to be too mechanical; but the discovery that economy always has fluctuations stands erect and very valid. For many years now, China's economy has been growing rapidly, and it has a strong inertia to continue moving at a high speed; but once it is greeted by the downward pressure, the situation is like this: It is easy to go uphill but difficult to go downhill. Inertia from the rapid growth period means that slowing down has taken a while. Because the effect of inertia from the rapid growth tends to lag, for example, during rapid growth everyone tries to hire more people, the labor salary goes up; everyone tries to acquire land, the land price also rises. In short, the more fierce the competition for resources, the sharper the price hike. The government also becomes more ambitious as tax revenue also soars. But when the downturn comes, not all the indicators go down at the same time. Nowadays no few enterprises are having a hard time because the sales price of their products has gone down while their costs have not gone down correspondingly. With high costs and plummeting sales prices, the enterprises are getting squeezed; so how can they survive?

The answer to break the siege is by innovation.

The economic logic is that the same cost has different meanings if we produce different products. To produce old products with old methods, the cost will be prohibitively expensive. But, if you add innovation, the cost burden of new products or new processes will be lighter. The engineers hired by Steve Jobs are not inexpensive, but he is able to afford it; not only this, he also made huge profits. What is the secret? The answer is to rely on innovation to absorb costs. The story of Huawei is also the same. I visited the company in 2014, and they proactively raised the salary for new hires. They also have cost pressure; why can they can afford it? This is because they rely on innovative products to continuously maintain competitiveness.

Obviously, the risk of innovation is very high. Of today's new products, new technologies, new models, and previous new ideas from entrepreneurs of different eras, probably even God does not know which one will gain the foothold in the market. To this end, we need to have an appropriate system to complete the arduous task of screening. Nowadays, everyone understands that this system is nothing else but the market economy system.

The market economy is a system that provides the most opportunities for innovation and entrepreneurship, a system that let consumers pick the products to the maximum extent, and also a system that protects the innovation function of entrepreneurs. The space is vast, regardless of the background or the age; we can always give it a try if we have "ideas." Even if other people don't believe us, but do we believe ourselves? Do we have the capability to convince all sorts of investors to support us? Creative ideas can be converted into products, products need to be tested by the competition in the market, and the principle is the survival of the fittest. Viewed from the current perspective, after the demand for food and clothing is satisfied, the only way to cope with the very uncertain fluctuations in the economy is to follow this type of method. My understanding of this is that we should build a platform, call the "brave warriors" together, ask them to change the creative ideas that might be generated during the continuous process into business plans, into products and services, and then have them tested by the market.

Because the risk of innovation is extremely high, the prize must be super. As we see, so many young people became sleepless watching Alibaba going public. Without a super prize to motivate people, the mobilized resources will be limited anyway. The reason is, as the Chinese saying goes, "it takes thousands of lives to make the fame of one general." We can't only look at those few successful people; the success of one general is often accompanied by the loss of numerous heroes. On the average, the "profit" from innovation is not so high. If we encourage more potential entrepreneurs and business adventurers to improve quality and lower the cost in the competition, the benefit will eventually overflow to do good to all the consumers and the society. Certainly, it would be even better if the super prize winner, now becoming super rich, can devote more to public welfare.

Gather the Concentration of Innovative Elements[28]

Since setting foot on Israel, the country of innovation, I did not see quite as many innovations as I had expected. Was there any difference in airport service or the way for shuttle bus driving between Israel and China? Was the admission-by-ticket method at the Old City of Jerusalem any different from China? What about vendors in Old Tel Aviv, and the restaurants where we ate at and the hotels where we stayed? All things were kind of exotic, but they still seem to be quite the same as in China. As a matter of fact, for the majority of things that can be perceived or experienced, there is nothing new, and most of the technologies used daily here are not that much better than in China. In this sense, isn't the title of the bestseller *Start-Up Nation* (Chinese translation published by Citic Press in September 2010) an overstatement?

Sure enough, staying a few more days and listening to some presentations left us with a new impression. Surprisingly, this country, with just above eight million people in 2013, has 38,000 scientists! Their high-tech sector contributes to 10% of their total employment, 15% of their total economy, and 50% of their exports. Their research and development expenditure accounts for as high as 4.2% of the GDP, and this is the highest in the world. The country is also a world leader in terms of other indicators, such as the number of start-ups, the amount of venture capital, and the number of NASDAQ-listed companies. What's most remarkable is that whichever institution or organization you visit, the host can proudly take out a long list and tell you which "world-changing" key technologies originate from Israel's R&D centers, Israel's innovation enterprises, and Israelis.

But when you get back onto the street, if you do not intentionally remind yourself that this is a country built in the desert and surrounded by strong enemies, you wouldn't easily feel that Israel is more exceptional than many other places of the world; it is even rather moderate measured by the per capita of USD 35,000. It's just that the graffiti is ubiquitous in Tel Aviv, just like in Manhattan, indicating that this place which strictly follows Jewish commandments has more tolerance for individuality than other places.

This leads me to guess: Innovation is actually the activity by only a few people. Innovation starts with new ideas, but it is always difficult for new ideas to gain responses from the majority of people. People would generally follow the

28 This section was originally published on *Caixin Weekly* (now *New Century Weekly*), the 22nd issue, 2015.—Editor's note.

crowd and do whatever is prevalent or what are they are used to. "Unusual" things definitely go against the majority. It is difficult for new ideas to pop up; people laugh at them after their pop-up, and no one supports a try-out. If this is the case, "innovation"—the conversion of new ideas into exploratory activities—cannot take place. It is probably necessary to admit that most people's daily life is far away from and on the opposite side of innovation. This is where the difficulty of innovation lies. If no one responds to an innovative idea, it will fade away over time and everyone sinks back into mediocrity.

Under what conditions will "innovations" become forceful? From experience, it might be to put all the forces which support innovations together and reach a certain minimum concentration. I've always been thinking, what would happen if Israel had not been founded as a country to gather Jewish people from around the world in 1948? Possibly the Jewish people distributed in different parts of the world in the diaspora would still be terrific—which is the result for them to gather together in those places—but probably there would be no chance for the formation of the "Start-Up Nation." Bringing together people with ideas who are willing to take the adventure and reaching a minimum concentration should be the most important condition of all.

Historically, all innovative actions in science, art, technology, and even handicrafts are the result of similar people coming together to reach a minimum density or concentration. People studying the classical age of the West will definitely mention Greece, and the actually refer to only the few city-states (poleis). The Renaissance is inseparable from the city of Florence, Italy. Actually the Scottish Enlightenment, which generated David Hume, Adam Smith, Thomas Reid, and many thinkers influencing the modern world, was concentrated in a few universities, taverns, and cafés in Edinburgh. This seventeenth-century small town had only several dozen thousand people and lots of traces of barbarism, but precisely because a small environment was put together to form an atmosphere, there was the mushrooming of great thoughts, figures, and works in many fields. The story of the contemporary world is the same. When we say that the United States' scientific innovation is terrific, we are actually talking about the Silicon Valley, which is not a big place around Stanford University. When the elements for innovation build up and reach a sufficient concentration, new ideas and new findings will gush forth like water from the spring.

As for the majority of city-states in ancient Greece, many European cities other than Florence during the Renaissance, and most Scottish towns other than Edinburgh, they were nothing special. The United States also cannot do innovation anytime, anywhere. I had my hair cut in America and I didn't find that the barber there was really any better than their peers in a small county site in China. The only difference is that the American hairdressers' salary is much, much higher, and this is because they're lucky to be able to get a share out of the overflow of the benefits from innovations such as those from the Silicon Valley.

What does this mean for us? We face lots of choices when we make corporate decisions: which industry to enter, which products to make, where to get financing, and where to open the store. But the most important thing is what kind of environment do we place the enterprises into? If you are determined to build an innovation enterprise, probably you must put yourself and your company into an environment that is responsive to innovation. From a country-wide perspective, the opening and reform policy has been implemented for more than thirty years, but in terms of innovation environment, only a few places have taken shape including Shenzhen and Zhongguancun in Beijing. The reason is nothing more than that these places have a higher degree of responsiveness towards innovation, and they have more "weirdos"; they wouldn't make a fuss of weird things, and more time, energy, and money are concentrated day and night to seek innovation.

When will people work with increasing enthusiasm as they go? It is when they have buddies? What is a buddy? A buddy is someone who, first, is willing to listen to your idea, even if it sounds crazy; second, echoes and responds after understanding your idea; and third, pays attention to for and recognizes your efforts even if he can't respond. Sometimes the thoughts and actions of a person are only for the limited few specific people to listen and to watch. After listening to your idea, a hand-clapping is an encouragement; to give some comments and have a discussion is an even bigger encouragement. On the other hand, if you are motivated by others' ideas and encouraged by others' behaviors, then the place is a promised land for innovation. It's really quite strange that many, many people of the world gather together, but they would not listen to each other let alone motivate and appeciate each other. In such an environment, even if someone comes up with a new idea, it is easy to be seen as heresy, and the idea will die away with time.

Therefore, the most important part of innovation is to gather the same type of people, when the concentration of like-minded people reaches a certain required level, it will be enough to generate new ideas, which can be changed into actions, discoveries, and products, which then will obtain all sorts of supports. Birds of a feather come together; to perform innovation it is a must to have a innovation crowd where people can frequently inspire and motivate each other. Only after we have the crowd and the concentration exceeds the critical value can we have many chemistries and come up with pathways that we have never thought of before. If there is only one individual making the call and no one responds, it will be difficult for him to achieve something no matter how strong he is. Viewed this way, when entrepreneurs and enterprises choose positions for themselves, the position is not only about the physical location of the sites, but also about with whom entrepreneurs will exchange, and about mixing themselves into which type of groups or crowds with which kind of ideas, namely the position of their social networking, which might be more important than anything else.

In summary, we should not think that a country is innovating at any time at any place. Even Israel, as a country with a few million people, cannot do this. They also have to gather the several universities and research institutes, some innovation industrial parks, a number of venture capital funds, and a batch of innovation companies. It is even less possible for a big country to innovate in every place and at all times. But for both big countries and small countries, it is possible to first put things together in a few places with adequate concentration and adequate density to form a few groups or clusters. Our entrepreneurs should pay sufficient attention to the choice of the "groups," see it as a variable for their decision, and join the group that suits their future development.

The Attitude toward Knowledge: A Feel from a Visit to Israel[29]

Israel attaches great importance to education. Actually many countries including China also attach great importance to education. Then, how is the education as emphasized in Israel different from other countries? During this visit to IDC (a business school in Tel Aviv), a rabbi (meaning "sage" in Judaic) was invited to lecture to us. His topic was "How Education Has Shaped Israel's History." He used only a few PowerPoint slides to make himself clear.

As he first told us, all Jewish people need to receive education from two books since their childhood: one is the Bible written in Hebrew, and the other is Talmud. The latter is the interpretations (with 2.5 million words, the book is a very thick palimpsest) to the Hebrew Bible by generations and generations of outstanding rabbis over the past 2,000 years; and it also records a great deal of folk wisdom.

29 This section is adapted after the author's speech at a discussion of the Experts Advisory Committee for the Thirteenth Five-Year Plan.—Editor's note.

This rabbi also tells us that Jewish people learn from these books since their childhood and they need to read them over and again for their whole life. The first responsibility for all Jewish moms is to educate their children, and this is their holy duty. Generally starting from the age of 1, children begin to listen to stories from these two books told by their moms or grandmas. And at about 5 years old, Jewish children have listened to virtually all stories from these two books. Then they will go to school and follow rabbis for the formal learning. The rabbi lays emphasis on the rituals: Children going to school for the first day must wear new clothes, so they know learning is a happy thing. New classmates are welcomed by a hand-clapping. The very first class is about how to read. The letters are written on a clean slate using honey. After reading the letter, the children can lick it off from the slate; or alternatively, each child is given a candy before they start learning—so that children will understand that to learn is sweet.

What's even more important is that the Jews use a discussion-style learning method at school—two students read the same text and raise questions to each other, such as for the question of "what is the meaning here," you have your explanations and he has his, the two of you need to discuss. Doubt is allowed and even encouraged, and this includes doubt about God, the Bible, and the rabbi. Students are encouraged to raise questions and challenges. The Jews are used to the discussion and critical style education since their childhood rather than mechanical memorizing, still less do they have blind faith in authority. Many Jewish people later become successful in science and technology; what is so strong about their education is first the way of thinking as the focus of their education.

During the visit, we also invited Professor Aaron Ciechanover, the first Israeli to win the Nobel Prize in Chemistry, to give us a speech. He said that ever since he was a little boy his mother had told him: "Walking into a river, people can go downstream, or they can go upstream; you should forever go upstream." This also laid the foundation for his attitude of life. There is a sentence in the Talmud to the effect that "difficult things are easy to accomplish." To go along with the river current does not take much effort, but many people take the same approach, so it gets quite crowded and it will be more difficult to stand out. To go against the current, it is, on the other hand, easier to make a breakthrough because there are fewer competitors.

The suffering of the Jews has convinced them that land can be deprived and wealth can be taken away, but knowledge forever stays. To put this into the modern language, what they trust most is the investment into human capital. It seems the theory of human capital has found Israel to be a very thorough testing ground.

Israel is a country that requires all citizens to perform military service; national defense is the first priority because this country surrounded by strong enemies. Because the army mainly relies on discipline and obeying orders, I initially felt it should be difficult for them to be a culture to encourage innovation. This was then one of my questions, but in the end, I found the answer.

First, to turn all the citizens into fighters, Israel's state fiscal resources sponsors the military R&D system to a large extent, and the funding is sufficiently assured. This is because without high-tech, Israel has no way to survive in the harsh environment.

Second, their military R&D system is led by their best professors. For all the top four universities and research institutes in Israel, the military science research projects are chaired by first-rate professors.

Third, all Israeli senior high school graduates must join the military, and the best of them are chosen to enter the military R&D system. The proudest thing for the first-rate young students is not to be admitted by prestigious universities such as Harvard and Yale but rather to be chosen by the Israeli intelligence service or the military research departments.

Fourth, militia is the part of Israel's military people, so the hierarchy is not so strong in the formal army. The R&D people in military uniforms generally do not mind too much about ranks or seniority, and people in the front line have a big say; for project establishment, namely what on earth should be done, it is not fully a top-down decision, but the combination of top-down and bottom-up is also encouraged.

Fifth, after three years of military service, Israel also has a reserve service system—people return to the military for one month every year—which further disrupts the hierarchy: You might be a senior executive of a company, or a department head in the government, but when you return to the reserve forces, your leader might be your previous subordinate. This also helps to spark innovative thinking between them because they are not shackled by the hierarchy. Innovation needs this kind of atmosphere.

It is said that American technology giants in Silicon Valley have a love and hate relationship with their Jewish colleagues at their Israeli R&D Centers. They deliver performances, but it is not an easy job to be their leaders, who often get asked: why are you leading me rather than the other way around?

Some people ask: Don't their leaders hate this? The answer is that they deliver, and in the end, they produce innovation results aren't their leaders aware of this point?. In fact, this is also one of the necessary conditions for innovation. Therefore, we should not attribute the success only to the Jewish smart brains. The answer is not fully their brains. What's more important is whether or not there is an atmosphere and environment that can bring the wits and capabilities into play. If this is absent and the wits are used elsewhere, innovation will be difficult.

The Future in the Eyes of an Economist[30]

Uncertainty Is the Best Known Answer

Economics is often seen as a gloomy branch of learning, because its view on the future is not so clearly optimistic. Adam Smith was relatively clear; he believed that as long as there is sufficient economic freedom, the invisible hand will lead mankind towards a better economic growth. In his time, the British Industrial Revolution was thriving, and experience also supported an economics with a clear and optimistic view about the future. The greatest prediction made by Smith in *The Wealth of Nations* was the judgment that the American economy would be very promising; this view was later validated by reality.

But after Adam Smith, with all the conflicts caused by the rapid spreading of capitalism, many economists became not as optimistic. The most well known of them is Thomas Malthus, who believed that population growth would outstrip food growth; therefore, the future would be full of troubles and the rebalance would be built by famine, natural disaster, or even war. His ideas put a melancholy mark on economics.

By the time of the *Communist Manifesto*, the view became, on the one side, very optimistic and gave full affirmation to the capitalist mode of production for its liberation of productive forces that surpasses any previous era in human history; at the same time, it predicted, based on the explosive growth of the socialized productivity, that the capitalist production relationship would inevitably die out. Since then, this major judgment has been constantly tested. The tension between the claim that capitalism would surely die and the fact that it still has not perished has become an earworm.

30 This section is adapted from the author's speech at Lenovo Star WILL Conference in Beijing on July 9, 2016.—Editor's note.

The Soviet Union had a few decades of optimism. They not only proved that "socialism can be built in one country," but also decided "to complete the construction of socialism in one country." Their most glorious period was World War II, as their industrial capabilities mobilized by the planned system became the material basis for the fight against fascism. After the war, they were even more optimistic; Khrushchev declared that "the construction of communism will be completed in one country." Unfortunately, his promise did not come true. The Soviet Union not only failed to win the peacetime competition, the theme of which was to satisfy people's growing need for material and culture, but also sank into to a stagnant economy and an ossified system, leaving absolutely no heritage of viewing the future with a clear and optimistic mood.

China started its construction out of poverty and blankness. The first move was to learn from the Soviet Union; China was similarly optimistic and likewise set the goal of surpassing Britain if not the Unites States. Unfortunately, the Great Leap Forward ran into difficulties, some adjustments had to be made to stabilize the footing, and then China switched to the political route of treating class struggle as the outline, and the "Cultural Revolution" pushed its national economy onto the brink of collapse. Backed into a dead corner, China had to liberate its mind and implement the opening-up and reform policy. To reform and opening-up also meant China was optimistic about the future. Deng Xiaoping believed the world would have twenty to thirty years of peace, which would allow China to focus on economic development. In 1980, China set the goal of doubling the output twice within twenty years and delivered it, and its economy doubled another time in the first ten years of the new century and became the world's second largest economy. However, looking back to the 1980s, the starting point was really very low. For people like me taking part in rural investigation and research after university graduation, the actual situation to face was that "800 million people are in agriculture, but there is not enough to eat." Therefore, we needed to reform. The reform is no easy job; a number of new problems will pop up after we solve one, and even up till today we cannot say that we have put everything in the right place for the reform. How should we see the future—should we be optimistic or pessimistic? Frankly speaking, with so many problems entangled together, people do not have time to think deeply about the future.

Teaching economics will touch on the topic of anticipation and illustrate that people's behavior is influenced by their view on the future. I know that the best theoretical answer about the future is "uncertainty," as was proposed by Professor Frank H. Knight in his 1921 book (*Risk, Uncertainty, and Profit*, published by Renmin University of China Press in November 2005). What is "uncertainty"?

Uncertainly means even empirical probability is unable to figure out what will happen in the future; perhaps we can plainly interpret it as "unpredictability," meaning an accurate prediction cannot be obtained. Then how should we deal with the world of uncertainties? Economics has what seems to be a valid conclusion up till today; namely, we cannot do without a set of systems: the rule of law, the market, property rights, and contracts, especially equity contracts. Why do we want "the market to play a decisive role in resources allocation?" The reason is that the future is uncertain when we dive deep down to the bottom.

"Get Ready for the Future"

The above answer is reliable, but not perfect. First, there seems not much more to say about the uncertainty and unpredictability of the future; this leads to overlooking "the influence on people's current decisions and behaviors from how they look at the future," and it reduces the ability to understand and explain human behavior. Second, the unpredictability suggests that "the unexpected might happen at any time," this easily leads people to think about the bad prognosis—as if uncertainty means always means a disaster is coming. But in fact, the uncertainty could also be a pleasant surprise rather than unilateral misfortune.

Therefore, some explanations can still be made to the "uncertainty." In this regard, I am inspired by Peter Thiel's *Zero to One: Notes on Startups, or How to Build the Future* (Chinese translation published by Citic Press in January 2015). The author takes the way people look at the future, builds a two-dimension by two-dimension matrix (definite/indefinite, optimistic/pessimistic), and obtains four quadrants: definite optimist, indefinite optimist, definite pessimist, indefinite pessimist. Then he takes "the way of looking at the future by all the countries" and puts it into this cognitive matrix. Of course, this is not exactly accurate because "every country" encompasses a large number of people who sees the future in a different way. So at most, his book is a summary of the mainstream views of all the countries, plus some of his own subjective impressions. The conclusions are not so rigorous, but still I am inspired, and the impact is not a small one.

For example, he believes that "from the seventeenth century all the way through the 1950s to 60s, the prevailing belief in the west was the definite optimist view about the future"; and that "the United States in the 1950s to the 1970s" has been a typical representative of this "definite optimist" throughout its history. Is his statement reasonable? Steamships, railways, the telegraph, large-scale mechanization, the wide application of chemistry, cross-sea tunnels, subways, other onshore infrastructure construction, and the excavation of Suez Canal and

Panama Canal; are all these great feats summoned by magic? As a unique British colony in North America, the United States is endowed with abundant natural resources; the population is also quite small. Simply by reclaiming wastelands, selling cotton, tobacco, and lumber, the life of the early generation of European immigrants would already be quite comfortable. Then, why did they still invent the factory assembly line, build the Empire State Building and the Golden Gate Bridge, implement the Manhattan Project, invest in interstate highways, and even implement Project Apollo? Not to mention the crazy ideas and daredevil actions of countless people. In short, none of these things are "purely natural," as they are all artificial. Before doing things, people are always dominated by the way they look at the future. No wonder Thiel has no hesitation in putting the United States before the 1980s into the first phalanx of those who are "definitely optimistic" about the future.

However, the author believes that the subsequent United States has turned "indefinitely optimist." The traits are: people feel both "optimistic and puzzled"; financiers have replaced scientists and engineers to become the God's chosen few, and financial expertise gets more limelight than science and technology; people overvalue "opportunities" and underestimate "planning" and perseverance; there low savings, low investment, and high consumption. All of these traits have placed the uncertainly optimistic tune onto finance, politics, philosophy, as well as life; no one cares whether or not this will last. Obviously, the author believes that the situation for "current Europe" is even worse as its mood is dominated by "indefinite pessimism"; Europe is just muddling along; every country of themselves sees the big trouble, but they only talk about it for a long while and nobody really sets to fix the problem.

What is most irritating is that surprisingly this little book lists "today's China" as the representative of the "definite pessimist"! In order not to misinterpret the author's original intention, consider this quote:

> A definite pessimist believes the future can be known, but since it will be bleak, he must prepare for it. Perhaps surprisingly, China is probably the most definitely pessimistic place in the world today. When Americans see the Chinese economy grow ferociously fast (10% per year since 2000), we imagine a confident country mastering its future. … From China's viewpoint, economic growth cannot come fast enough. Every other country is afraid that China is going to take over the world; China is the only country afraid that it won't. (*Zero to One: Notes on Startups, or How to Build the Future*, p. 87).

What is the basis of this?

> Every senior Chinese leader experienced famine as a child, so when the Politburo looks to the future, disaster is not an abstraction. The Chinese public, too, knows that winter is coming. Outsiders are fascinated by the great fortunes being made inside China, but they pay less attention to the wealthy Chinese trying hard to get their money out of the country. Poorer Chinese just save everything they can and hope it will be enough. Every class of people in China takes the future deadly serious. (ibid. pp. 87–88).

Whether or not you agree or disagree with Thiel's assessment, I was quite touched by the reading. As for myself, I should not be put into any of the four quadrants. If categorization is a must, I would put myself into another alternative type—"too immersed in observing and interpreting experience and phenomena so that no time is spared to think about how to look to the future." When anyone asks me a question about the future, "uncertainty" becomes my universal answer. Shouldn't I be a bit introspective over such a long-established stereotype thinking?

Enlightenment from Israel: Difficult Things Are Easy to Accomplish

I was even more moved by the two study trips since last year. The first trip was to Israel. It was organized by Z.H. Island Business Academy, and I was invited to go together with a team of young entrepreneurs. The duration was short; counting the time that I spared towards the end of the trip to see a Kibbutz[31] in the desert, the whole visit was only eight days, but it was a big shock to me. Before departure, I did some reading about Israel, which is described as the God's "Promised Land" and "a land of milk and honey." I didn't realize that this is not fully the case until my arrival. The statutory area of this country is even smaller than Beijing (the actually controlled area is more than 20,000 square kilometers, which is slightly larger than Beijing). Their natural resources are extremely scarce; 60% of the country's land is desert, and they only have 6,000,000 *mu* of arable land. The annual rainfall is less than 200 mm for half of the country, and even less than 30 mm for its southern areas. But, today Israel is "Europe's fruit and vegetable basket." One Israeli farmer is able to provide for 400 people in 2014 as compared with fifteen people in 1955. Large volumes of high-quality, high-value-added

31 A Kibbutz is an Israeli collective community which—in the past—was primarily engaged in agricultural production, but now also in manufacturing and high-tech.—Editor's note.

agricultural products are exported. Their drip irrigation technology and products are world leading, and they even export fresh water and desalination technology.

Even more impressive is that despite a total population of only eight million, they have more than 7,000 technology start-ups. After the United States and China, they have the greatest number of NASDAQ-listed companies—and, their per-capita amount of venture capital is higher than the United States or Europe. In 2014, Israel's per-capita output was USD 35,000, with the high-tech industry contributing to 50% of the total export and 10% of the employment.

What's the secret for them to be able to achieve all this? It is the people; in particular, the excellent capability to convert knowledge into technologies and products. Where do they get the capability? It originates from education. We Chinese also value education, but comparatively speaking there is a difference in the focus. First, their education places lots of emphasis on faith, and generations after generations of Jewish students firmly believe that they are not only the children of God but also that they are born to be able to "wrestle with God"; so they are never afraid of any hardship. Second, even with staunch and pious belief, and with a high degree of esteem for the rabbi, they are encouraged since childhood to dare to ask questions, to cast prudent doubts, and to challenge authority. When a Jewish child comes home from school, the mother does not ask about exams or their grades, but rather asks: "Did you ask a good question today?"

At the Peres Center, I attended a lecture by Professor Aaron Ciechanover. As a little boy, he was taught by his mom that when a man walks in to a river, he could go with the current or against the current, but "you should always go upstream against the current." This also drew the trajectory of his life in advance: Once he attained sufficient success in one field, he would go against the current and open a new field. After being academically well established in his home country, he went to the United States to challenge himself. After becoming a tenured professor, he found himself discontent and returned to Tel Aviv to tackle difficult research projects. In 2004, he was awarded the Nobel Prize in Chemistry, becoming the first Israeli Nobel Prize winner. His experience mirrors one of the parables in Talmud, namely "difficult things are easy to accomplish."

Another terrific sharing was the lecture by Brigadier General Danny Gold, former Head of Weapons Development at the Israeli Department of Defense, and the story was about the development of the "Iron Dome." The backdrop was the Second Lebanon War in 2006. Israel's neighbor fired about 4,000 rocket bombs into northern Israel, killing forty-four civilians and forcing 250,000 people to be evacuated and some one million people into air raid shelters. At the same time, in southern Israel, nearly one million people were under the threat of

Qassam rockets, which had a longer range. In 2007 the then Defense Minister Peres decided that "Iron Dome" would be the way to deal with the problem, and Danny Gold was picked to lead the research and development. Six years later, the real war deployment with the "Iron Dome" was completed. In just the three years from 2009 to 2012, it successfully intercepted 245 incoming rockets. During the presentation, the former brigadier general played a short video: A large group of Israelis are having a wedding. The air raid siren sounds. No one scrambles to the air raid shelter. Instead, everyone holds their mobile phones up to take photos of the sky as they watch the intercepted rockets dispersed into pieces scattered in the sky, like fireworks of congratulations from a foreign country! After retiring from the military, Danny Gold started a technology company which develops a miniaturized rocket to break up blood clots in the human body.

No wonder Israel becomes a country of innovation, whose level of innovation is completely out of line with its natural resources and its population. It was after arriving in Israel that we learned that Microsoft, Intel, Apple, Google, Facebook, and all other well-known Silicon Valley technology giants have—without fail—all established scientific research centers in Tel Aviv. The number of Israel-developed key technologies that truly change human life can be put together to form a very, very long list. Once again, what is the secret do they rely on? It is their wisdom and their inexhaustible persistence; it seems that the belief in God of this nation has been translated into the belief in human ingenuity and capability, and they dare to explore the unknown from the known knowledge. Suppose we ask the crowd of Israeli entrepreneurs how they see the future; I believe the ultimate mainstream will be "definite optimists." Otherwise, why do they always choose to think about things that others dare not to think about and do things that others dare not to touch? The success of pathfinders inspires their followers, so more people will believe that the opportunities in the uncertain future are unlimited.

Be Audacious in Thinking and Down-to-Earth in Doing

The second trip took place not so long ago. Several of us teachers, colleagues, and a handful of alumni organized a trip to the United States to survey innovation. The story originated from a forum organized by Peking University National School of Development in 2015. The forum invited Wang Yuquan, founder of a Chinese venture capital company, to share their experience in investing into American scientific innovation projects. He also invited a number of entrepreneurs and scientists from American technology startups to deliver presentations, give demonstrations, and answer questions. Some joint discussions were held on what Wang Yuquan summarizes as "American-style modular innovation," which was an eye-opener for the participating teachers. Afterwards, Professor Xue Zhaofeng, one of my colleagues and a participant of the forum, came up and organized the tour on the topic of modular innovation. He also co-authored *Modulized Innovation* with Wang Yuquan. The book explains in detail how the 1980 *Bayh–Dole Act* (also known as *the Patent and Trademark Law Amendments Act*) passed by the U.S. Congress works in concert with other economic and legal systems and policies to facilitate the effective combination of resources such as federal research funds, non-profit universities, professors and doctors, venture capitalists from all walks of life, and entrepreneurs, how this combination would allow innovation in very different technical and economic directions, and the significance for China's manufacturing and China's innovations.

I listened to all the presentations and remarks of the forum, and I have read the full text of Wang and Xue's book. Over the years I have developed the habit of on-the-spot investigation when I hear interesting things. After I learned about the trip, I signed up to join the two-week study tour with more than thirty colleagues and alumni sharing the same preference. The key point of modular innovation is to create the connection between the ideas in the academic ivory tower and products, markets and industries. Therefore, this study tour was in the San Francisco Bay Area and the Boston Corridor, and most visits centered around the two top universities. I had been there before and heard the motto was "Die Luft der Freiheit weht" (German for "The wind of freedom blows") for Stanford, and "Mens et Manus" (Latin for "Mind and Hand") for MIT. What I did not know, though, was that the brain energy of America's best universities had long gone beyond their unfenced campuses and been integrated together with the elite force from the market and industry.

I will still use a few impressive examples to answer how people working at the forefront see the future. The first example is XCOR. About ninety miles north of Los Angeles, a "gateway to space" was erected in a semi-desert area, and this gateway is the Mojave Air and Space Port. XCOR is a technology start-up based here. They are developing engines for vertical takeoff vertical landing spaceships. In an inconspicuous warehouse-style factory, more than forty scientists and technicians have kept themselves busy with the project for a dozen years. Other than the presales of a few tickets of space travel (USD 96,000 per ticket; there are Americans who paid the bill for it), XCOR has earned zero revenue, and it relies on burning the money from its investors for the development of one model of space engine after another.

How do these plain individuals who we have met look at the future? It is said that the small town of Mojave has gathered quite a number of space enthusiasts. Their basic consensus is that the Earth is overburdened by humans, and so it is necessary for us to fix the roof before it starts to rain and get ready in advance for our future migration to outer space. They are talking about sending two million people to Mars first, and this is only the elementary target; to truly bring it into reality, it is necessary to schedule daily shuttle trips. This is why we need "returnable spacecrafts," and thus space engines that we never had before.

Let me move on with Hyper Loop One; they are absolutely determined to build super high-speed trains. The idea is to pump all the air out of a large tube to form a vacuum, and then drive the train with maglev technology, the speed of which can reach 800 kilometers per hour. After we found the company in a graffiti-filled neighborhood in Los Angeles, its CEO spent a little more than half an hour to give us a brief yet very clear explanation of their dreams, progress, achievements, and aspirations. It sounds like they have raised a total capital of only USD 100 million to do this great seismic job, and it is said that they have completed the demo test in the Las Vegas desert; already customers have come to place orders, and the future is very promising. The work of dozens of engineers is in full swing. Many of the people do not draw salaries—in fact, the company does not have much money to pay them—but they convert their work hours into the company's stock, "just in case the company succeeds."

The future of these two things is highly uncertain. Are the people doing the work not aware of this? Why would they have such crazy ideas? And they also do not feel that things like going to space or building super high-speed trains should only be considered and pushed forward by the nation. Their people have no limitations in thinking, and their "concept of a nation" is different from ours in that their concept also encompass all the citizens including themselves rather than only the "government," still less just the "officials." Apart from the bold thinking, they are also able to motivate quite some people to dedicate themselves to the job and work on the single project for seven or eight years or even a dozen years. This certainly will be totally impossible if a system is not put in place in the background, as repeatedly emphasized by Xue Zhaofeng during this study tour. However, the way how people look at the future seems more like a hidden cost. Had they not been definitely optimistic about the future, they could just as well invest the money, the human-power, and the resources into anything; am I right?

We also visited a company called WiTricity. The founder was a physicist at MIT, whose research topic is wireless charging. After being granted the license by the university, he found some venture capital and managers and created this company. Now their demo laboratory product is ready. To demonstrate their product, they took out the charging mat and placed several mobile phones or a laptop on it; the charging immediately started, and not single wire was needed. With this technology, electric cars do not need charging poles. What's more fascinating is that it can penetrate through the human body and be used to charge pacemakers within the human body. The company structure is also interesting. The professor serves as academic advisor while the entrepreneur runs the company, and they share the equity.

There is another enterprise near Boston called 1366, which develops silicon solar wafers. The current technology cuts a silicon block into thin slices, and half of the costly silicon material is lost during the cutting. In 1366's new techniques, the silicon wafer is formed in one step, no cutting is needed, so the cost can be saved by half, to bring down the solar electricity cost down to similar levels to thermal power. I asked the CEO: when you begin mass production, will you consider going to China for manufacturing? He said no, they had already selected a site in upstate New York State to build a plant. However, the finished silicon wafers would be shipped to the Pearl River Delta for final assembly and then marketing.

Wicab—the first investment project for Wang Yuquan—is located in Wisconsin; but the CEO came all the way to San Francisco to give us the presentation. They discovered we actually do not "see" the world with our eyes. Instead, we use our eyes to transmit external picture to our brains where the imaging takes place. As per this principle, the blind only have problems with their eyes as the signal receiver; as long as their brains imaging function is there, if information input can be achieved through other channels, their sight can be recovered. So they invented a device called Wicab (also called "electronic lollipop" or "electronic popsicle"). By holding it underneath the tongue and using this other channel to transmit the image signal to the brain, blind people are now able to see!

On the road I brought with me *The Nature of Technology: What it Is and How it Evolves* by W. Bryan Arthur (published in Chinese by Zhejiang People's Publishing House, April 2014). It is not an easy book to read. However, after visiting more than ten high-tech projects, I have a better understanding. What is new technology? It is "a technology that adopts new or different mechanism to achieve an existing purpose." Then what is "mechanism"? Mechanism means to "make use of a certain phenomenon, concept or theorem," and technology is nothing more than the "capturing of a concept and putting it to use." What is even easier to understand, is that "novel technologies are shaped by social needs; they often come from experience outside the standard domain; they originate better with the exchange of knowledge; and they are catalyzed often by networks of colleagues." (ibid. p. 120). Isn't this what we are seeing every day during this learning tour? If we are to probe into the attitude of American engagement in innovation towards the future, we will notice that they all believe that scientific principles can be discovered and used, and there are always solutions to all sorts of problems in front of mankind—the definite optimism is coming at us.

Let Pragmatic and Definite Optimism Rise

Let's come back to the basis of Mr. Thiel's assertion that we Chinese are "definite pessimists." I think his most reliable reason is not the fixed stereotype thinking left from the long history of civilization but rather the inability to look ahead and see clear prospects. Just look at the following quote:

> The easiest way for China to grow is to relentlessly copy what has already worked in the West. And that's exactly what it's doing: executing definite plans by burning ever more coal to build ever more factories and skyscrapers. But with a huge population pushing resource prices higher, there's no way Chinese living standards can ever actually catch up to those of the richest countries, and the Chinese know it. (*From Zero to One: Notes on Startups, or How to Build the Future*, p. 87).

What does this mean? It means that with the current technology neither our resources nor our environment can support China's total population of more than one billion to have the same standard of living as the western developed countries. We've long since had a saying: if the whole world is to have the same standard of living as Europe, we will need three Earths; and to live the life of Americans, we will need five Earths. However, where can we have three (or five!) planet Earths? The conclusion is that this is impossible, and this is the origin for Chinese to be "definitely pessimistic."

The key point is that it might perhaps work for a couple hundred million people to copy and imitate the technologies from countries with the advanced way of living, but it will definitely never work for a billion or several billion people to do the same. The environment has already given us warnings. Supposing all of the environmental costs of economic development were to be "internalized" into the price of goods, then modern enjoyment would be far too "expensive" for most people. But who has the ability to persuade people to be content with the traditional life "where plowing must use the ox and lamps must use oil"? We need to admit that the current technology, although already advanced, is not advanced enough to continue to push the modernization further forward. In order to satisfy human's increasing modernization demand, R&D and innovation cannot be stopped. In order for Chinese—plus Africans and other people—to have "definite optimism," it is not enough to go from zero to one; the capability to change the one into *n* within the capacity of the environment is still needed. This *n* is not a small number as it involves a population or one, two, or even three billion. If I've not read things wrong, this is the core concept of the book *Abundance: The Future Is Better than You Think* (Zhejiang People's Publishing House, April 2014). Peter Diamandis, the author, is a Harvard medical doctor with an engineering background and also a leader in the commercial development of outer space in the United States. Reading this book and having some discussions on the road during the study tour is a perfect combination, and I really recommend it to everyone.

It seems that we have to face a closed loop. A definite optimistic outlook for the future is the spiritual premise for the doers of all economic and technological revolutions. However, only when most miraculous technologies are able to demonstrate a realistic prospect for most people to be able to live an affluent life can the general public have a positive attitude towards the future. Do we have the chicken first or the egg first? The old question wants a new solution. We have felt one point from the study tour and would like to share it with everyone: The optimal doer of innovation and entrepreneurship is neither all the people of a super large organization nor any single-handed prophet. The optimal innovation organization is a "group" of the right size, not so small and not so big. It is easy for the same type of people to reach consensus, to admire, learn from, and inspire each other; and when the organization cost is affordable, they will move in the same direction. When the different groups interact with each other and a positive outcome is obtained, more people will be affected. Just like life, it can be born out of nothing. Starting from the "pot of primordial soup," active molecules join together, get simmered, and interact at high frequencies until a new structure is grown. From this viewpoint, the embryology for revolution, reform, and construction is the same.

In conclusion, I'd like to summarize a few of the points for sharing: First, the front-line innovations in developed economies are worth our attention, and Chinese people might be able to find some treasures from them. Second, ideas are more important than resources, because usable resources of all the eras are determined by what we think. Third, bold thinking and doing has a positive meaning, but it has a premise; namely, to believe the future will be better. And fourth, the crowd of innovators and entrepreneurs need to get rid of anxieties around them—about growth, about transformation, about education and culture, along with other indescribable anxieties. But just anxiety alone cannot help them out. To let the pragmatic definite optimism rise in China, let us start with the crowd of innovators and entrepreneurs.

Let More People Benefit from the Internet

Many paths can be taken toward economic development: industrialization, urbanization, marketization, commercialization, what was called agricultural mechanization and electronization and now called Internetization. I propose the following: All of the "-izations" must benefit a larger number of people; any method that does not cannot be called an "-ization."

Lessons from History

For some time economic construction (in China) was called "industrialization." Industrialization was a very correct target because it was difficult to gain a foothold in the world with just agriculture. But for quite some time it was difficult for the industrialization to bring benefit to all the people. For some time, the farmers, accounting for the majority of the population, did not benefit from the national industrialization. They were only making contributions through supplying grains to the state at very low prices but benefiting very little from other aspects: The urban–rural gap was huge in terms of education, medical care, and social security conditions.

This is a lesson from history. It seems to be a realistic path of development to make the farmers life a little harder life by requiring them to use their grains to support industrialization. But, when the industry gets built, to whom can the products be sold? If the majority of people are impoverished and do not have purchasing power, the industrialization cannot be carried forward any more after reaching a certain level. Later this mode is called self-circulation of the industry, and this road was also later on reformed. After reform, a big difference has taken place in terms of benefiting the majority of the people. The household contracting system, rural enterprises, private economy, and then the opening-up to the outside world has involved many people into economic activities and made China into the world's second largest economy today. A report by the International Monetary Fund (IMF) using purchasing power as the evaluation criteria even says China is already the largest economy. Indeed, what this IMF report uses is the purchasing power, the calculation of which involves lots of details and conditions, but all in all there is no denial about the rise of China's economy. Therefore, the historical lesson has taught us that we must cast our eyes on benefiting the majority of people in doing anything.

The Two Most Important Groups in Today's China

So, in today's China, how do we classify the majority of people? There are two very important groups. One is the young people, such as those born after the 1980s, after the 1990s, and the post-millennials, who are the biggest part of the demographic pyramid. What's even more important is that not only they are the largest in number, but also they represent the future. This is something we need to highly emphasize in adopting any economic pathway.

The second group out of the majority of the people which we must follow are the Chinese people who live in places at or below the county level. For now and a long time yet to come, these will remain the places with the largest population for China. Certainly, the bustling urbanization might bring about some changes as big cities, metropolises, and metropolitan areas will unstoppably expand; but when we look at statistics, by household registration 65% of China's 1.3 billion people are rural residents. Some of the rural residents have moved into cities or towns; now more than 200 million rural residents have moved into cities and towns, and of them quite a large number migrate to county sites. This is why the rural population living at or below county-level places, especially those living in below county-level places, must be considered when we set the next target and want more people to benefit from economic activities. We should not just focus on Beijing, Shanghai, Guangzhou, and Shenzhen. For sure, it is important for China to develop these metropolises, but the scope is not wide enough to have the "-izations"; to do that, we must also take places at or below the county level into account.

Bring Benefit to More People via Internet

What will be the problem if we put young people and the people living in places at or below county level together and see them as one group? In counties, and especially in places below the counties, there aren't very many young people, and the number of productive young people is even lower. With industrialization and urbanization over the years, large numbers of young people have left their hometown. Currently, the population living in places below the county level accounts for more than 50% of the total population, but most of them are middle-aged or senior people, or children, and the number of productive and educated young people is very low. This constitutes a problem for China's current development. This is because developing the economy and creating new industries, especially e-commerce, needs young and skilled people. However, the rapid urbanization and industrialization brought about by more than thirty years of reform and opening-up have moved many young people from rural areas into cities. Looking at the global picture, this has become a big challenge for China's economic development. So, how can we solve it? Effort on the part of the government is one aspect; every year the central government researches into rural issues, including rural reform and rural development. There's another aspect as well; namely, we need to have efforts from all sectors of the society.

Alibaba has made useful explorations in this regard. The Alibaba Group was established in 1999, and I still remember what Jack Ma said at Peking University on its establishment. Investors from all over the world were in the audience, and internet heroes were talking about what they wanted to do at the podium. When it was his turn, Jack Ma said that he didn't know exactly what he needed to do, but he only knew that his investors needed to give him more resources, and you could not expect a child to have a great future if he is talking about making money. At that time, I was in the audience listening and felt: game over! He didn't explain what he wants to do, how will others give him the money? It was very interesting. Masayoshi Son took a fancy to Alibaba and gave the investment to Jack Ma, who chose to serve China's small and medium-sized enterprises and made his way.

A dozen years ago, some people at Alibaba were already studying the internet and trying to understand whether or not it could radiate into rural areas, and into the rural areas which I just mentioned—with not so many young people but still a quite large population. From the current perspective, we probably cannot claim that this is a wide-open and very workable road, but compared with the explorations more than ten years ago, more people can be more confident about moving in this direction. Internet technologies provide this ability. Of course there is a threshold, and a little training is needed to cross it. However, as everyone is aware, farmers in rural areas, including the older and the less educated, are able to stride across some technical thresholds, because mobile phones have already become quite popular and the development of telecommunications, the distribution of base stations, and the spreading of Wi-Fi has significantly reduced the cost. Therefore, we will be able to blaze a path for the villages and counties to leverage internet to benefit more people.

Mobilize the Vast Number of People

How to bring benefit to these people? The way is to satisfy their needs. This is not a slogan; everyone has needs. The youth, senior citizens, urban residents, and rural residents all have their respective needs. These needs are always multifaceted, from multiple aspects and at different levels. We have now discovered that the internet is able to activate many of the unmet needs in the past, which is encouraging. Great changes have taken place in the countryside since the opening-up and the reform. Looking at national statistics, the net income of the rural population has grown exceptionally fast these past twenty or thirty years; but, how can this money be spent? There are still many difficulties to overcome; many goods and services still find it difficult to penetrate into the countryside, and many kinds of information have been unable to spread into the countryside. Still, this is a field where the internet economy has a very strong motive force.

In what ways is the internet powerful? It can mobilize more people to satisfy more people's needs. It does not rely on a few companies or manufacturers, but rather it mobilizes the vast number of people and entities.

Suichang County, for example, does a good job although it's far from big cities. What is the secret? Today's villages are no longer the traditional villages. As roads have been built to each and every village, the network of roads, electricity, and telecommunications has been built, and the farmers' income is increasing, many demands are yet to be satisfied and activated. They have built online marketplaces, and this is amazing. Going to the fair is a traditional business model existing in China's rural areas for more than 2,000 years. People would travel for an hour to the east for the township fair for Monday today, and go northwards for an hour for another fair for Tuesday tomorrow. This was the way to connect commerce and agriculture for the traditional countryside, and it was a hard work; I know this quite well because I was once assigned as an educated youth to the countryside as a farmer and I also went to these fairs. Now young people are going to the Suichang's online marketplaces, and rural people are able to understand the concept because going to the fair is the China's tradition and now it is just that new technical measures are adopted. A one-hour walk is no longer necessary, plus the type of goods are no longer limited as in the case of the physical marketplaces; consumers can choose products from all over China and all over the world.

We should not look down on the farmers; they're no different from city folks. Indeed, their income on the whole is still lower, but they also want to consume more. Still many rural resources are yet to be brought to the market. For example, some online rural merchants are capable of selling ten million RMB of clean, green, and organic agricultural products, which are most preferred by urban residents.

More than twenty years ago when I was studying rural issues, I paid a visit to Japan. At that time, I didn't really understand two things which were introduced. The first thing was what we called "fax agriculture." Under this model, millions of people in Tokyo had their contact points with rural families in Japan. Once a week they would send a fax asking for, for instance, 2.5 kg of rice, then it would be packaged and delivered to the contact point. Then, I didn't get the idea because, according to the experience in China, it was difficult to understand why each individual household can place the order. Because in China, agricultural products needed to go through state purchase, the supply and marketing cooperative, and then third tier sales station to reach individual households.

The second thing that I didn't quite understand was their return to traditional agriculture with no chemical fertilizer or pesticide. They asked us to taste their cucumbers and tomatoes, and sure enough the taste was like what I ate during my childhood.

Viewed now, once the economy grows and the income of urban residents increases, these demands become real. First, people want personalized things. How to satisfy the personalized demand? In the past, we didn't have internet, so personalization was difficult, because the cost was too high, but now it becomes possible. Second, people want things to be organic. People are becoming more and more demanding on nutrition and safety and are more willing to pay more. But the question is how to get products out of less developed and pollution-free areas? The internet can provide a great deal of help. We need to bear in mind the idea of serving the majority of people and bringing them the benefit; this is worth much commending.

Research Deep into the Objective Law

To benefit most people and meet the demands of more people, we must study the laws. Motivation alone is not enough. Whether a given matter can be accomplished or not can only be tested by the outcome.

The job will be difficult. The population in rural areas is very scattered; although the cost of information dissemination via the internet is already very low, logistics is quite difficult. And this is why just now I said the online marketplace model is very interesting. So the key is still to find a gathering point. In the past, for China's revolution to gain victory the strategy was to encircle the cities with the countryside. But my viewpoint on this matter (i.e., the development strategy) should not be for the countryside to encircle cities but for the cities to radiate the rural areas. We must research into the nodes because internet would become a flat surface without nodes. Every point can be interconnected over the internet, but when things get offline, the distribution and delivery is a problem. Therefore, we have to do good research as to how large to medium-sized cities and county sites can extend downwards and what kind of model can enhance the radiation intensity of this extension. This involves many costs, one of which is a question for the internet economy. If only one package needs to be delivered to a remote village, who will do it? There is always a tipping point. Once that tipping point is crossed—for example if there are 100 packages a day for a village—many courier companies will be willing to accept this business because the operating cost has been reduced. But can we grow the number of daily parcels from one to 100? By not charging anything? Offering a service for free allows the service to cross the tipping point; if the tipping point is not passed, no one can make money. The reason why many things are free online is because the aim is to foster the demand to surpass the tipping point.

According to my research, the government is the earliest adopter of internet thinking. What did the government do in the past? They built roads with fiscal funding to build roads, and many roads were toll-free. Why toll-free? Because after the roads were built the economy would develop and the government could levy taxes. The government should be the party that needs internet thinking most, as many things done by the government are to spend fiscal resources on public construction. So, in this round of development, how can government financial funding help with developing the rural internet and reaching the tipping point? My view is that to have one player is not enough. It is not enough to have only businesses, enterprises, industries, and industrial alliances; probably the government force should be added and aligned together with the efforts of all players to surpass the threshold and find the path. If after one or two or even ten parcels we are unable to further grow the volume, it will be a big trouble. Currently, the 1,000 Counties and 10,000 Villages Plan is underway. China is a very large country, and so to speak, a large country needs some big trees to provide shade or benefit to a larger population. But, when planting these seedlings and growing them into large trees, we need to study the laws of nature to press smoothly ahead. We need to take advantage of the existing gathering and distribution, and we also need to study China's current rural layout at and below the county level. The prefecture and county system was established by the first emperor of Qin Dynasty, but the current counties are not the same as before. Different counties are at the same administrative level but they might have different levels of aggregation. The routes and strategies should be different for different aggregation levels. It simply would not work to use brutal force, so we need to follow the trend. Also, we must have internet thinking and act at certain stages to raise the demand, invest money, and make the services free so as to foster the demand first. These are all important aspects which we must pay attention to.

Today, owing to expansion of cities, many areas of the county have become encircled into cities. I've had investigative trips to many urban villages, where population density is much higher than traditional villages; however, their life, production, consumption, schooling, and investment have not yet attracted much attention. Many of our city managers regard urban villages as the targets for demolition and renovation; however, as someone who studies urbanization and who knows that Rome cannot be built in one day, I believe the half urbanized and half rural state will stick around for a long time. The people living there, if viewed as farmers, are higher-income farmers and lower-income rural residents. They should also be the targets of our service because of many unmet demands. Geographically they stay very close to cities and towns; this is also worth studying.

New Challenges from the Internet

The internet has many advantages, but it also brings many new challenges. Counterfeits have already become one of the main troubles over the internet; this is different from shopping at brick-and-mortar stores where customers can see and feel the product and they can easily reject it. Many online merchants going to villages must be aware that because the rule of law and the conditions for safeguarding rights are limited in the rural areas, if we are not thoughtful for them the farmers' rights would be impaired in certain circumstances. Their income is already low; if they get fake products from online shopping, this will be against our intention. We must have consensus on this question and take product quality and quality supervision seriously from the very outset. The counterfeit problem also has a threshold; and if it is passed, things will be very difficult to handle. Therefore, you must not think that strengthening a certain kind of management will necessarily be detrimental to the positive development of this field. We should have dialectical thinking, and we should encourage supervision. At the same time, we should set the rules for necessary management from the start so as to establish good norms. We have gone on investigation trips to many remote villages. Those people have limited awareness of laws and regulations.

Sometimes they just accept the loss or the suffering as it is, but later on they will have misgivings and be hesitant. Now the development of online shopping has come to the point of extending down to the nodes at or below the county level, and we must take these kinds of factors into account for these nodes.

I am a layman on this question; but after seeing these stories I feel inspired and feel that it is feasible in China to let the internet and e-commerce benefit more people. A good beginning has been achieved for this road, but we need to make joint efforts to make the road wider and more steady to benefit more people as well as China's national economy.

The Production of Ideas[32]

Over the last couple of years, one of the keywords that I have been focusing on is "ideas."

First, let me talk about where the question come from. The life that we have become accustomed to is not necessarily the way it must be. Nowadays we travel by plane, we get connected to lots and lots of information with our mobile phones, many people no longer need to farm or to work in factories. All of these are not inevitable things, but they are all formed out of different behaviors through gradual changes; and the origin of these behaviors and changes is ideas.

Therefore, over the years, I have started to do some exercises: every time I see interesting things, devices, or phenomena, I would try to figure out where it came from, who thought of it first, and who turned the ideas into actions.

This type of exercise isn't very hard to do.

Why Did Gottfried Wilhelm Leibniz Re-Invent the Calculator?

First, I would like to share with you my trip to Germany in November 2016 to see Industry 4.0. The first stop was Hanover, where I was most impressed by Leibniztempel (Leibniz Museum). Leibniz passed away 300 years ago, but the museum fully reflects Germans' respect for knowledge and for scholars.

Leibniz is regarded by the Germans as an academic master. He designed many things and made many great contributions. His manuscripts are being collected by several hundred scholars, and it is said that the work will not be

32 This section is adapted from the author's speech on December 18, 2016, at the inaugural Peking University National Development Summit.—Editor's note.

completed until 2018 when all of his extant manuscripts are put together. The museum showcases a calculator invented by Leibniz. He spent twelve years on the job and changed the French-invented calculator which was only able to do plus and minus calculations into a device capable of doing all four mathematical functions (i.e. addition, subtraction, multiplication and division). Our delegation was very lucky to have invited a 90-year-old professor who studies Leibniz all his life to give the explanations, and he specifically talked about this machine.

The operation of this calculator seems simple today, but it was anything but simple more than 200 years ago. Via an interpreter, the professor told us how Leibniz came up with this idea: people should not do this kind of repetitive calculation, a machine should be used to liberate them. In order to bring this idea to fruition, he invested twelve years. Just imagine, the price of our labor did have an obvious increase for very, very long time; when did it start to become more expensive? Labor does not naturally become more expensive because the economy has developed. Instead, the story goes like this: someone invents the machine, then people are equipped with the machine, the productivity gets improved, and then the opportunity cost for other types increases as compared with this particular type of labor. Thinking of this point, I suddenly understand what Industry 1.0, Industry 2.0, Industry 3.0, Industry 4.0 are all about.

Taking the thinking further, why did Leibniz have such an idea? At that time Germany was not industrialized, manpower was very cheap, and calculations was a good job without being exposed to the burning sun or getting wet in the rain; but Leibniz just felt that was not the way it should be. Therefore, what's so valuable about this idea is that he wanted to liberate people as he felt that people should not do repetitive labor but should instead be freed for creative work. This is what we refer to as "putting people first" today.

However, Leibniz is not an isolated genius; long-term changes of the whole of society are like a stream and he is part of the stream. This stream dates back to the origins of European civilization, such as the cultures of ancient Greece, of China, and of ancient Egypt, and it is the succession and revival of the civilization for generations and generations. In Europe, the first great movement was the Renaissance, followed by Newton's scientific revolution, and the Copernican theory of Heliocentrism. Via the Renaissance, the Religious Revolution, the Scientific Revolution, and the Enlightenment, step by step people broke away from the suppression of humanity of the medieval times and regained respect: People should not do repetitive work; instead, people should do more creative work. The stream of this idea is carried forward up to the present day.

Today's vogue topics, such as artificial intelligence and interconnectivity, have posed new questions: If all work can be done by machines, what should humans do? This is not essentially a scientific but rather a philosophical question. Lots of work which should not be done by humans was performed by humans under the then historical conditions; then humans were gradually replaced as the conditions matured. Will humans have a future or not? This is a philosophical question. Distinct thoughts mean distinct results.

This was the what I felt from the brain exercise during this visit to Germany.

It Is Inseparable from Innovation to Go from Zero to One and From One to N

The second exercise originated from our trip in 2016 to the United States with Professor Xue Zhaofeng and some of the alumni at Peking University National School of Development. We were visiting some twenty to thirty high-tech companies in Silicon Valley. Along with all the visits my thoughts were constantly provoked by the following question: What on earth is new technology? An economist once wrote a book to discuss the nature of technology and he says: new technology is to achieve the existing targets by using new or different principles.

During the stay, we saw a type of "electronic eyeglasses," created by BrainPort Technologies (at Wicab, Inc., as mentioned before; the product is also nicknamed "electronic lollipop" or "electronic popsicle"), which can help the blind "see" the world. To be able to do so, we need to figure out clearly the principle behind things, identify the real causal relationship, and then use the discovery principles to solve certain practical problems. These technologies for the blind is a perfect example.

First, scientists discovered that people see the outside world not through the eyes; the eyes are just external receivers of external data. The actual image formation takes place inside the brain. The eyes of blind people have lost their functionality so they cannot receive external images, but their brain's imaging function still works. So they started to think whether or not the information can be sent to the brain through other organs. The process was first to discover the mechanism and then probe further. They discovered that beneath the tongue is the most sensitive part of human body. In the end, they came up with an electronic sensor, which could be held under the tongue of the blind person to solve the problem of receiving external images and enable the person to "see" the outside world. For sure, there are countless details in the whole development process; but what is even more important than the details is to have the idea, and only after having the idea will people think about how to find a solution.

The third exercise was in Israel. Israel is a small country, with a minimum width of only 50 km, and it is surrounded by Arab countries. Because it was often attacked by rocket bombs from all directions, there was no assurance of the safety for life and property, let alone its economic development. A brigadier general from the R&D department of Israel's Defense Forces proposed the idea of an anti-rocket system. But to bring it into reality, three key issues needed to be resolved: first, accurately calculate the location of enemy rockets; second, manufacture faster rockets than the enemy's; third, choose an optimal angle to knock down enemy rockets without creating any threat to the lives and property of citizens. But none of these key issues had existing technological solutions, so at the very beginning, his leaders disapproved the idea. Later, he sought out support form the then Israeli Prime Minister Shimon Peres to get the R&D project established. Not long after, a well-known anti-rocket invasion system was born in Israel. It made a big difference: in the past, Israelis would rush into air raid shelters at the alarm. After this system was deployed and put into use, the alarm did not cause people to run away or hide; instead, they would take out their mobile phones to shoot pictures in the sky because they knew the rockets would be knocked down. What's even more interesting is that this same brigadier general was able to improve this system and modify it into a miniaturized missile to break up blood clots in blood vessels. Therefore, good ideas require particularly good abstraction abilities, and they can also inspire additional ideas in a few or even many different fields.

The fourth exercise is related to a best-selling book, *From Zero to One: Notes on Startups, or How to Build the Future.* According to the author Peter Thiel, there are two types of economic growth: one is to go from 0 to 1, meaning to invent things that didn't exist before; the other is to go from 1 namely the invention to ten, a hundred, a thousand or even more. There is a saying that only going from 0 to 1 can be called innovation because it is vertical, whereas going from 1 to *n* is horizontal so it is replication. In fact, there is still innovation in the process of going from 1 to *n*. The razor is a good example. Originally the razor was a folded knife, and the owner could not shave himself without a servant or helper. For this reason, many people could not afford to shave because it was too expensive. But why didn't the razor eventually disappear completely? Then a man by the name of King C. Gillette (founder of Gillette Corporation), a salesman for Baltimore Bottle-Cap Company, appeared on the scene. Around 1900, his industry started a revolution of using disposable packaging. While shaving, King Gillette was inspired and came up with the idea of splitting the razor into two parts, making the blades disposable and selling the holder generally at lower-than-cost prices to customers. Then people would buy blades every week, and most men now could afford to shave. At the beginning, he managed to sell fifty holders and ninety-one razor blades. Everyone thought this idea would be unsuccessful. Later he responded: "As long as men's moustache grows, there is a chance for my idea to work." Then, opportunity came during the Second World War. The United States sent troops to the frontline battle; he saw the opportunity and gave the razors to the military at cost with the freight paid by himself. When the army returned from European battle fields with the razors, they became the salesmen for this product. Currently, Gillette occupies 70% of the American razor market.

Hence Gillette created a marketing model. As it turns out, many products can be disassembled into different pieces for separate sales. This is what we now call the "handle and blades" business model. Subsequently, HP sells its printers and inks separately; today the personal computer has become a simple terminal held by hundreds of millions of people, and large computing capabilities are put on the servers and the cloud. Actually behind these business practices is the sign of this same idea.

The fifth exercise comes from Swiss watches. Back then, after more than a century of success, the Swiss fine watchmaking industry was almost wiped out by Japanese companies. The Swiss were unmoved by the development of quartz timepieces, and although Japan was a newcomer, their cheap and new-style products were very popular with the market. After some years, Japanese companies began to acquire Swiss watch core factories. At this time, leading entrepreneur Nicolas Hayek stepped forward and led the restructuring of the Swiss watch industry. He reversed the situation with an idea. Hayek was of the opinion that people's watches are not only used to tell time but also constitute part of the wearers' overall image. He was the first person to propose that a watch's functionality needed to be integrated together with such elements as beauty and fashion. Later his company, Swatch, became very well known throughout the world. Today they have a flagship store located at the Bund of Shanghai, and they are using such expensive places as their global art center. The center has offered a prize: Creative people from all over the world can send them their ideas; if a ideas is selected, the artist will be invited to live on the Bund for up to six months for liberal creation with all the fees paid by Swatch. All they ask from the artist is to leave one thing behind, such as a pair of slippers or a bowl that he has used. Relying on the combination of creativity, fashion elements, and precision Swiss manufacturing, Swatch won back the sales in the Asian market. Asked how many watches a person needs, they would usually answer: How many styles of neckties do you have at home? Watchmaking is one of Switzerland's pillar industries, Nicolas Hayek himself never made a watch, but he made this watch revolution happen by his idea and his perseverance.

The sixth exercise is the design of urban architecture in Manhattan, New York. New York has many tall buildings. However, the old tall buildings had the problem of blocking the sunlight of other people. Some good ideas are born out of acute social contradictions; the person leading the idea was the then mayor of New York City. In 1916, he incidentally found that Gothic-style architectures often have a pinnacle, which allows sunlight to shine down from both sides. Later he formulated a regulation to limit the heights of buildings for the commercial, industrial, and residential areas, stipulating that the height of buildings should not be more than one to two times the width of the streets. If the height is bigger, they must taper inwards in the Gothic fashion. After 1916, a large number of buildings with this style got built in New York. However, with the ongoing aggregation of population, improved construction technology, and improved elevators, the model of twice the height of street width or tapering came into conflict with the market needs. The mayor had no choice but to allow for some modifications to the regulation. Then lots of special cases and exceptions were put in place and the thirteen-page, regulation became 1,300 pages. And further later, the Mayor had to adjust the management method, proposing the concept of "control via incentives."

The idea stemmed from the story of an insurance company who hired a German architect to build a headquarter building. This architect was determined to follow his design and refused to have his building tapered. How was this problem solved in the end? He chose to let light in at the bottom of the building instead of at the top. He relinquished half of the land space of building and made it freely accessible to the public. In such a way, the problem of light and air was solved and the original design for the upper section of the building was maintained unchanged. Based on this experience, the mayor revised the 1916 regulations and created a new idea: privately owned public space (or POPS, which was a new term). The regulation says that for every square foot of land given to the public, the developer can get three square feet of public space from the government. In China, when developers want to increase the height of their buildings, they have to do lots of work and play lots of tricks. Why can't we work out an idea to strike a balance and establish a connection between different interests?

From a Flash of Inspiration to Systematic Production

The seventh exercise is also related to the United States: how to change the "rust belt" into a "brain belt." What do I mean by this? I started to take notice of this matter from a certain private manufacturer in Wenzhou. Domestically the company produces fast food tableware and drinking straws, both with low value addition. Straws are hollow, so the cost of shipping would be too high to transport to the United States, so they wanted to open a factory in the United States and found Pennsylvania after investigation. The factory site was a discarded steel company. In the United States, a very serious after-effect of the decay of many industrial enterprises is that the sites of many iron and steel mills are now vacant. They call these areas the "rust belt"; the darker the color on the map, the worse is the situation.

How to change the situation for the "rust belt"? The United States has a plan to use brain power to revive the productivity. The basic model is to bring in venture capital to areas around universities, research institutions and laboratories; at the same time, the government will pay for the formation of a new cluster of diverse and high-density businesses. For example, there are 55,000 companies densely located around the campus of the University of Texas at Austin. And in Albany, capital of the state of New York, a science park has been formed to integrate universities, state and federal government agencies, and private and public institutions. Germany also has similar models. Via new forms of creativity and consolidation, the original "rust belt" is transformed into an innovative "brain belt."

The biggest difference from previous exercises is that the generation of ideas is no longer a flash in the mind of a single smart person; instead, it is a systematic production process.

To wrap up, ideas seem to be ordinary and everyone has ideas, but some thoughts can become significant *ex post*. Under what circumstances will these ideas become an important force to transform the industry, the market, and even the economy and the society? There following conditions are necessary.

First, high density, especially the gathering of a group of people with similar minds. If this condition is absent, ideas will be scattered hither and yon.

Second, when can the ideas form an atmosphere? There absolutely must be a small environment and a community, where all people believe the subject matter is worth doing and encourage the doers not to be afraid of failure but instead to rise up and try. This is a very important condition.

When lots of ideas pop up, polishing, screening, and refining must be performed to sort out the meaningful ones. This is one of the key factors in knowledge-driven growth.

To gradually convert originally spontaneous and scattered ideas into a systematic production process, an atmosphere must be formed to allow continuous ideation and then gradually arouse many people. With the joint efforts of all the people, ideas can be converted into actions, and actions into products, and eventually into a pathway to a life style.

Upward and Downward Innovation[33]

Scientific and technological innovation is highly overlapped with economic growth. The further we look into the future, the more the two of them will blend together. Therefore, to research the economy, we must heed innovation. This academic tradition has longed been established in economics. Currently, when we talk about innovation, it is quite easy to talk big. This has the advantage of attracting widespread attention and mobilizing more resources into innovative activities. However, if we tout too much, it wouldn't help us much in the understanding of the meaning of innovative behavior.

Exploration, Discovery, and Trial Have Long Been Part of Human Behavior

According to *Records of the Grand Historian*, when Qin Shi Huang, China's first emperor, was searching for an elixir of life, an alchemist named Xu Fu catered to his desire by saying that there are three holy mountains far out into the sea and that he was "willing to look for the elixir for the emperor." The emperor was overjoyed, and assigned 3,000 virgin boys and girls to Xu Fu to go overseas for the drug, but no news was fed back. Nine years later, the emperor asked again, the alchemist reported that he failed last time because there were giant fish blocking the way in the sea. So the emperor sent royal archers to join Xu's team. However, this time Xu Fu led the fleet and ran away. It is said that he arrived at Ryukyu and even the main island of Japan, "proclaimed himself a king," and never came back.

33 This section is adapted from the author's speech at Tencent Research Institute on January 13, 2017.—Editor's note.

This story seems irrelevant with innovation, the topic for today. But is there not a small element in it? I think there is: people try to look for and discover what they hope to have but is not available from the reality. This element probably has been there since before recorded history; not to exaggerate, it is perhaps innate in humans.

Unable to find the ready-made elixir, would people give up the thoughts on longevity? No, people started to practice alchemy—since no ready-made drugs could be found, they tried to invent and make something. Records show that, as far back as the Eastern Han Dynasty, alchemy was already quite developed in China. Some contemporary scholars believe that "alchemy is the origin of modern chemistry."

From search to discovery to invention, this type of activity has been continued up to the present day. I started with these two stories to illustrate that the creative element of innovation has long been a part of human behavior, only that it has been very difficult to distinguish it from superstition or absurd fantasy; and that the primary method of exploring the unknown is to rely on experience, on ongoing trial and error, on summarization. The same is true of the West, and by records their ancient civilization is not as good as the same of the East.

Take sailing as an example. On land, a compass is enough to give directions, and it can also be a makeshift for coastal navigation. However, to successfully achieve trans-ocean sailing, people need to know not only the latitude but also, more importantly, the longitude. In 1714, the British Parliament passed the famous Longitude Act, which set out a huge prize for a "practically usable" method for longitude measurement. There were two technical pathways. The first approach was to navigate via the stars, namely to locate the fleet in the ocean through astronomers' understanding of the star positions. The other approach was through accurate time keeping on land; namely, clockmakers needed to make an accurate clock, which would then be used to determine the longitude of the fleet by accurately calculating the time from departure. The key here was how to make an accurate clock that could report the correct time during the bumpy sailing. Eventually, watchmakers moved ahead of astronomers. The British watchmaker John Harrison spent thirty-two years and invented H4, the most accurate clock of its time, and solved the key technical problems of ocean voyages.

To compare the H4 clock and the alchemy of the old times, we will see that these two activities are both based on experience; the method is to start from the actual problem and continuously explore and test until a solution is found. In term of cognition, the two methods actually belong to the same category. But afterwards, the scientific cognition methods represented by astronomers started to rise to the central stage of scientific cognition.

From a long-term perspective, population growth is inseparable from technology-supported economic growth. The human population had always been very slow to grow, but this changed around the times of ancient Greece and Rome. Why is that? A new element appeared in the Greek city-state (or *polis*) where scholars abstracted concepts, put forward propositions, and guessed the essence of the world so as to understand the causal relationship between phenomena through logical reasoning, dialog, and debate. This was the sprouting for scientific discoveries, which initially had nothing to do with technological inventions or their application, but implied a non–experience-based new source for technology inventions. The Romans advocated the Greek reasoning and raised the ancient civilization to a new level. In point of fact, this was at about the same time as China's Spring and Autumn or the Warring States Period, when hundreds of flowers were blooming, hundreds of schools of thought were contending, and the academic thoughts was amazing. However, in both the orient and the occident, science-driven innovation was still far from being popular.

It is really only after the sixteenth and seventeenth centuries that the population curve started to rise significantly. The corresponding time was the outbreak of the second agricultural revolution, the Industrial Revolution, the steam engine, railroads, airplanes, the discovery of microorganisms, computers, atomic energy, and personal computers, followed by the genome and internet. The acceleration of innovation by science and technology can be summarized as one point: scientific discovery has replaced experience to play an increasingly decisive role in innovation. Currently, when we talk about innovation, we would generally add "science and technology" as the attribute, so the full name becomes science and technology innovation; the phrase starts with science, and that explains a lot.

Rightly at the critical juncture of moving from experience-based to science-driven innovation, China was left much behind West Europe. An Australian scholar wrote a book called *The Shortest History of Europe* (Guangxi Normal University Press, January 2011), which says two periods are very critical for Europe to step out of the depressing medieval times.

The first was the fifteenth century: the Renaissance, for which Greek thoughts are the root.

The Renaissance was a reflection on the trends of thoughts of the medieval era. In the medieval times, the church, the pope, and the unification of the state and the church were shackling people's mind and people had to be obedient to authority and to God. Some scholars and artists gathering in Italy were dissatisfied with this way of thinking, and via studying the works of Greek sages they found a way to emancipate the mind; this movement was called the Renaissance. The implicit meaning was that the insight of ancient Greek scholars was so great that it is no more necessary for everything to follow the will of the God, or of the Pope, or of authority.

The second period was the seventeenth century: the Scientific Revolution; the Greeks were wrong.

The Renaissance boosted mankind's confidence about ourselves and our ability to think. Following the Greek thinking for a very long time also caused people to think seriously about whether or not the ancient Greeks were fully correct. This way the Scientific Revolution got started: any proposition and any conclusion can, should, and must be and tested only by experiment! People discovered that a lot of what the ancient Greeks said was wrong. For example, they guessed that the essence of the universe was water and earth, and Greek astronomers believed that the sun goes around the earth. This opened up the tradition for science: no matter who says what, or whatever is your own guess, it must be repeatedly checked through designed tests and be revised or overthrown if it fails the test; only in this way can we approach truth.

People with this belief gathered together to form a community of scientists and a scientific tradition. In spite of different opinions, these people shared the same cognitive norms, namely to use experiments to test their laws or conjecture (causality). This approach has a methodological difference with the ancient experiential innovation: observation is used to find the problem; people are not dependent on summarizing experience, but they cut in from abnormal phenomena, leverage the advantage of human brains to make imaginations, conjectures, and extrapolations, and then go through strict tests. Along with this comes another type of capability for humankind to understand the world, known as the Scientific Revolution.

There was also an episode. What to do if scientific discoveries—such as the earth goes around the sun—go against the popular belief, especially the geocentrism endorsed by the church? This was the problem that many scientists of that time felt most reluctant about. Because the much-squeezed Christian religion, which up till then had stayed within its small paradise, later joined hands with the secular power to form an alliance, and it became the unquestionable imprisonment for human spirit and the protective umbrella for the vested interests of the church power across all parts of Europe. At that time, the church took advantage of its control of the right to interpret the Bible and developed the "indulgences." Anyone who bought the coupon could use it to atone for his sins and to avoid going to Hell after death. Later on, the Church even started to ask believers to buy "indulgences" for their families and for their future generations. As a result, large amounts of private wealth flowed into the church to support the corrupt and extravagant life of the Holy See. A man by the name of Martin Luther appeared on the scene. With his German uncompromising spirit and perseverance, he studied Greek and Latin to read the original Bible and found that the Bible did not authorize the church to monopolize the right of interpretation, nor did it indicate that going through the church was not a must to believe in God. He broke the church's monopoly on the interpretation of the Bible and initiated a religious reform. This reform not only deconstructed the old political and social structure of medieval Europe, but also added momentum to the spirit of the Scientific Revolution. Just imagine—to innovate, having new ideas and bringing them up is a must. Shouldn't doubts on popular beliefs be allowed? If people dare not to cast their doubts, where can the innovation come from?

Upward and Downward Innovation: Principle–Technology–Product

In November 2016, I made a visit to Germany to investigate and study Industry 4.0, and the time happened to be the 300th anniversary of the death of Gottfried W. Leibniz. A super scientist of his time, Leibniz is given by Germans the honorary title of the modern Aristotle. Calculus, discovered independently and respectively by Leibniz and Isaac Newton, is still a compulsory knowledge for worldwide higher education up till today. At a lecture held at Leibniz University in Hanover, a 90-year-old professor introduced Leibniz to us. He told us that Leibniz invented the first calculator capable of doing addition, subtraction, multiplication, and division. While giving the demo, the old professor explained why Leibniz, who valued his time so much, would spend a dozen years in developing what seems to be a simple calculator today. He showed us a paragraph of the original German language writing by Leibniz, and it turns out that Leibniz believed that people should not do monotonous and repetitive work like calculation. This was the perception by a German scholar 300 years ago! For people to engage in creative work, the primary job is to discover the laws of the world and to understand the principles of how nature and the society work.

Then, the next things to do is to invent technologies in order for scientific discoveries to benefit mankind. This is because the understanding at the principles level is admittedly important, but a series of difficulties must be overcome to use the principles to solve actual problems and satisfy actual demand. Humankind has long aspired to fly after watching the birds flying freely in the sky, and later on grasped such principles as aerodynamics; but to be truly able to fly, we still needed to overcome countless technical problems. After technical problems have been solved, the next step is to combine technologies into products to meet people's needs. In this way, principles, technologies, and products constitute the three links of innovation and they form a closed loop of reciprocating motion.

So what do I mean by upward and downward innovation? If we start with the needed product, look upwards for the technology; there is no readily available technology to arrive at an invention, we need to work upwards and figure out the mechanism and eventually drive a scientific discovery at the principle level. This is the upward road. There is also the downward road: we start with curiosity, or do science just for the sake of science without knowing whether it will be useful or not; we first perform and straighten out the thinking at the principle level, then invent usable technology, and finally make the product.

Next let us look at one example of each to see what is upward and downward innovation.

The first example is atomic energy and atomic bomb. For atomic energy, the paper came first; a German scholar published a dissertation in 1937. Previously, explosives were based primarily on chemical changes, but the atomic structure, especially the nucleus, remained unchanged. But, as scholars discovered, if the nucleus gets changed, an enormous amount of energy will be generated. So first the scientific discovery was made on nuclear fission and fusion, with the principle written down. Is this discovery tenable? The academics would be the first to discuss the question. As for whether it can be used or not, it depended on some conditions: France and Britain were busy dealing with Hitler, their atomic energy scientists, and Jewish scientists fleeing Germany eventually came to the United States. They convinced President Roosevelt to establish the Manhattan Project, and only with this project were the technical problems solved. In the end, the first-generation product was the Little Boy, which was dropped onto Japan and accelerated the ending of World War II. This is a classic example for going from the principle to the product and downward innovation.

The most classic example for upward innovation is of course Apple. Steve Jobs is not a scientist, but he may be the best product guy since the beginning of the Industrial Revolution. He has a great sense of human needs and of the potential needs of people which even they themselves cannot clearly articulate. Especially he upholds product quality and user experience and would never give up until the ultimate level is reached. In Apple's model, they starts with the product, look for technologies and parts, which drive technology inventions and scientific discoveries at the level of principles. So it is going upwards.

Because innovation can be upward or downward, innovation behavior can make a choice to go downwards or upwards. As mentioned before, ancient Chinese civilization was great, and the academic thoughts were also amazing. Unluckily, China did not experience the two periods which Western Europe underwent after the Middle Ages (i.e., the Renaissance and the Scientific Revolution), and it especially lacked the scientific tradition. This led to China's lagging behind and being bullied in modern history, so China becomes a latecomer in modernization. This also determined that our innovation focus more on starting with needs, products, and results and looking upwards for technologies and principles. On this learning trip to Shenzhen, I found that most of the innovation stories began with products and then explored upwards; or in the words of Gao Yunfeng, Chairman of Han's Laser Technology, they fall into the category of "reverse innovation." It is more or less the same case with Tencent, right? However, Shenzhen is also starting to show some new signs of going from principle to product. For instance, Royole, which we are going to visit, is a place where the dissertation—namely, the principle-level discovery—came first, and the technological problems were solved later to make the product. Looking into the future of China, the upward innovation will remain hot while the downward innovation will start to germinate, and I expect that there will be more and more interesting stories coming.

Four Major Driving Forces, None of Which Is Dispensable

In fact, the motif behind the behaviors in scientific discovery, technological invention, product design, or product manufacture can be traced back to the four drivers described by *Abundance: The Future Is Better than You Think* (Diamandis and Kotler). The first driver is curiosity, which is contained in human nature; as the smartest of all creatures, humans are borne with this preference. The second driver is wealth. If developing a product or a technology or discovering a principle can bring about wealth and freedom, it will become a common but powerful driver. The third driver is fear. The book mainly uses national security for discussion. Why did Roosevelt carry out the Manhattan Project? Because of fear—If Hitler had mastered the atomic bomb first, the result of World War II might probably have been different. In point of fact, the arms race is a competition of economy, and at the same time a competition of science and technology, and it is also a very important force to push forward scientific innovation. The innovations in Israel, Silicon Valley, and Boston are targeted at demands not only from the market but also from national defense. The fourth driver is the meaning of life. This is more about feelings. People want their life to have meaning, and they want to leave something meaningful to the world.

If scientific and technological innovation is to gain momentum, none of these drivers should be absent. Scientific discovery is fundamentally supported by human curiosity; but, scientists also need to eat and live, to have equipment to do the test and to have long lasting investment before they can make discoveries. So it is necessary for wealth to mobilize large numbers of people into discoveries and inventions. As for the so-called fear, it is actually the by-product of the competition between different groups and countries. Its direct starting point is not to create wealth but rather to assure for safety and have effective deterrence, and to strive to own a Sunday punch that others do not own. And last, after the first three motifs are satisfied, there will always be some people who pursue the meaning of life and want to make valuable contributions to the world, such as discovery and invention.

These four major driving forces, strong or weak, exist everywhere; only their allocation, role, and state of combination are different as a result of limitations from specific conditions. When we talk about unblocking the artery for scientific and technological innovation, we must first—under the constraints of reality—allocate the drivers properly and choose the right combination. In this respect, we also need to draw on the experience of other countries. For example, Israel's area and population are very small, but their educational foundation is solid and they have many exceptional talents in science. So they focus on discoveries at the principle level and the development of key technologies, and they have established a firm foothold in cutting-edge fields of research; their products and industries target large markets such as the United States and China.

I made a visit to Israel in 2015, and before departure a question came to me: the Israelis believe in God so much, how can they at the same time become a world leader in science and innovation capabilities? We went to an explanation given by a rabbi. It turns out that the Jewish Bible says the Jews are chosen by the God to wrestle with God. That means they grapple with God rather than just kneel down to worship and bow to God. This is the spiritual source of Israel's innovation capabilities. They all value education, but what they focus most is not the answer but questions, or the exploratory spirit of asking audacious questions and chasing down to the root. It is said that Jewish mothers would ask their children returning home from school: "what good questions have you asked at school today."

As a powerful country of innovation, the United States has a more comprehensive allocation of the aforementioned motive powers. They have many first-class universities, strong scientific research strength, abundant capital, and sound financial services, plus they have formed a national super pursuit for science and technology for global predominance, and have the ability to attract young people who have dreams of science and technology from all over the world. In places with abundant motivations from curiosity, wealth, and fear, there will be more people pursuing the meaning of life. If you look at Elon Musk, Tesla's CEO, he is a quite young person, but all of his chosen business directions are related to the fate of mankind. In summer 2016 I took part in an in-depth study on American modular innovation organized by friends, faculty, and alumni from Peking University National School of Development. We visited more than twenty science innovation enterprises in Silicon Valley, Los Angeles, and along Boston Route 128. On coming back, I put down impression on the visit as: "Be audacious in thinking and down-to-earth in doing." As we all know, the motto of Stanford University is "*Die Luft der Freiheit weht*" (meaning: the wind of freedom blows). It was after arrival at the site that we felt that the wind blows not only within the campus but also inside and outside campus to cover the space between universities, enterprises, key national laboratories, and financial markets to blend them into an entirety. Therefore, for a big country to be a strong innovator, it seems to be a must, apart from having all the drivers, to have an unobstructed artery system to connect everything into an entirety. How can this be done? The answer is gathering and aggregating such that the high-quality molecules can energize and interact with each other under the high concentration and the high density.

Top Enjoyment and Public Affluence

To go all the way from the principle to the product, the job is not done yet. Under the market economy, a good product is not necessarily equal to a good commodity, nor will it necessarily be popular and become the trend. That means the product has not brought benefit to mankind or changed the world. To convert products into commodities, we need to research the laws of the market.

In the past, we talked out product life cycle, which is actually a time process of commodity production to go from development, launch, big sales, peak, and all the way to decay. Do scientific innovation products also have life cycles? The answer is probably yes. For example, the emergence of the internet can achieve a network effect, which might change the pattern of the curve for the product cycle.

Let's return to the first story about why Emperor Qin Shi Huang sent people out in search of the elixir. Ordinary people also wanted to achieve longevity, but that longing was in vain because there was no financial strength to support the realization of such an aspiration. Therefore, as the general law has it, when a commodity is first launched into the market, there is no economy of scale, so the price must be expensive and the product can only be enjoyed by wealthy people; then the technology becomes mature and the production gets scaled up, and the product penetrates into the middle class; and further later the technology becomes even more mature to allow for mass production, and the product becomes popular among the class with mid to low income.

From this perspective, there is another kind of upward and downward movement for scientific products to enter the market. Going upward here means to create top enjoyment and ultimate experience and bring about the joy of consumption that has never been experienced before. In point of fact, this is something for which the best craftsmen have been working hard throughout human history. However, regrettably, they always serve only a small group of people, namely the royal families, the nobles, and the super wealthy. Yet in terms of technology, craftsmanship, and quality, these pursuits have tapped the potential of human imagination and craftsmanship. France is the home of many top luxury companies. According to *The Essence of Style: How the French Invented High Fashion, Fine Food, Chic Cafés, Style, Sophistication, and Glamour* (SDX Joint Publishing Company, February 2012), this mainly originates from the extravagant Louis XIV the Sun King. This great French king had a trick that the equally lavish and degenerate Chinese emperor did not; he allowed the royal craftsmen to open stores in the market and to sell "Tailor-Made for the Royal Family" as a method of branding. As history has progressed to today, we have heard about the shopping rush for bags by Chinese aunties at Champs Elysées, but never heard about Frenchwomen going to Dashilar to buy things used by the Empress Dowager Cixi. In this respect, Japan seems to have followed the same path as France. I have visited Inden-ya, a company specializing in deerskin products for thirteen generations. Historically, the designated supplier to the Japanese Imperial Palace, it is now a top luxury brand comparable with its French peers.

The key is that after the modern Industrial Revolution, the middle class has risen, more and more total wealth has accumulated, but the income distribution shape has changed from the "a pyramid" to "a gourd" or "an olive." After the food and clothing demand is satisfied, a very large population also would like to seek fresh and high-quality enjoyment. At this point, care should be taken during commodity development: Should we provide even more sophisticated, more refined, and more ultimate products and services, or take the products and services originally only available to the rich and the powerful and made them accessible to the general public?

American companies did a good job in this respect in the age of industrialization. This is perhaps because the United States did not have the social hierarchy of old Europe; there was no emperor, no aristocracy, and no innate lineage at birth. Under such a social structure, American entrepreneurs were good at producing enjoyments which were previously tailor-made for a small number of European royal families and nobles; via mass production, the cost and price were revolutionarily brought down so these products could penetrate into the daily life of the general public. Next I will give two real examples.

The first one is about razor revolution. The old-style razor was a very sharp folded knife. It must be made of good steel, and the price was certainly quite high; plus men could not shave themselves, and they needed to have a barber or a servant to do it for him. But in the twentieth-century United States, a salesman named Gillette came up with a cross-boundary innovation and split the integrated razor into two parts: the handle and the blade. Consumers only needed to buy one handle at cost, after which they could buy a blade once a week, and put them together to shave themselves. The disposable blade needed to be replaced once a week; the unit price was not high but the margin was nice, so this was a very smart business. As a result, the huge working class of the United States no longer needed to go to the barber to get a shave because they now could solve the problem at one-tenth of the cost. Up till now, Gillette is still the main razor brand for European and American markets, and China's urban and rural convenience stores are also full of Gillette products.

The second example is Ford's form of production, as everyone is familiar with. The world's industrialization is inseparable from assembly lines, right? This was a virgin invention by Henry Ford. More than a century ago, the entrepreneur had an idea. If every blue-collar worker could afford a car, the total sales volume of cars would be astounding. How then could the car become affordable for workers? The unit price and the manufacturing cost of cars must be brought down significantly. He had this idea before he invented the assembly line. It is said that when Ford's assembly line first reached 10,000 cars a year, all other shareholders were very happy, but Ford said that "my goal is to build 10,000 cars a day!" Low unit price, mass production, and good quality. Back then Ford's Model-T could adapt to the worst road conditions, otherwise it would not have been able to shape the market.

To summarize, upward and downward innovation has double meanings: one is about the cognitive pathway—should it be to go from discovery of the principle and the invention of technology to product production, or to start with the product and trace upwards for technology and then the principle? The other aspect is about translating the product into a commodity that leads the market trend—should the method be to go upwards to seek top quality product and experience, or to change to the opposite direction and make what is supposedly enjoyed only by the upper class accessible to ordinary families? In both dimensions, to move upwards and downwards are all scientific innovation behaviors that need drivers. For a big country, all drivers are indispensable, and good combinations are also quite necessary to get the artery mutually connected for both types of upward and downward movement.

5

Distinguishing Online Ride Hailing

The Innovation of Online Ride Hailing Originates from Extralegal Activity[34]

Before discussing the hot topic of online car hailing, let's first discuss a cold topic. A society always had all kinds of different people, and people always have different ideas, different beliefs, different interests, and different demands. With so many differences, how can people stay in harmony, and how can their disputes be properly settled? This in itself is a permanent question.

For this purpose, the law sometimes has to get involved. On origin of the law, there are many theories. In the 1990s there was a shocking case in the United States where sports star O.J. Simpson was accused of murder. His chief defense lawyer was a law professor at Harvard. He did not believe that rights come from God. For example, God will not be able to answer if He is asked about the rights of internet. He discussed the genesis of the law, and concluded that the Bible is often contradictory, and does not show consistent legal norms, as it is not a problem to kill people in certain circumstances in some biblical stories.

34 This section is adapted from the author's keynote speech given at the 23rd Edition of Tencent Internet Lecture Hall on November 24, 2015.—Editor's note.

Therefore, his belief is that the law does not come from God, nor does it come from human nature. Human nature has multiple facets, and there is both good and evil; if human nature has only its good side and no evil side, we do not need to have the law. He believes that the law originates from experience, especially from the experience of events which causes great harm to other people or to the society; because the society gets hurt and it wants to prevent the recurrence of those evil events, the law is born.

This is a very interesting doctrine. Today, if we look at innovation from this point of view, we have a problem. Some behaviors have no experience, or not enough experiences, so people do not know whether it is good or bad, whether it will cause damage or bring benefits, or they have no way of knowing how much damage or benefit will be caused. How to deal with this kind of problem?

The internet has this problem. All over the world, the internet is developing very quickly. And there is no consensus even to this moment on what on earth the consequence will be. The emergence of the internet has moved the original pattern and changed the way of life of the people, and it has also touched the original concepts and vested interests, making itself a hot topic for a certain period in the society.

In point of fact, with the acceleration of innovation in human society, we do not have enough time to experience many things; for instance, no one fully knows what on earth is the consequence of transgenics. The time to check and test many new technologies is very long; how should we deal with such innovative activities during the testing period? Therefore, when should a rational order be formed to allow the society to continue innovating at the lowest cost? This has always been a question.

The emergence of cars caused an uproar. In fact, to drive a horse-drawn carriage is more complicated than to drive a car. A car is not only simple but also fast and stable and capable of carrying more people. It was obvious that cars would replace horse-drawn carriages which required lots of skills. The then environment was very similar to where we are today when we discuss the internet. London passed the well-known Red Flag Law (the Locomotive Act), stipulating to drive the car there must be a man holding a red flag in front of the car to guide the driving, and the speed of the car cannot exceed the horse-drawn carriage, otherwise it is improper competition.

People argued over Taobao for some time because there is no tax for online transactions so it is unfair for offline physical stores. With regard to Didi, many people challenge that the online car hailing company has stolen businesses from traditional taxis because the monthly income of taxi drivers has reduced a lot since the launch of Didi's Premier Service.

If the creation of the law stems from summarizing malicious behaviors in real world, then how should we deal with events for which we do not yet have sufficient experience? How to establish the rule of law for this process, and what measures should be taken to allow innovation and at the same time to solve the problems that might be brought about by the innovation?

Since its inception, the internet has been accompanied by negative effects, such as the "dark web" as a headache for the security departments of all countries, and the "convenience" provided by the internet to terrorist activities. That is also a type of Internet+. Although the internet makes communication more convenient, not all conveniences are used solely for good; evil actors will also try to make use of them. There is always a trade-off.

My viewpoint is that innovation should be given a trade-off period. During this period, because we won't have immediately reliable evidence to judge whether the innovation is used for good or for evil, or we do not know yet which restrictions should be added to ensure that the usage is for good and prevent it from being used for evil, we need to have an appropriate trial period. During this trial period, we should adopt the principle that "things are doable if they are not prohibited or restricted by the law" so as to encourage innovation and experimentation. For possible damages during the trial period, we should, as much as possible, make the ruling using the existing law—to deal with online sales of fake products in the same way as for physical stores, and give the same punishment for running the red light to Didi premier hailing service cars and to the taxis. It is important that this trade-off or trial period be seen as an essential part of the rule of law.

Next let us move on and discuss the online car-hailing service. In fact, cities have had taxis for a long time, but the existing taxi operation model has many problems that have not been resolved over the years. For example, every day Beijing has several dozen thousand taxis, but according to the survey about 40% of the mileage is without passengers. Because the drivers and passengers can't find each other, the taxis have to "scan the streets" to try their luck. This results in more exhaust gas emission, gasoline burning, the consumption of drivers' energy, and leads to passenger complaints about being unable to find taxis. The mischief here is actually the information cost—metropolises have big populations and people are always moving, no one knows when who will go where. In this time of telecommunications, the transportation departments also promoted the "call for a cab" model where people can book a taxi via a telephone call. But at that time, mobile internet was yet to become popular, so people had no choice. To make the phone call was already inconvenient, and it was difficult for the two parties to exactly locate each other. As a result, the "call for a cab" ended up nowhere, and it remained difficult to get a taxi.

The arrival of the mobile internet era gave birth to Didi Taxi, and precisely, all previous pain points now become a rare opportunity for online car-hailing to win the market share. You will know this if you use it: the customer sees from the mobile phone how many empty cars are in the vicinity. After sending a request, he immediately knows whether there is any driver grabbing the order, and he also knows the surname of the driver and in how many minutes he will arrive. The taxi driver also knows the location, name, and even the car-hailing credit records of the passenger.

As the old saying goes, comparison kills. As soon as online car-hailing comes, the shortcomings of traditional taxis immediately get exposed, and the market demand follows the more convenient and more efficient new model; is there anything strange about this? Indeed it takes away businesses from taxis and arouses attacks, outcries, abuses, and even strikes or demonstrations, which are not so difficult to understand. However, the mobile internet was not invented by Didi, nor is it exclusively occupied by this previously unknown emerging company. There are so many urban taxi companies out there, why didn't you yourselves invent an "internet + taxi" model earlier?

Didi taxi becomes so popular that Didi Premier also picks up momentum and emerges. And this time, the disturbance is huge; because now illegal cabs, which were quite active in urban transportation for years, also leverage the momentum and they are about to go from illegal to legal with the support from mobile internet technology. Under this circumstance, urban transportation administration authorities, whose main job was to crack down on illegal cabs, now have lots of work at hand.

Is it legal or illegal for private cars to offer urban taxi services? I believe that a trial period should be given and it is unnecessary to reach a hasty conclusion. We should take this opportunity and reflect on why "black taxis" or illegal cabs can not be eradicated for so many years. Would it be possible to use system and organizational innovations in the new technical environment of mobile internet, and find a long-term viable solution in for the difficult-to-solve urban transportation problem under previous technical conditions? Giving the big controversy, it is indeed no good if the competent authorities do not have its attitude for a long time. Would they consider putting forward a few principle opinions to encourage innovation and trial, and to face and solve the new problem? China is a big country with hundreds of cities. We can start with cities and let different places adopt slightly different measures according to their actual situations. When the opportunity is ripe after trying for some time, the central government can summarize the experience and formulate sound national policies and regulations.

In short, the innovation starts from outside the law; to worry about this is useless. From the perspective of governance of the country and the society, we should never recklessly give the "black" cap to behaviors that are still able to meet market demand and not proven to do any harm to the social benefit. Instead, we should try our best to include the behavior of more people into the legal framework, otherwise it is very difficult to achieve the rule of law.

The Barrier of Interests for Innovation[35]

Nowadays, it seems no one is against innovation, but to implement it needs to cross the hurdle of interests. This is no easy barrier, because once a change in technology or business model is applied to real life, it will inevitably move the existing order along with the corresponding ideology and vested interests.

Vested interests are formed by history. Taking taxis as an example, its birth was also an innovation, which touched the then vested interests. The full name of taxi was taximeter, which means a "mobile distance recorder." The story took place in New York in 1907. After dining in Manhattan, a Mr. Allen and his girlfriend took a hansom cab on the street and went home, but they were charged five dollars for a mere 0.75-mile (about 1.2 kilometers) ride. At that time, the common practice was for the coachman to "haggle" with the customer, and the coachman could take advantage of price discrimination to drain the consumer surplus[36] completely; this practice was quite normal. Allen had to swallow the loss, and he made up his mind to kick overcharging hansom cabs out of the market. However, his solution was neither to weep to regulatory officials and make complaints, nor to use his fists and kicks. Instead, he created a new taxi company and used cars to replaced horse-drawn hansom cabs; he installed a taximeter

35 This section is adapted from the author's speech given on December 8, 2015, at the Shanghai Innovation and Practice Forum on the topic of "Ride Hailing Models."—Editor's note.

36 Consumer surplus refers to the difference between the highest price consumers are willing to pay for a certain commodity and the actual market price of that commodity.

on the car to clearly measure the distance, and the taxi cab was born. The new model was transparent and therefore very popular with passengers. What about traditional horse-drawn carriages, then? As an outdated vested interest, they just faded away.

The taxi mileage is transparent; should the fare also be transparent? The fare does become transparent, and it is fixed––the base fare is price A, and for each kilometer after an initial distance the price is price B. There are also adjustments; for instance, the price for very late at night is price C. Why are price fluctuations and bargaining not allowed, like buying and selling cabbages and radishes in the vegetable market? The answer is that bargaining in the free market is not free in and of itself; once the cost grows too high, the market will find another way to set prices. The reason why urban taxis do not allow haggling over the price is because the cost of occupying urban roads is too high. Supposing that it is permissible to flag down a car on the street and bargain on the fare right there; probably the traffic system of the whole city will be paralyzed.

Therefore, the mileage meter (taximeter) also becomes the price calculator, and it records both the distance and the fare according to fixed rate. This price is usually determined by the municipal authority or via the price hearing procedures. The little box holding the taximeter is not something that can be installed randomly by the driver himself. There are also some cheating drivers playing tricks on the meter, but to do so is a crime. The supervision has long been put in place to cover each and every taxi.

Now the visible hand administers the price, and with this it also restricts market access. Otherwise, when differential pricing is prohibited and unified price control is adopted, the profit of taxis will be squeezed by the pressure of competition to near zero; would anybody be willing to invest and operate the industry? This leads to the logic of regulation: When you control the head, you must also control the feet; in the end, the regulator must be fully responsible for the regulated. This is rightly the meaning of the "capture theory": The regulated has the advantage of industry information relative to the regulator, so that the latter is eventually captured by the former. Once the regulator has raised the market access threshold, and the incumbent operators get the sweet flavor of "ensuring reasonable profits," it is really hard to tell who is managing whom. The extremely high market value for taxi licenses throughout the world shows that the regulation itself is just an administratively monopolized business. For sure, the reasons given are always safety, fairness, and order. Indeed, if there are no regulatory authorities to control the qualifications of taxi drivers, gangsters can drive passengers to "Sweeney Todd's barber shop" and rip them off. This obviously cannot be allowed.

Slowly, the taxi industry evolves more and more into a sound and "mature" industry. Have you ever noticed that every country's laws and regulations on taxis are more or less the same, and there is truly a lack of country specific characteristics? "The control all over the world is a copy and paste"—all happy families are similar. The price is that it is not easy for the system to adapt to changes in the environment. In the United States, the country that invented the modern taxi, private cars are still the predominant method of mobility for its urban residents. Why did Uber get started in the United States? One of the important inducements is the poor-quality taxi service in this global leader. Currently, every city is upholding "priority to public transportation." Aren't taxis a kind of "public transportation"? Why couldn't they become well developed with all the priorities?

In China, the impact is even more sudden. When people were poor, they couldn't afford to take taxis. After the opening-up and reform, however, urban mobility became a big issue. When Zhu Rongji served as the mayor of Shanghai, his first well-known move was to rectify the taxi industry: Foreigners or non-locals coming to Shanghai found that the taxi service was too poor; refusing to carrying passengers, taking detours, and overcharging were in fact the byproduct of the serious short supply of taxi services. After 2000, waves and waves of immigrants, as a result of urbanization, flocked to Shanghai, and the permanent population of Shanghai increased by almost 40% during the ten years from 2000 to 2010. The "mature" taxi industry did not have much adaptive elasticity, so it got punished by the anarchy of the market––the rise of "black cabs." Black cabs are private cars used as taxis, which are not permitted by law or by policy. From time to time, the authorities resolutely crack down on them, but the demand is strong and the lawful taxi supply is insufficient. The government claims that the cracking down is carried out to protect the consumers, but the consumers seem ungrateful and they keep spending money on these illegal cabs.

As mobile internet became increasingly common, online ride hailing services sprung up practically of their own accord. But the regulatory thinking of the relevant departments remained the same: taxis are taxis, private cars are private cars, and there is an insurmountable barrier between the two. Can any private car be operated as a hire car? First the driver must apply for a license and be granted the qualification of taxi operation through approval. Otherwise, "private cars can never become taxis," as expressed in the astonishing comments of Transportation Minister Yang Chuantang during the Two Sessions in 2016. From a onlooker's perspective, the minister's remarks seems to suggest that he does not know much about urban transport.

For cities, especially metropolises which large numbers of population would like to flock into, one of the features of urban traffic is not only that roads are quite scarce but also that their use is not flat. Experience has given us two important knowledge points: one is that urban road construction generally cannot keep up with the pace of the increasing number of cars; the other is that no matter how many urban roads are built, it is inevitable that they will be jammed during rush hour and empty during slack periods. It is thus no wonder that under these constraints comes the panic for people who uphold the dogma that "no one is allowed to engage in taxi service unless the operation if licensed." Think about it. If too many taxis are approved, it will add to the congestion during rush hour, and after the rush hour there will be too much idle time, so no one can make money. On the other hand, if too few taxis are approved, it will make movement very difficult for middle class locals and business people from elsewhere. Interestingly enough, the supervision authorities tend to prefer granting fewer licenses to more licenses. In metropolitan cities, the increase in population is completely out of proportion to the increase in taxis. Why is this? According to the "capture theory," the lower the supply of taxis is, the higher the power rent becomes from approving taxis. The medallion can cost hundreds of thousands of RMB (The price in New York is even more expensive; the transfer price for one taxi license in the market was USD 220,000 to 260,000 in 2003). As for the other derivative tricks, it takes very hard work for discipline inspection authorities to figure out. If passengers cannot get a car, that's not the focus of attention for regulatory authorities. Otherwise why couldn't people see transport officials meet the press, speak words of iron, and keep themselves so busy with revising the regulations before there was "disturbance" from ride hailing?

In my personal opinion, "black taxis" contain some reasonable elements to ease urban transportation. Isn't this correct? That some private cars provide rental services at some locations during certain hours is the right cure for the illness. Anyways, during rush hour or in the remote city corners regular taxi services are unable to satisfy the demand; what is the problem for informal, part-time private cars to come and give a helping hand? Speaking more generally, it is perfectly normal for private cars to participate in public services under certain conditions: when an FBI agent chases the suspect, he or she stops a private car and uses it as a government car; is this allowed? When we deal with disasters such as SARS or earthquakes, private individuals, private cars, and private meals all participate with no hesitation in the public service; shouldn't this be allowed?

Therefore, the "forever impossible" for private cars to act as taxis is just a fuss made by some officials.

To have crackdown as the sole and only policy on "black taxis" is to miss out on the opportunity to release the reasonable elements. Admittedly, there are many disadvantages with illegal taxis, and they might even cost the life of the passenger in the worst case. However, people do not see the supervision authorities spending efforts to figure out the statistics in weighing the pros and cons, let alone to carefully study the measures and methods to preserve the pros and remove the cons.

Online ride-hailing provides a new opportunity. With information cost significantly reduced by the internet, and the real name registration system for mobile phones, the mobile internet has enabled more flexible, more convenient, and more reliable ride rental contracts to come into reality, which fits well into the mobility needs of urban residents; finally, this leads to the birth of a new model which traditional taxis cannot be compared with and "black taxis" cannot catch up with: the booking is made online, there is no need to occupy the road haggling over price; the driver and the passenger are transparent to each other with the real name system; plus the vehicle is monitored real time on the platform, the route is very clear, and the passenger also knows where he is heading by just looking at the mobile phone. We can't just go about at random saying that this is illegal, as the Contract Law of the People's Republic of China recognizes and protects the property owners' right to sign and perform contracts with each other—as long as it does not interfere with public interest. The online hailing cars are based on the appointment for a trip, and they are no longer the traditional taxis invented in New York City in 1907, which would stop when the passenger waves his hand. Therefore, both in theory and in practice, the taxi management regulations formulated when we had no idea at all about what is online ride hailing service are not applicable. "Things could be done if they are not prohibited by the law"; when taxi regulations were originally enacted, who would have had the foresight to know that online ride hailing services would emerge?

Online ride hailing will certainly lead to new problems. Of course, we must face these problems and properly manage them. However, when managing new things, we must accumulate experience and new skills from practice step by step. There house is not on fire, so why rush to formulate new rules; do they truly have the confidence to solve the problem? The claim might be that taxi drivers are not happy and they will make trouble. But in point of fact, these men and women have been unhappy for a long time about the high hand-in, long working hours, and the asymmetry between their rights and obligations. The criticism has been there for years, yet no one is seen to have found a nationwide solution. Each region and each city are just dealing with their own taxi systems, right?

Taxis and online hailing cars are, in the end, an item of urban affairs. China is very big; it has several hundred cities, and each city has its own actual conditions. A comparison on fares, medallion fees, market structure, and market regulatory rules of different places will obviously show that China has no uniform nationwide taxi market. This being the case, wouldn't it be better to let mayors and urban transport departments try out some local methods and local regulations first, draw experience from each other, learn from each other's strengths and avoid each other's weaknesses, and then come up with a national regulations when the conditions are ready? Final conclusions for all matters should only be made after experiments are conducted. This is the case with traditional economy, but is it not also needed for innovations?

Viewed from this perspective, the current issuance of the first license for online ride hailing service by Shanghai Transportation Committee (hereafter referred to as STC) is a momentous decision. First, with 24 million people, the cosmopolitan area of Shanghai is equivalent to a massive laboratory. We will be able to see whether there is any positive effect in providing more convenience for urban mobility, easing the city disease and improving the environment if some private cars are converted into a constituent part of the public transport via online sharing. Second, STC have managed Shanghai's traditional taxi industry for many years; of course they understand the rational of taking all stakeholders into account, of course they will pay attention to the convergence and complementarity in the competition between new and old enterprises, and of course they will look carefully for the balance point of interests and strive to achieve a big innovation and progress with a low friction of interests.

Perhaps this move will also uncover significant treasure. Over the years, popular meanings of economic growth have included that everyone is now able to enjoy more things. In 1928, when Herbert Hoover ran for president, he promised that "the United States will be closer to the final triumph over poverty than ever before." And the symbol? "A chicken in every pot and two cars in every garage." This is the American dream, which has also affected the whole world. To measure whether there is improvement in life, the criteria in China start with the "three old items" of a watch, a sewing machine, and a bike, followed by the "new three items," the "new three items," and then an apartment and a car for every family. By the time we own more and more things, we find that we have less and less time to enjoy them, yet they are taking up more and more space; plus the objects consuming lots of resources tend to be idle most of the time. All households in

Shanghai have at least one washing machine, and the space it takes up is expensive with respect to the housing price! But how much time is the machine actually used; is it one hour per day on the average? This is true not only of washing machines, but also true of other appliances, and even of houses and cars.

Consumers only find enjoyment from buying and owning the item because they want to have the convenience—they can use their own washing machine at any time they want. If several families are sharing the same item, it will be awkward if you want to use it while others are using it. Actually this is an information problem here; if it is easy to know when each household will use it, one washing machine could be shared by multiple families. Of course, what needs to be communicated is not only the sharing time, but also other preferences. During my study in Los Angeles, I found that a carpool lane is reserved for private cars carrying multiple people (i.e. carpoolers) so as to mitigate the congestion. That means car sharing is encouraged. Much to my surprise, still some Americans did not use carpooling for no reason other than carpoolers' different preferences for the onboard music. In other words, it was because the information cost to find carpoolers with the same music preference was too high. Today, this is no longer a problem; people can shake the mobile phone and find as many people as they want with the same hobby.

It is possible that the sharing economy might become very popular owing to the greatly reduced information cost by the mobile internet. This is what we call a transformation of the growth mode: It is unnecessary to consume so many resources to produce so many idle objects, and unnecessary to put so much pressure on the environment; but the consumption enjoyment of people can equally be improved. With such a prospect, we shouldn't have said that "private cars can never provide rental service," in the future, there will be an increasing number of shared private items. Uber's market value is said to be as high as USD 50 billion, and Airbnb's is USD 25.5 billion. Why is that? The secret is the rise of sharing economy. Some experts predict that the license issued by STC may lead to explosive growth in the sharing economy in Shanghai, or even in the whole China, and we hope this prediction come true.

Coming back to the topic, it is difficult for innovation to overcome the hurdle of interests. What is more difficult is whether or not the spontaneous innovation activities by the market can be included in the legal institutional framework. This step taken by STC not only provides Shanghai with an opportunity to be the first to try but also greatly increases other places' costs of resisting the change. In a country where the slogan of "mass entrepreneurship and mass innovation" is deafening, because Shanghai government has already issued licenses to online ride hailing services, will other places and departments be thick-skinned to block them every day? As has been reported in the news, Premier Li Keqiang has asked various ministries and departments of the State Council to conduct grassroots-level surveys after the 2016 National Day holiday and take a look at the innovative practice. I really do hope that the head of Ministry of Transportation will come down from his lofty perch and take a look; it would be best if he could experience the online ride hailing services for himself, and then make some new remarks that are different from what was said before the survey. At the very least, he shouldn't be headstrong and use his power to create difficulties for the innovation, right?

Urban Transport Problems Are Exactly the Opportunity for Mobile Internet Application[37]

On Urban Transport Control

In the big context of the internet era, urban transport reform faces a series of different thoughts and conflicts. The government, consumers, taxi companies, and taxi drivers all have their own considerations, but they also face some common restrictions.

Taxis are a form of urban transportation. What is special about cities? The simplest and most straightforward feature of cities is that lots of people gather in a limited space. It is not a rural society where everyone knows everyone quite well. Urban societies gather strangers together; the population is large and people are constantly moving, so they do not know each other and it is difficult to establish trust. But, because of the high degree of division of labor, urbanites badly need to cooperate with each other. This is the first point. The most fundamental reason for so many strangers having to gather together is that they can get higher income. This also means that urban residents' time costs more and their space is very limited. This is the second characteristic. The third characteristic is that urbanites' time distribution is very uneven. They need to be on time to get to work, to go home, to go out on a date, to travel on business, or even to go to entertainment; but these time nodes are unevenly distributed, and there is a very big difference between peaks and troughs. As everyone knows, in terms of traffic,

37 This section is an excerpt of the author's speech at the Internet and Urban Transport Policy Seminar in March 2015.—Editor's note.

cities have the gridlock during busy hours and get wide open during idle hours. These characteristics are the constraints for solutions to urban traffic problems.

Why are taxis regulated? The first reason is safety. If any vehicle is allowed to transport people, it might become the tool for criminal purposes. It seems easy to liberalize operations, but the right will be immediately taken back if something goes wrong; this goes back and forth and, in the end, the "balance" point is identified by the control. The reason behind this is that safety is the premise for the mutual service between large numbers of strangers in cities.

Because the government is exercising control, it must be responsible for the regulated; at the very least it must guarantee that the regulated companies and drivers can feed themselves. Owing to the uneven time distribution of traffic, it is very difficult to determine the optimal number of taxi medallions. If licenses are issued based on the peak demand, many drivers will have no business after peak hours. Therefore, it seems difficult to achieve supply-demand balance for taxi licenses. It is not impossible to adopt a floating price for peak hours and let the highest bidders to get the taxi first, but the question is how to achieve this? Supposing passengers were allowed to stand on the street and haggle with drivers, then the city congestion would be even deadly worse during rush hours. Before there is a suitable technical method to deal with these problems; insufficient supply of taxi licenses and price control are the normal state of this industry. When I first travelled to Washington, DC, I noticed that its taxis have many different colors, and taxis of different colors go to different districts, and no cross-district operation is allowed. Later, as I studied regulatory economics, I learned about the "capture theory." As the government implements regulation, it also becomes controlled by the regulated. In any case, each side has its own bargaining chips.

The New Air from Mobile Internet

Currently, mobile internet is being added to traditional urban taxi services; the progress is very rapid, and this poses many new problems that are worth studying.

First, mobile internet provides a powerful tool for building trust between strangers. On the traditional internet, it was difficult for people to know the identity of the other party. As the saying goes: "On the internet, nobody knows you're a dog" (*The New Yorker*, July 5, 1993). However, mobile internet is based on mobile phones, and each mobile phone corresponds to a certain specific person under the real name system. This is a revolutionary progress in building trust between strangers. For example, via the service platform, the driver knows who the passenger is, and the passenger knows who the driver is. Real-time monitoring to track the car throughout the journey is also not difficult. Why is mobile internet invincible in so many industries? My understanding is that this is because it has the capability of lowering the cost of building trust and breaking through the barriers between urban residents' need for cooperation and the difficulty to establish trust. This point deserves adequate attention from mayors, transport authorities, taxi companies, drivers and consumers alike.

Second, mobile internet–based taxi service can reduce the unloaded ratio, release urban road resources, and alleviate the city's biggest constraints during certain hours. Why are cities so congested? It is because the cost of making cars is low and the cost of building roads is high, and the pace of road building can never catch up with the pace of car making. Taxi services connected to the mobile internet can significantly reduce the unloaded ratio, and this is equivalent to increasing the supply of road space. Also, drivers do not have to prowl about and look for customers, and both fuel consumption and emissions can be reduced; these are all very desirable outcomes.

The only "problem" with mobile internet–based taxi is that it has brought about an impact on the original order. In point of fact, all technological advancements face this sort of situation. Years ago, the invention of automobiles impacted the business of horse-drawn carriages and caused protests. Some local governments even stipulated that cars were not allowed to drive faster than carriages. But, in the long run, new technologies and new models will always be irresistible.

As urban transportation modes are constantly changing, the "premier hailing service" which we are discussing now may also become a vested interest themselves in the future. Recently, a group of people in Japan are advocating for "car-free cities," and the idea is to use safe and convenient trams to replace cars. I don't know what the future will hold. But once the innovation is implemented on the ground for further development, all cars, including the currently popular "premier hailing cars" and taxis, will face challenges; this is the correct meaning of "progress."

Obviously the current situation is that there are a great many taxi drivers and a lot of practical interest is involved, so the government does need to handle the situation properly and with care; once the existing pattern is substantially changed, it will step on the vested interests. The premier hailing cars cannot be the only provider to satisfy all the urban transport; taxi service will still be indispensable in the foreseeable future. Therefore, the problem here is, as the old saying goes, that "both the palm and the back of the hand are flesh." You cannot choose between one or the other. I hope that all parties can take a step back, return to common sense, look at the overall constraints for urban transport, and explore how to improve urban mobility under the impact from the new technology and the new business mode so as to face the reality and be future-oriented.

Pay Attention to Procedural Rationality

In the past when we discussed questions, we focused a lot on the inherent rationality; namely, the most reasonable state of things is the way they should be. However, the problem of travel in modern cities is that space, population, time, and new technologies are all muddled together and each of them has completely different interests and angles; this makes it difficult for people to arrive at a completely consistent intrinsic rationality, therefore special care must be given to procedural rationality. Procedural rationality means that even when it is difficult to quickly reach an agreement on inherent rationality, there should be a set of methods to face the practical problem and push for improvement to the actual problem.

From the perspective of procedural rationality, I would recommend to consider the following points on the emergence of mobile internet–based ride hailing services.

First, adopt an inclusive regulatory policy. China has a large population, limited space, and insufficient experience in urban management. There will be no way out if we do not rely on new technologies. Years ago the impact on traditional telecommunication form IP telephone use was also initiated by small private enterprises entering the market, but they were knocked down all at once. The situation was improved later—the attempt to charge Wechat users two years ago was a near miss. We must have a consensus among all the people that although new technologies will impact the old order, they will bring greater long-term benefits if we are inclusive. Inclusive regulation should emphasize open minds, nimble methods, and some room for flexibility. In layperson's terms, at the very least, "a gentleman can talk instead of fight." Discussions are discussions, any opinion could be expressed, but we simply should not rashly kill new born things.

Second, empower cities. Taxis are a highly localized urban business, with very little cross-city interactions. China has more than 600 cities, and they may vary in the degree of congestion, the available road resources, the concerns of the transport administration bureau, and the supply and demand of mobility. This is a very good environment for innovation by a large country such as ours. We should delegate the suitable power and the corresponding responsibilities to each city and let them solve the mobility problem rather than make an immediate nationwide response. Many different solutions will be generated when internet and the traditional taxi business are combined together in several hundred cities. The Ministry of Transportation can evaluate each city, select and commend good cases, and then develop a national legislation by referring to their experiences. To let urban affairs be decided by the city, legislate when the time is mature: First legislate at the city level and then gradually escalate to a national law; this is a more reasonable process for solving the problem.

Third, things can be done if they are not prohibited by the law. If we talk about reasons, all sorts of opinions are somewhat reasonable. But when it comes to the law, which provision of the existing laws and regulations says that it is illegal to use the mobile internet to hail a cab? This sentence certainly is not included in any of them. To be explicitly clear, mobile internet–based ride hailing service is not any type of taxi service as defined by the existing law, and it is impossible for the existing law to have the such an amazing foresight as to pre-include mobile internet ride hailing service into its scope of control before the emergence of these service. We should not expand the scope of applicability of the law willy-nilly. If there is no prohibition by the law, things ought to be doable; this is the most important institutional assurance for innovation as well as an important aspect for procedural rationality. Obviously, people will always worry about the negative effects from new technologies. Then we should go ahead with information collection and analyses and provide the findings to legislators and law amenders as a reference. Currently, the ability to call a cab using the internet has not been around long enough and the number of trips taken is insufficient; no one is able to claim that nothing can go wrong. However, if the premier ride hailing results in personal or property damage, there is the governance by the criminal law; if fraud is involved, there will be a verdict on the behavior by the laws related to contracts and fraud. Whatever the tricks are, as long as the safety of other people's lives and property is being endangered, there is always a law to follow. So long as the behavior damages neither others nor the public interest, it should not be rashly prohibited. The impact of new businesses on old businesses during competition is not a "damage." Otherwise to open more buses, build more metros, and develop new urban transport system will all impact the income for taxis, and there will be no market economy if demonstrations and protests are made at the drop of a hat. If people are constantly marching and protesting, there will be no market economy. The Frenchman Frédéric Bastiat wrote a fable: the candle-makers want to sue the sun because sunshine is free and it reduces the market demand for candles. But the problem is, has the sun truly encroached on the candle-makers?

For governance in ancient China, one principle was that if there is no whistle blow from civilians, there will be no investigation by the government. At present, for many things without reporting by the general public, the government still must chase down. I thought they could easily be determined as "illegal business." In the past, the state arranged everything and every person was an employee of the super state company; the government would make certain arrangement for people if they were not allowed to do certain things. Now most businesses are private enterprises. The government must be very cautious if it does not allow them to do this and to do that but does not provide them with food. Every time the private sector finds a new way in the market, it will create jobs and pay taxes, and this is related to the overall situation for the national economy.

A Four-Year Review of Online Ride-Hailing Services[38]

The Development of Ride-Hailing Services Follows the Same Logic as the Experience of Reform

Online ride-hailing services first appeared in Beijing and Hangzhou as far back as 2012. Its development has gone through four years up to the current promulgation of *The Interim Measures for the Administration of the Operation and Service of Online Hailing Cars* (*The Interim Measures*). I think there are two points worth commending from this process: First, online ride-hailing service emerged on the streets first and the administration standards came in later; second, in an environment full of controversy, the opinions of all parties were widely heard and digested, and the government regulation method was formed with the participation of all stakeholders.

The first point is particularly commendable. To look back, online ride hailing first showed up in San Francisco in 2010 and then in Paris the next year. If some people wanting to provide the same type of service in China had opted for another pathway—for example, if they had applied to government authorities to organize expert justification before granting them a license, or if they had only called for China also to have online hailing through the public opinion—then after the same amount of four years, would we be able to see today this administration method that recognizes and regulates online hailing cars? It is difficult to answer a definite no, but the possibility should be close to zero.

38 This section is a reprint of the author's speech on August 3, 2016, at a policy seminar on the topic of *the Interim Measures for the Administration of the Operation and Service of Online Hailing Cars.*—Editor's note.

Fortunately, China has not taken this "road to innovation." What actually happened was that while other people still had no idea about what online ride hailing is all about, a group of young people had written their own software for ride hailing. They went to the streets to instigate taxi drivers to try the new method and acted as online hailing passengers themselves with their mobile phones. In short, they started doing and trying first. By the time our superstructure took much notice of it, the online hailing service had already been experienced by quite a lot of people, and it had even taken a foothold in urban mobility. Just taking Didi as an example: On the publishing of the for-comments draft of the Interim Measures, the number of daily orders generated by the company increased from seven million to ten million. The coverage of online hailing was even bigger if the figures for other companies are added.

True knowledge comes out of practice. As I have noticed, during the controversy people who vote for or against online hailing both use the online hailing cars as the object of analysis and the basis for their arguments. It is probably difficult to arrive at a conclusion for the debate without talking about the online hailing cars, and it is even more difficult to identify the minimum level of consensus.

The more important significance of allowing the trial first is that this new industry will have an opportunity to constantly modify and improve itself. Probably only when someone traces back the history of this innovation in the future it can be made clear that many changes were taking place in the business model, service norms, technology, and internal control of all online hailing providers from the birth in China in 2012 to the promulgation of *The Interim Measures*. The internet economy itself has the intrinsic largest capability of "fast iteration," which means that passenger experience can be taken into account and—with the active participation of users—the service quality and business model can be continuously improved. Had the opportunity for iterative improvement in the trial not been given, and the very original business model was used as the basis for submission and approval, then it might be even more difficult for this kind of innovation to stand on its own feet.

The experience of online hailing services shows that the model of "trying first and standardizing later" is a realistic path to initiate and then implement the innovation. This method is consistent with China's previous reform experience. From household contracting responsibility systems, to private enterprises, to opening up to the outside, all the way to the rise of internet e-commerce, and courier delivery, all of them started first with experiment and the regulations came in later. Supposing that this tried-and-tested logic is reversed, and we stipulate that the baby's name should be given first before people are allowed to have the baby, then definitely no reform will become possible and innovation can also not be achievable.

The question is, how can we more clearly affirm this experience? Coming back to online hailing services, I'd like to ask a question: Before the promulgation of *The Interim Measures* by the government ministries, what was the legal status of the online hailing cars on the streets of China's large and small cities during the four years? Legal, illegal or "grey," which means neither legal nor illegal?

I tend to choose "legal." The reason for this is because online hailing cars are not the same as the original taxis, and their activities are not the "business operations" as defined by the original laws and regulations. Because there were no such activities at the time of their promulgation, it was impossible for legislators to determine in advance whether or not the subsequent online hailing service must fall into the category of the original "business operations." This is a case about the knowledge that "white horses are not horses." After the advent of online hailing services, including the controversial question of whether or not private cars can be operated as a premier rental vehicle, a legal procedure is needed to see whether it is legal or illegal. Before initiating relevant procedures, and before the already-initiated defining procedure concludes that "online hailing cars are illegal" or "the operation is prohibited," the online hailing cars are legal. When we say "things are doable when they are not prohibited by the law," of course they are doable only when they are legal.

In fact, this kind of state was quite common throughout the course of China's reform. Nothing good would happen if we knock down new things before understanding them. If we encourage bold experiments and bold breakthroughs but easily put an "illegal" hat on their heads without legal basis, how could there be reforms and innovations?

The experience of online hailing services shows that the model of "trying first and standardizing later" is consistent with China's previous reform experience.

Some people might criticize this and say that if things go this way, wouldn't there be too much freedom, and wouldn't the world be put into chaos? I think they really are overthinking. Because this only applies to "behaviors that are not expressly prohibited by law." As for behaviors explicitly prohibited by law, the due banning, punishment, and financial penalty are still in place, so how can this lead to chaos? As common sense has it, to see online hailing as legal before it is determined to be illegal by a procedure does not mean that anyone can use online hailing to do harm to the lives and property of other people or to damage public interest; should this happen, the existing criminal law, property law, contract law, and the regulations on maintaining public order can be leveraged for effective control. For example, if an online hailing car hits someone, will the police ignore it? The accident will be handled in the same way as for private cars, taxis, buses, and public cars crashing into a person.

Not until sufficient evidence shows that the accidents for online hailing cars are not limited to a few persons in question, but have an inherent connection with this type of business operation, should we launch the review and approval procedure so as to determine whether it is necessary impose universal restrictions on online hailing cars, or prohibit them and list them as illegal based on the actual effect from their occurrence. Logically, if the situation is not serious, there is no need to rush the creation of legal restrictions or prohibitions. On the contrary, if the situation is serious and it is impossible to prevent it with other regulations, new universal legal constraints will be promulgated.

That is to say, the tolerance for new business models from adopting the principle that "things are doable if they are not prohibited by law" will not enlarge the threat to the freedom, life, and property of other people and to the public interest.

What I do not endorse is the following popular concept of "the rule of law"—any kind of economic activity, any behavior by the general public to meet the market needs, even it is just a single move, a single form, or a single action, must be approved by certain administrative organs and must have provisions and obtain permission from the legal text, otherwise it must bc illcgal. What kind of rule of law is this? In the past, dogmatism could easily ask for "the text book"; now we are asking for "legal provisions." If the system becomes so ossified that we "would not go outside without checking the almanac first," there will be no innovation society to speak of, and the crowd will burst into laughter and break up in a uproar.

This point is worth emphasizing because China's transformation is far from complete. Back in the old days, why did the Xiaogang Village want to reform? Because the old system did not provide enough food to farmers but it still tightly tied their hands and legs. Reform is a breakthrough: Is it feasible to allow farmers to take care of their meals by themselves? Practice proved this works, so the reform was extended to non-agricultural fields. The state could not give a job to every one, but it could let people start their own businesses, set up factories, do business, and work for industries. It was just this simple, and it turned out to be a promising road. Now that China's economy has made great achievements, we should never go back to the old road of managing people's head and legs without giving them meals, and indiscreetly announce things which are not prohibited by law as illegal.

Based on the above understanding, online hailing services which first appeared on China's streets in 2012 are legal since their birth. What, then is the significance of *The Interim Measures* issued by the relevant government ministries four whole years later? I believe that the role of this regulation is to "make it clear that online hailing service is legal, and to standardize the management after confirming the legal status."

Legal in the First Place, Why Still Should Online Ride Hailing Be Made Clear as Legal?

To begin with, online hailing is legal; why take the additional trouble to clearly stipulate that it is legal? The answer lies in China's national situation. After all, China is at most in the initial stage of the rule of law. The concept that things are doable if they are not prohibited by law is very new to many people, and they have lots of misgivings. People seem to be more accustomed to the concept that things cannot be done unless they are announced as "legal," and some people even believe that "things said to be legal may not necessarily be doable." In the face of this kind of reality, it is probably not superfluous to add "expressly stipulated as legal" to the "originally legal."

More importantly, for a new industry that grows rapidly in a short period like online hailing, there is indeed a need for standardized management. Not all lawful behaviors need special management norms. Many things in daily life are lawful, but they do not need administration norms, such as the volume of TV sound of neighbors, how late the aunties can dance at the square, to whom you will sell your old bicycles, and whether or not I charge my friends a small fee for taking them to the airport. When added up, these daily behaviors amount to a big number and they are just regulated by ethics, customs, and community conventions. Just in case something big happens, the general civil law principles should be sufficient.

Online ride hailing is not such a kind of affairs. It is novel, uses the state-of-the-art technology, and it can make quite many people confused and they only know the answer without knowing the reason. It has a very strong network effect; once the tipping point is crossed, it can quickly gather tremendous amount of supply and demand. It is especially active in big cities and large towns where the population is concentrated in a narrow space, with a high frequency of interaction and a big influence on the outside world. It also takes up urban street space, which is a kind of public land with an extremely uneven distribution of busy and idle hours, so it leads to some special problems with the competition for resources. Certainly online hailing was not born out of a vacuum. Since its birth it has been challenging the incumbent traditional taxis and trying to take a piece from their cheese.

With all the aforementioned characteristics as an incomplete depiction, it is not enough for online hailing service to have a lawful status. Practice soon brings up new questions: From within and outside the online ride hailing industry, will a lawful freedom affect, hinder, or even infringe on the appropriate and lawful freedom of other parties? Empirically, between municipal management organs and the platforms for online hailing service, between the platforms and drivers, between drivers and their passengers, and between online hailing cars and other mobility businesses competing for street resources, one freedom often has frictions with the freedom of others.

Academically, people generally agree that what the law should protect is the freedom not infringing on the lawful freedom of others. This is of course correct. The problem is that—in the real world—it is not easy to define whether a freedom has hurt the freedom of others or not. In particular, when the law and economics reached the ideological height of *The Problem of Social Cost* by Ronald Coase in 1960, which says all infringements of rights have a certain two-way nature, we have to switch from pursuing the inherent rationality to relying more on procedural rationality to find an answer to this question.

Over the past four years, the actual practice of online hailing service was required to make its legalization clear and to form a set of management norms. This ensures that this major innovation in China's mobility can be turned into a stable reality in the daily life after all sorts of controversies and run-ins. This leads to the creation of *The Interim Measures*; no wonder the main public opinions all give it a thumb-up and express their welcome. After carefully comparing the differences between *The Interim Measures* and the for-comments draft ten months earlier, Xue Zhaofeng believes that the new regulation, "as the first national level regulation on online hailing in the world … will write a new page in the history of science, technology, and commerce." Obviously, there are also concerns about how to complete the registration in 2,800 different places, and about whether or not the implementation in so many places will result in improper control and excessive control in disguised forms and hinder fair market competition.

Because this involves the role of city governments in reform and innovation, I will elaborate a bit more. During both the discussion in 2015 on the experience of China's first city to recognize the legal status of online hailing, and the discussion on the for-comments version at Langrun Garden of Peking University at the end of the year, I proposed to put how to standardize the management of online hailing service into the authority of cities and recommended that mainly the city governments should assume the responsibility of implementing the specific norms after several guiding principles have been set by central ministries.

The starting point of emphasizing the power of city affairs is because with the development of intercity rail transit, the old and new taxi business has become the internal affairs of cities, there is no need to cross the city, let alone nationwide administration norms. Even more importantly, it is a delicate job to delineate appropriate boundaries between multiple freedoms as described above. Only after experience and information are collected from the several hundred largely different cities can it be possible for online hailing services be properly handled in the city's overall mobility landscape.

Things like bureaucratic inaction and rent-seeking from approval power will always exist to some degree. Therefore, both the central government's guiding principles and the top-down scrutiny and promotion are indispensable. Additionally, there is a competitive relationship between cities. In terms of solving the difficulties in hailing a cab, in mobility and responding to public concerns, the competitive pressure faced by local governments will also facilitate the implementation the new policy. Nowadays the number of places with readily available courier services has by far exceeded 2,800 administrative units. Wouldn't it be stupid and ridiculous to find trouble with and block courier services?

Looking at all these several aspects, we can at least say that even though the devil is in the details, there is also the hidden angel. We can always try our best to let "angels" subdue more "devils" and create more useful experiences. Again, what the future will be like depends on the actions of all parties.

Should Urban Services Only Be Provided by the City's Permanent Registered Population?

A Question to Beijing, Tianjin, and Shanghai's For-Comments Draft Regulation on Online Car Hailing Service

Beijing, Tianjin, and Shanghai have released the for-comments draft of their regulations on the management of online car hailing and asked for public opinions. This suddenly aroused lots of public outcry and criticism. Public governance involves the interests of many different parties, and so it is quite normal to have different views. Because they are openly seeking comments, it obviously shows that they are still seeking the balance point. Therefore, it is people's right to express their view points, and it is also their opportunity.

I have attended several seminars on online car hailing services, and my personal opinions have not changed, so I do not need to repeat. In the current controversy, there is a common point for the to-be-promulgated regulations of the above-mentioned cities (i.e., the person to engage in online car hailing service must be a permanent registered resident of the same city [namely, have a local household registration or *hukou*]). For a time, the screens frequently got bombarded by the phrase "Beijing people and Beijing cars."

On the provision that local *hukou* is a must, please allow me to ask a question that has always been on my mind these days: If all the products and services enjoyed by a city can only be provided by the registered population of that city, what will the city look like?

For example, if the vegetables, grains, fruit, and water eaten or drunk by Beijing people can only be produced, processed, transported, and sold by people who are permanent, registered citizens of Beijing, what will the capital city look like? And if the concerts and operas in Tianjin can only be performed by permanent, registered residents of Tianjin, will its cultural market be as hot as it has been in recent years?

To build all the skyscrapers on both sides of the Huangpu River, if people must have a local household registration to get involved in the production and transportation of building materials, the construction activity, and building management, what will Shanghai's skyline look like?

Indeed, it is not at all difficult for readers to keep adding items to this list of "what if." Perhaps a mischievous friend might ask: "if only people with the local *hukou* can have the qualification to serve as the Party Secretary of Mayor of cities, what would happen to the municipalities directly under the central government?"

Perhaps the officials of the transportation bureau were too hasty in drafting the new policy on online hailing cars to think about these "ifs" in the common sense. If they have more time to think about it, will they hesitate a little before writing down that "only permanent, registered residents of this city are permitted?" Or will they follow the example of Shenzhen, Chongqing, Chengdu, and Guangzhou in the new regulation on online car hailing? Or will they at least be more lenient and set the limits to "the resident population of this city"?

And my question to the latter is: Other products and services consumed by the city, ranging from eating, drinking, sleeping, to all the daily necessities and even making decisions on urban public affairs, are not limited to the city's permanent, registered residents; why is such special attention paid to online ride hailing services?

The most probable answer is that "online hailing cars are special." The word "special" sounds very familiar to me as I have participated in the discussion of regulation or control for many years—the telecommunication industry is special, the emerging strategic industry is special, healthcare is special, courier is special, education is special, big cities are special, and so on and so forth. In point of fact, everything in the world is special, but among all these specials, there are always abstract generalities and commonalities. I hope the taxi management authorities in these cities can answer this question: What is so special about online ride hailing that it is really necessary to stipulate that "drivers cannot engage in it unless they are permanent registered residents of the same city"?

Postscript

Rise from Abstract to Concrete

Wang Dingding

I borrow Karl Marx's proposition of rising from abstract to concrete, which is also frequently quoted by Mr. Wang Yuanhua. The most thought-provoking word here is "rise." Most of today's young people are used to rising from reality into theory, but they seldom think about how to "rise" from abstract to concrete. In his early years, Mr. Wang Yuanhua immersed himself in the study of *Carving a Dragon in the Core of Literature*. In his middle age, he experienced a catastrophe owing to "Hu Feng's Case." Just like King Wen of Zhou Dynasty who deduced the theory of the Eight Diagrams during his imprisonment in Youli, Yuanhua read *Shorter Logic* during his imprisonment; and like Confucius who read I-Ching so many times that the cowhide rope connecting the inscribed bamboo slips broke several times, Yuanhua read *Shorter Logic* so many times that the book was worn out and broken. And from this Mr. Yuanhua, who always advocated integrating life into knowledge, doubted and criticized about whether or not Georg Hegel's logic and any logic (or principle) can encompass the real world.

The editor invited me to write testimonials for this book of Qiren Zhou. I wrote back telling them that I would write a book review after reading each of Qiren's books. Qiren is like my elder brother, my book review cannot be the foreword, and it should serve as the postscript. But there is a more important reason for my respect for Qiren, which is shown in the title of this postscript. Over the years I have become familiar with or considered to have read a wide range of theories, but I know deeply the intrinsic defects of the self-consistency of theories and of any logics. On many occasions, such as at a China Center for Economic Research (CCER; namely, today's National School of Development of Peking University) new student orientation, the focal point of my speech was the intrinsic defects of theories. I believe Mr. Jin Yuelin's summarization is the best: "The theory reveals the intrinsic causal relationship, but the momentum does not necessarily lead to what is supposed to happen unless all the conditions are met." The most puzzling part for young people here is the "momentum," which is to a certain degree in line with the theory but may not necessarily take place. Li Ling's summarization of the basic principle of China's ancient strategists is to follow the momentum not the people, which is different from the Confucian idea. Therefore, "the situation speaks louder than people." In one of his essays included in this book, Qiren expresses that he is not interested at all in the superb theory construction capacities demonstrated under the constraints of imagination, and that he only follows real-world problems. However, every time that I introduce this set of his viewpoints, students often ask what the "real-world problems" are. Students have real-world problems in their eyes; they are often guided by the mass media, and they have their own "common sense."

Mr. Jin Yuelin expressed a classical opinion on the relationship between logic and reality, which I also often quote: "The set of all realistic possibilities is a subset of the set of all logical possibilities." In recent years I cited this viewpoint from Mr. Jin to explain why creativity cannot be encompassed in the set of all logic possibilities. My reason for this is that the logic possibility for creativity, in essence, is demonstrated only in the future, but any set of logics can only cover the total possibilities of a static moment. What Qiren follows is, in essence, possibilities that are yet to be generally perceived—in terms of this book, it is the institutional innovation detected from his social surveys, to have the possibility of being politically accepted in the future. It is not randomly visible innovation activities, but the kind of innovation activities that he comprehended as the momentum in the mega-trend. In other words, the "possibilities of reality" as discussed by Mr. Jin Yuelin do not include the possibilities of reality that have not taken place or have not been realized. Coming back to Mr. Jin's concept of "momentum," the etymology of the Chinese language suggests that the word has a close relationship with "*ji-wei*" (几微in Chinese). The character "*ji*" is the source for the Chinese translation of "*ji-he*"(几何in Chinese), meaning something is going to happen but has not happened yet. If you are a student of sciences, you should not underestimate the Chinese character "*wei*," meaning tiny or subtle. The first classical literature of sinology, *Book of Documents* (in Dayu's *Strategy to Govern the Country*), says: "People always change their mind, the essence of Tao is to find the truth from subtle phenomena." One of the abilities of saints is to be able to "know how things will develop from their tiny beginnings," as a falling leaf heralds autumn. In maintaining the health of the society, the method of going from outside to the inside is called to "prevent tiny things from becoming a big trouble." There is another method of going from outward appearance to inner essence; as the traditional Chinese medicine puts it, "the best doctors do not only cure the diseases but take preventive measures before their illness." In other words, Western medicine is inferior because it sinks down to treat the disease and forgets that the cause for the illness before its occurrence is the root cause (Western medicine acknowledges today that this is sub-health). Then, how to cure the diseased society of China? There are still two ways. The method from Western medicine is to take stop-gap measures—"treat where the pain is, be it the head or the foot"; namely, to treat the diseased person. The idea from traditional Chinese medicine is to cure the patient before he is ill and look for the root cause. I have observed Qiren for a long time, and I believe this is also his idea (see Chapter 4 of this book). However, to cure the disease before its occurrence, we have to face the possibility "that the momentum might not necessarily come." This is because what we are facing here is the "*ji*"; namely, things that suggest a coming trend that has not arrived. Why is it so difficult for many students to learn the insight of Qiren after following him in the survey over the years? My explanation is, Qiren's social surveys are not social surveys in an ordinary sense. What he is focusing on is nothing else but the "*ji*"; namely, the little tiny signs.

The logic of the reform echoes with Zhang Weiying's *The Logic of the Market*, in which Weiying emphasizes the core importance of entrepreneurs to the market economy. In this book, Chapters 1 and 2, and even Chapters 3, 5, and 6, Qiren is emphasizing once and again the core importance of "political entrepreneurs" such as Deng Xiaoping to the evolution of China's politics and economy. When we discuss entrepreneur activities, as determined by the essence of innovation of these activities, we must put the possibilities of reality that will be generally perceived only in the future into our analysis framework; then, just as stated before, this will have an intrinsic conflict with the original meaning of "logic." Therefore, the "logic" in the title of these two works is an analogy in colloquialism rather than the system of self-consistency in the academic sense.

Under the constraint of imagination, it is possible for each one of us build many systems with logical self-consistency, just like what we can see from the day-to-day work of every undergraduate of math. However, Bertrand Russell, a master of logics (he is also a philosopher, a social theorist, and a political activist) made it clear: "In any system of logical self-consistency, there is always one or two (or more than two) parameters known as logical constants that are most important; this is because these parameters are the common sense-based boundaries between the logic system and the real world." When we follow the real world, only very limited few possibilities out of the numerous logic possibilities existing under the constraints of imagination in the self-consistent logic system are closely related/relevant with the real world. Any overseas student having participated in economics seminars often hears such comments from participants as "this is irrelevant." This is a severe criticism, because it is such a deadly blow if you develop a theory after more than ten years of hard learning and then it is seen as "irrelevant with" the real world. Yes, economics is a social science between liberal arts and natural sciences, and it is a must that it uphold the principle that it is related to the real world through at least one logical constant; it just cannot be irrelevant.

Apart from personal emotions, the main reason for my respect for Qiren is my theoretical viewpoint as described above—even if I am familiar with hundreds of theories, what I care about most is actually the ones that are relevant for the real world. This relevance, or the common sense–based boundary maintained by me with the real world, largely depends on whether or not I have carefully listened to Qiren's voice.

The method of rising from abstract to concrete was written by Karl Marx in Section 3, "The Method of Political Economy," of his *A Contribution to the Critique of Political Economy* (see *Selected Works of Marx and Engels*. "Manuscript on Economics, 1857–1858," People's Press, Rev 1, First Part of Volume 46). Marx points out:

> Population is an abstraction if, for instance, one disregards the classes of which it is composed. These classes in turn remain empty terms if one does not know the factors on which they depend, e.g., wage-labour, capital, and so on. These presuppose exchange, division of labour, prices, etc. For example, capital is nothing without wage-labour, without value, money, price, etc. If one were to take population as the point of departure, it would be a very vague notion of a complex whole and through closer definition one would arrive analytically at increasingly simple concepts; from imaginary concrete terms one would move to more and more tenuous abstractions until one reached the most simple definitions. From there it would be necessary to make the journey again in the opposite direction until one arrived once more at the concept of population, which is this time not a vague notion of a whole, but a totality comprising many determinations and relations.

Marx believed that previous economists adopt the first approach as described above; namely, to go from the concrete to the abstract as the method to construct their system of economics. But the scientific method strongly believed by Marx is the second approach as described above, namely what he calls to rise from the abstract to the concrete, without which economics cannot be understood.

Also in this section, Marx criticizes Georg Hegel's method of thinking and discernment. Perhaps he also felts the same eternal impulse as Mr. Wang Yuanhua, who felt that life shouldn't be logicalized during his imprisonment? Perhaps he also had an unstoppable enthusiasm for reading great works of literature like Mr. Wang Yuanhua? All in all, from Mr. Wang Yuanhua's reading notes, I have felt the important meaning of Marx's above viewpoints to my academic life.

In at least two sections in Chapter 1 of this collection, I have read Qiren's critique on Marx's entire value theory: "no one has pointed out that the foundation for the theory of surplus value is that the transaction costs is zero." This is a very pertinent criticism; zero transaction costs is one of the implied assumptions in Marx's value doctrine and the whole Marxist political economy. The well-known "Coase Theorem" (Qiren feels strongly about the "zero transaction costs" assumption in this theorem), as I have explained again and again, equates to the following statement in the broad sense: In a world where there is no transaction costs, institution does not matter. This is a basic social science proposition, which is very important to readers who wish to understand the profound meaning of this works of Qiren.

Had there be no transaction costs, it would not matter if China adopts a system of the centrally planned economy or a free market economy. The key lies in the reverse side of Coase's theorem; namely, a world where transaction costs cannot be neglected and the "real world" as described by Qiren and Steve N. S. Cheung. In such a world, the type of social institution almost always determines the fate of the society.

Qiren takes great trouble to tell the story of China's reform; his intention is to remind readers to pay attention to and think about the possible picture of China's future reform. Through his description, it is quite easy for readers to understand that by the logic of reform, China's future reform must involve the political system reform. I prefer a more direct expression: The key link to hinder the continuous growth of China's economic growth will be mainly political, but no more mainly economic.

The political system reform, as emphasized over and again here, is Deng Xiaoping's unfulfilled ambition. In contemporary China, as long as it publicly announces that its political program is to seek happiness for the people, any political party must choose the basic direction of political system reform as restricting power. This is because, just as any Chinese who has not totally lost common sense would know, the popular corruption originates from unrestricted power. Just as the wise remarks by Lord John Acton suggest: "All power tends to corrupts; absolute power corrupts absolutely."

This postscript could be quite long. I could have made my article longer owing to the richness in Qiren's writing and to the rich feelings that I have obtained through his perception from rising from the abstract to the concrete; but I will stop here and hope that it serves the purpose of the present postscript.

www.ingramcontent.com/pod-product-compliance
Ingram Content Group UK Ltd.
Pitfield, Milton Keynes, MK11 3LW, UK
UKHW021837100926
8556IPUK00004B/405

9 781433 172946